D1506647

# Farm Fresh

## GEORGIA

# *Farm Fresh*
## GEORGIA

**THE GO-TO GUIDE TO GREAT** Farmers' Markets
Farm Stands · Farms · U-Picks · Kids' Activities · Lodging
Dining · Dairies · Festivals · Choose-and-Cut Christmas Trees
Vineyards and Wineries · and More

## Jodi Helmer

The University of North Carolina Press    Chapel Hill

A **SOUTHERN GATEWAYS** GUIDE

© 2014 JODI HELMER. All rights reserved. Manufactured in the United States of America. All photographs were taken by the author unless otherwise indicated. Designed by Courtney Leigh Baker. Set in Whitman with Bellow and Gotham display by Rebecca Evans. The paper in this book meets the guidelines for permanence and durability of the Committee on Production Guidelines for Book Longevity of the Council on Library Resources. The University of North Carolina Press has been a member of the Green Press Initiative since 2003.

Library of Congress Cataloging-in-Publication Data
Helmer, Jodi.
Farm fresh Georgia : the go-to guide to great farmers' markets, farm stands, farms, U-picks, kids' activities, lodging, dining, dairies, festivals, choose-and-cut Christmas trees, vineyards and wineries, and more / Jodi Helmer.
   pages cm. — (A Southern gateways guide)
Includes index.
ISBN 978-1-4696-1157-0 (paperback : alkaline paper) 1. Pick-your-own farms—Georgia—Guidebooks. 2. Farmers' markets—Georgia—Guidebooks. 3. Farms—Georgia—Guidebooks. 4. Tree farms—Georgia—Guidebooks. 5. Vineyards—Georgia—Guidebooks. 6. Dairy farms—Georgia—Guidebooks. 7. Festivals—Georgia—Guidebooks. 8. Hotels—Georgia—Guidebooks. 9. Restaurants—Georgia—Guidebooks. 10. Georgia—Guidebooks. I. Title.
SB319.863.G4H45 2014   381'.41094758—dc23   2013021088

Southern Gateways Guide™ is a registered trademark of the University of North Carolina Press.

18  17  16  15  14   5  4  3  2  1

TO THE FARMERS
whose passion and hard work put food on our tables

AND TO MY PARTNER, JERRY PORTER,
who nourishes my spirit and encourages my farm dreams

# CONTENTS

## APPALACHIAN REGION

Dade

Catoosa

Whitfield

• Ringgold

Murray

Walker

Chattooga

Gordon

Floyd
Rome •

Bartow
Cartersville •

Polk

Paulding

Haralson

## ATLANTA METRO

Cherokee
• Canton

Roswell •

Cobb
Marietta •

Gwinnett

Douglasville •
Douglas

★ Atlanta

DeKalb

Rockdale

Fulton

Clayton

Fayette

Henry
McDonough •

## PIEDMONT REGION

Stephens

Banks

Hart

Franklin

Commerce •
Jackson

Madison

Elbert

Barrow

Clarke
Athens •

Oglethorpe

Monroe •
Walton

Oconee

Wilkes

Lincoln

Bostwick •

Greene

Columbia

Carrollton •
Carroll

Covington •
Newton

Morgan

Taliaferro

McDuffie

Heard

Coweta

Spalding

Butts

Jasper

Putnam

Warren

Hancock

Glascock

Meriwether

Pike

Lamar

Monroe

Jones

Baldwin

Troup

Upson

Harris
Pine Mountain •

Talbot

Crawford

Macon •
Bibb

Muscogee

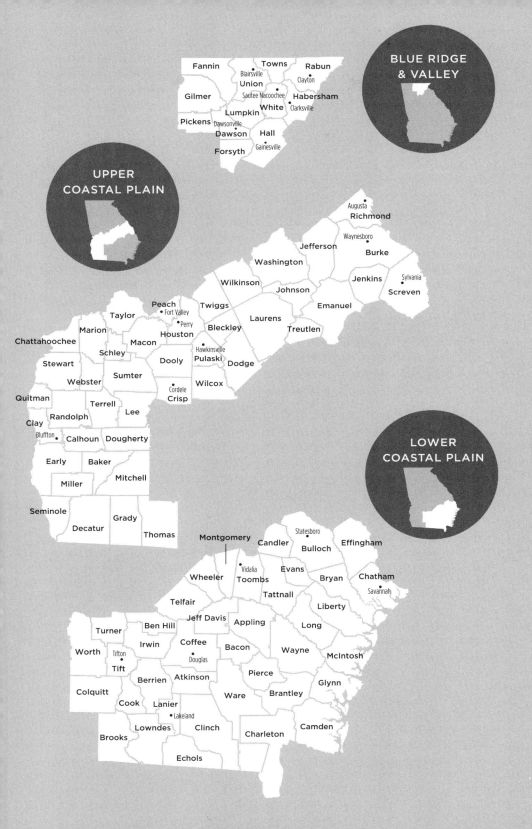

# INTRODUCTION

I grew up in the suburbs where flocks of kids played hide and seek between rows of brick houses and herds of station wagons lined neighborhood streets; milk came from cartons arranged in neat rows at the supermarket; and the closest we came to understanding the connection between cows and cutlets happened during school trips to the annual agricultural fair.

The first time I visited a farm, I was fourteen. During the weekend trip, I watched a Holstein give birth, pushing and straining without a sound until a calf slipped out onto the barn floor where momma used her rough tongue to clean her newborn.

Since then, I've developed a case of "rural longing," the desire to buy acreage, put up fences and spend my days feeding a tribe of goats and watching chickens scratch up their supper. There was a selfish motivation to writing this book: I wanted to spend time on farms, learn from farmers, get mud on my boots and fresh produce in my belly. The experience didn't disappoint.

In the course of researching *Farm Fresh Georgia*, I traveled 15,000-plus miles from South Carolina to the Florida line and from the Blue Ridge Mountains to the Atlantic Ocean, uncovering the best agritourism destinations in Georgia. Each time I set out for another research trip, I knew it would be a new adventure: I got a kiss from an alpaca, tried (and liked) sweetbreads, watched cheese being made while the cows grazed outside, cried during a tour of a Vidalia onion processing plant, fought off gnats, cheered at the pig races, slept in a tobacco barn, got lost in more corn mazes than I want to admit, and gave a belly rub to a sow named Lucy . . . all in the name of research. Along the way, I met some of the most gracious, passionate, hardworking folks around.

Not only were the experiences constant reminders that I have the best job in the world; they also reinforced the reasons that agriculture and tourism are the two biggest industries in Georgia.

The 2010 Georgia Farm Gate Value Report by the University of Georgia reported that agricultural production across the state topped $12 billion (an increase of $746 million from 2009) and agritourism helped bring in $640 million in revenues. It's the fastest-growing segment in either agriculture or tourism.

Georgia is the Peach State, and its reputation for producing some of the juiciest peaches in the nation is well deserved. More than forty varieties of fresh peaches are grown in Georgia, and packing sheds, farm stands, and celebrations to honor the state fruit abound. But there is more to Georgia than just peaches: Georgia boasts ten million acres of farmland and nearly 48,000 farms; it leads the nation in peanut and pecan production and is the second largest producer of cotton crops. The state agricultural industry has a total economic impact of $65 billion and created more than 351,000 jobs in 2008, according to the Center for Agribusiness and Economic Development at the University of Georgia. Agritourism plays a huge role in the success of state farms and the Georgia economy, generating $138 million in economic impact and supporting 1,756 jobs.

All across Georgia, farmers are eagerly throwing open their pasture gates and barn doors, welcoming visitors to experience their farms, dairies, U-pick operations, orchards, corn mazes, farmers' markets, wineries, and restaurants; some are even extending invitations to spend the night, setting up cabins in the pastures or converting barns into rustic farm accommodations. In Georgia, there is no such thing as an ordinary agritourism experience: Depending on the season and the region, it's possible to milk goats, sample fresh peaches, help on a shrimping boat, tour wine country, or learn how to make cheese—sometimes all in the same day!

As I learned while researching this book, the best part of spending time on a farm isn't the fresh air or the fresh food—though both are high on the list of reasons to have an agricultural experience. The opportunity to spend time with farmers, to understand how they turn sunshine, seeds, soil, and sweat equity into the foods on our table; to hear the passion in their voices when they talk about preserving the land and engaging in work that matters; to see the pride on their faces when they show off a crop of picture-perfect and utterly delicious produce—those are the reasons that agritourism is exciting.

It's not the production farmers who are growing commodity crops like soybeans and cotton or raising thousands of head of cattle in a feedlot who are welcoming visitors. The farmers who want to share their passion, their land, and their livelihood are often small-scale, sustainable farmers who are doing creative, innovative, exciting things on their farms.

As someone who grew up in—and still lives in—a city, it's exciting to see farms popping up in urban areas like Atlanta, Savannah, Roswell, Marietta, and Augusta; shoppers buying fresh produce from metro farmers' markets to cook up in their Midtown condos; and chefs using local ingredients to turn their cuisine—and their restaurants—into the best in town.

*Farm Fresh Georgia* is a celebration of the farmers who are living off the land and inviting others in to share the experience. Grab the book and a GPS, explore the farms tucked into urban neighborhoods or head out on the open road, take in the pastoral landscapes, stop at a roadside stand for a snack, and visit the farms whose pastures seem to stretch from the black-top to the horizon. Most importantly, get to know your farmers!

## HOW TO USE THIS BOOK

I organized this book around Georgia's six main regions: Atlanta Metro, Upper Coastal Plain, Lower Coastal Plain, Piedmont, Appalachian Region, and Blue Ridge and Valley Region. When it comes to finding agritourism activities, size doesn't matter; the Appalachian Region, the smallest region, has just as much to offer as the Piedmont, which is the largest region. Within each region, the listings are further divided into multiple categories (explained below) and alphabetized by county. If a farm fit into multiple categories, I chose the one that best represented it.

Each chapter includes a map of the region showing the counties and key cities. Many of these listings are in rural locations and might not show up on a GPS, and the towns listed in the address might not always be the closest town to the farm. In close-knit rural communities, finding the farm is often as simple as asking a local resident. A lot of the farms included in the book have taken advantage of a program offered by the Georgia Department of Agriculture that provides road signs identifying agritourism destinations. The green signs are posted along interstates, city streets, and rural roads, helping guide visitors to their destinations.

The farms, dairies, wineries, orchards, and other locations listed in the book are open to the public; some have set hours, while others operate seasonally or prefer that visitors make appointments or call ahead. Remember, these are working farms, dairies, wineries, restaurants, and shops. While farmers, cheesemongers, winemakers, chefs, and shopkeepers are often eager to share their stories and offer true agricultural experiences, their work must come first. In other words, feel free to ask questions but don't expect to spend all afternoon sipping sweet tea on the porch and talking about crop yield.

**Farms**

I define this category broadly: It includes working farms, historic farms, educational farms, and gardens. *Farm Fresh Georgia* lists farms specializing in organic, Certified Naturally Grown, or sustainable production methods as well as conventional farms that use pesticides. The farms range in size from one acre to several hundred acres. The book does not include factory farms or concentrated animal feeding operations (CAFOs). Some farms charge a fee for tours, so make sure you ask first. In most cases, the charges are nominal. It's a good idea to purchase goods from the farmers as a token of appreciation.

**Farmers' Markets**

There are more than 130 farmers' markets in Georgia, and new markets are popping up all the time. Across the state, the markets range from state-run affairs, where local vendors sell products alongside resellers hawking produce from other states and, sometimes, other countries. Instead of including an exhaustive listing, the book focuses on "producer markets," where farm and craft vendors sell only the products they grow, raise, or make, and markets that are in interesting locations or lively settings or feature unique offerings.

**Farm Stands and U-Picks**

Farms included in this section either invite the public to pick their own produce (the offerings range from strawberries and peaches to okra and corn) or purchase products grown and produced on the farm, which might include fresh produce, meat, cheese, milk, and eggs from stands located on the farm. Some of the farms included in this section operate on the honor system, trusting their customers to calculate the cost of their purchases and leave their payments in a locked cash box. It's a rural tradition that should be honored, not abused. Some farms that operate U-picks or produce stands also lead tours or host other activities. In those cases, notes about additional offerings are included with the listings.

## Dairies

Across Georgia, commercial dairies milk herds of cattle and ship the milk to processing plants where it's pasteurized, homogenized, and shipped to supermarkets. A growing number of smaller dairies are raising cows—and goats—for small-scale milk production. Some of the dairies featured in the book have on-farm stores stocked with dairy products, including raw milk, from cows and goats that graze outside the store, while others use local milk to produce farmstead cheese. Many of these smaller dairies offer tours to the public.

## Aquaculture

Georgia's location on the coast means that agritourism isn't limited to land-based activities. Captains of fishing vessels welcome guests aboard for a day of shrimping, fish hatcheries provide tours to showcase the process of growing fish, and trout ponds eagerly await guests ready to cast their lines.

## Choose-and-Cut Christmas Trees

Georgia is home to almost 100 Christmas tree farms, including several farms that offer choose-and-cut trees. The bulk of the Christmas tree farms are located in mountain regions where the higher altitudes and cooler temperatures are more conducive to growing evergreens. In terms of varieties, Georgia growers focus on Leyland cypress, Carolina Sapphire and Blue Ice cypress, Virginia pine, white pine, and red cedar. Many choose-and-cut farms also offer Fraser firs, which don't grow in Georgia but their popularity leads growers to ship trees in from Virginia and North Carolina. All of the farms listed in this section allow customers to trek into the fields to cut their own Christmas trees but also offer other activities to help inspire the holiday spirit.

### Apple Orchards

Ellijay is known as the Apple Capital of Georgia, and the glut of apple orchards in the Blue Ridge and Valley Region warranted a separate section to highlight the apple houses in the region. Most of the orchards sell fresh apples through an on-farm store, and several also invite visitors to trek into the orchards to pick their own apples straight from the trees.

### Vineyards, Wineries, and Distilleries

Georgia has a small but growing number of wineries. In the southern part of the state, most of the vineyards grow muscadines, which are used to make sweet wines; in North Georgia, vinifera grapes used to produce European-style wines like Merlot and Chardonnay are more popular. There is a divide between muscadine and vinifera growers, each believing their wines are superior. Instead of rating the wines, the book includes wineries that provide the best experiences, from outstanding locations and unique tasting rooms to excellent customer service. Craft distillers are becoming increasingly popular in Georgia. It's become a trend to use locally grown crops and traditional distilling methods to produce small batches of rum, whiskey, and vodka.

### Festivals and Events

Georgia loves to celebrate its agricultural heritage. Throughout the year, festivals celebrate peaches, blueberries, green beans, and shrimp and grits and events honor historic mills and new wineries. Listings in this section also include agricultural fairs, farm tours, workshops, and other limited-time happenings.

### Specialty Shops

In restored farmhouses, on historic squares, and, sometimes, in gleaming strip malls, stores stocked with locally grown, locally made products abound. The listings in this section feature stores such as community food co-ops, specialty food stores, and gift shops that carry farm-fresh produce or gourmet "Georgia Grown" items that are difficult to find elsewhere. This section also includes nurseries that specialize in native plants, medicinal herbs, and edibles.

## Farm-to-Table Restaurants

All of the restaurants included in this section are committed to using food from local farms. Some of the chefs have their own farms, while others grow gardens on restaurant rooftops, but all maintain relationships with local farms to source the freshest local ingredients to feature on their menus. Most farm-to-table restaurants are centered in urban areas and tend to feature more expensive menus than restaurants that don't use local ingredients. Every attempt was made to feature establishments in every region and a range of price points.

## Lodging

There is nothing quite like waking up to the cock-a-doodle-doo of the resident rooster. To offer a true farm experience, working farms, ranches, and wineries all over Georgia welcome guests to spend the night. The accommodations range from bunking in a Conestoga wagon and sleeping in a converted tobacco barn to cozying up on bunk beds in the saddle house on a horse farm.

## Glossary, Appendixes, Index

A glossary of farm terms appears at the end of the book to help make sense of words like "abattoir," "feedlot," and "organic," along with a list of suggested resources for further reading, watching, or web surfing and a county-by-county listing of sites to help locate all of the listings at a glance.

### Dining Price Key

| | |
|---|---|
| $ | Inexpensive; most entrees under $15 |
| $$ | Moderate; most entrees $15–$25 |
| $$$ | Expensive; most entrees over $25 |

### Lodging Price Key

| | |
|---|---|
| $ | Inexpensive; rooms under $100 |
| $$ | Moderate; rooms $100–$150 |
| $$$ | Expensive; rooms $150–$200 |
| $$$$ | Deluxe; rooms over $200 |

**Talk to Me**

Although I spent a year on the road researching the destinations included in the book (and, with very few exceptions, visited each of the places featured), things will change in the time between research and publication: Farmers will alter their courses, schedules will change, chefs will move on, businesses will close (or open). I'll continue researching in the hopes of updating any glitches, but if you visit a place you'd like to see included in the next edition, or if you see anything that needs updating, clarifying, or correcting, please let me know by writing to jodi@jodihelmer.com. Meanwhile, I will post all updates at www.farmfreshgeorgia.com.

## TIPS FOR VISITING FARMS

Most of the farms included in the book are farms first, tourist destinations second. For farmers, the first priorities are to the crops and livestock, not giving tours and posing for pictures. Remember to honor their hours of operation (if no hours are posted, call ahead) and avoid showing up early or staying late.

Do your part to support local farms. Many farms offer free or nominally priced tours. If you visit, consider purchasing fresh produce or other goods. Your support helps these farms operate.

Dress for an agricultural experience. Working farms often do not have asphalt parking lots or paved trails, so it's best to wear sturdy shoes that are suitable for trekking in barns, pastures, and fields; rubber boots can be hosed off in case of an unfortunate encounter with animal-produced "fertilizer" are a safe bet. Be prepared with bottled water, hand sanitizer, sunscreen, and insect repellant.

A lot of agritourism destinations have petting zoos where visitors are encouraged to interact with livestock to collect eggs, bottle-feed a calf, or nuzzle a goat. But not all working farms have the same policies. Before reaching out to touch a buffalo or chasing down a barn cat, ask the farmer if animal interactions are allowed.

Keep a close watch on the little ones, keeping them away from farm tools and equipment and monitoring their interactions with animals.

Assume all fences are "hot" or electric. To keep livestock in their pastures, farmers keep their fences turned on. Don't touch the fences (or attempt to crawl between the wires to get into the pasture) or you'll get shocked.

Leave pets at home. No matter how well behaved Fido and Fluffy might be, pets do not mix well with cows, ducks, goats, chickens, sheep, pigs, alpacas, and the farm dogs trained to protect their charges.

Have fun! Visiting a farm is a great opportunity to see where your food comes from and connect with the farmers who grow and raise it. Ask questions, take pictures, make memories, and show your appreciation for their work and their time.

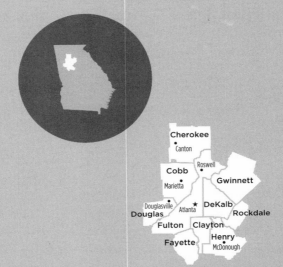

# Atlanta Metro

Atlanta is the biggest city in Georgia, and its metro region is home to award-winning restaurants, creative chefs, farmers' markets, farm stands, and small-scale farms. It has all of the trappings of a typical urban environment from skyscrapers and city parks to freeways and traffic jams, but roots of farming culture are alive and well in The ATL. Urban farmers tend raised beds overflowing with tomatoes, peppers, okra, and collard greens; parks and parking lots blossom into farmers' markets on weekends; and chefs design restaurant menus around seasonal bounty.

## FARMS

### Cagle's Family Farm

The Cagle family has been farming in Cherokee County for five generations. The farm still operates as a working dairy, and the cows are the main attraction of agritourism activities: In the animal barn, small hands clutching handfuls of hay are thrust at calves, followed by giggles of glee when fuzzy ruminants accept the offerings. There are more excited squeals in the milking parlor where a patient Holstein is hooked up to a stainless-steel milking machine for a demonstration. In an effort to live up to the tagline, "Even the fun is fresh," Cagle's provides all of the trappings of a traditional agritourism operation: In the fall, the farm offers a corn maze, hayrides, a haunted barn, and a pumpkin patch, and there are enough goats, sheep, pigs, ducks, and chickens to make the farm feel like a petting zoo.

362 Stringer Road, Canton (Cherokee County), 770-345-5591, www.caglesfamilyfarm.com

## Joyful Noise Acres Farm

Mary Beth Sellars grew up in rural Georgia but moved to Atlanta in the 1990s after she got married. Her husband, Chip, was a real estate agent whose clients wanted urban homes and condominiums. After eighteen months in Atlanta, Mary Beth tired of the hustle and bustle and longed to return to the country. She convinced Chip to trade his BMW for a pickup truck to join her on a farm. "He didn't know what he was getting into when he married me!" she jokes.

Mary Beth wasn't sure what she was getting into either. From a small homestead with a vegetable garden and a few chickens, the couple expanded to a twenty-one-acre farm where pigs and chickens roam the pastures and the demand for pork and eggs led the couple to set up farmers' market booths and open a farm stand. Instead of driving clients to showings in a luxury sedan, Chip drives the tractor on farm tours.

"There is such a huge push in the local food movement to see where your food comes from, and we wanted to open the farm to visitors, to show them how their food is raised," Mary Beth says. "We are not a fun outing like a pumpkin patch or a corn maze—but the little kids love chasing the barn cats. This is an educational tour, a chance for people to see the farm and learn about the source of their food. The best part of the tour is seeing the looks on their faces when they see the animals up close."

The tours, offered by appointment between March and November, have proven popular. For Mary Beth, finding a partner who shares her passion for living off the land has made achieving a lifelong dream to own a farm even sweeter.

620 Allison Lane, Ball Ground (Cherokee County), 770-861-5935, www.pasturedmeats.com

## Ross Berry Farm and Apiaries

After fifteen years as beekeepers, Terry and Jeannie Ross lost most of their 100 hives to colony collapse disorder. Instead of giving up when the 2009 devastation occurred, they started all over again. With forty-five hives on-site, Terry and Jeannie opened up their honey house to sell sticky sweet honey straight from the hives. To promote pollination, the couple planted blueberries, blackberries, figs, grapes, and other fruits and flowers where the bees can feast on nectar. As a result, Ross Berry Farm sells several different varieties of honey, including tulip poplar honey, wildflower honey, sourwood honey, and tupelo honey. A passion for the bees and their honey led Terry to share his beekeeping experience through on-farm classes. The beginning beekeeping course is offered in spring and summer.

159 Watkins Road, Canton (Cherokee County), 770-776-6094, www.rossberryfarm.com

## Tanglewood Farm

Between the bleats of dwarf goats and brays of diminutive donkeys, the sound Michelle Bolt hears most often at Tanglewood Farm is, "Awww, they are so cute!" The ten-acre petting zoo is home to more than 100 miniature animals, and the open-gate policy—visitors are invited to step into the pens to cuddle, nuzzle, and adore all of the animals—led *Atlanta Magazine* to name Tanglewood Farm one of the best attractions in the metro area.

Tanglewood Farm is much more than a petting zoo: Bolt started the farm in 1998 to perfect miniature breeds. "There is a conservation aspect here, too," explains Bolt. "We want to promote, preserve, and protect these rare breeds."

Langshan chickens, an endangered breed from China, are raised on the farm along with miniature Jersey cows (there are just 100 in the world)! Tanglewood Farm is also home to Tiny Bubbles, the smallest registered miniature horse in the world. Most of the miniatures at Tanglewood Farm are part of a breeding program and available for sale, which means the second most common phrase at Tanglewood Farm is, "Should we take her home?"

171 Tanglewood Drive, Canton (Cherokee County), 770-667-6464, www.tanglewoodfarmminiatures.com

## TheArtBarn at Morning Glory Farm

When Susan Shaw needs inspiration for an art project, she doesn't have to look farther than her barn. Her chickens, horses, pigs, and goats are the subjects of most of her work. In search of a quiet place to raise a few animals and operate her graphic design business, "Farmer Sue" bought Morning Glory Farm in 2000. She turned the barn into a studio but found the farm so inspiring that she began hosting art classes in the barn, turning it from a quiet office into a raucous Art Barn. Almost overnight, Shaw went from an entrepreneur to an accidental farm girl. "All of this happened by accident," she says. "I feel like the luckiest girl in the world because I never set out to do this and ended up with such a happy job."

Susan Shaw, better known as Farmer Sue, takes a break from chores at Morning Glory Farm to cuddle up with her favorite chicken, Vera Bradley. Photograph by Amy Hunsinger, courtesy of Farmer Sue.

Farmer Sue knew the barn was "a magical place that inspired creativity." Instead of working in the barn alone, she threw open the pasture gates for school groups and summer camps. Her goal: to incorporate agriculture, education, and art. Wearing her trademark overalls and straw hat, Farmer Sue shows off the vegetables growing in her organic garden, describes the relationship between animals and nature, and introduces the animals: Goats bleat from a rooftop, and a hen named Vera Bradley poses patiently for pictures without so much as a cluck. After exploring the farm, it's off to the barn to create works of art. With simple instructions like "draw a swoosh" and "add a half circle," the brightly colored paints on the farm table start to resemble a chicken. Farmer Sue signs hers: "Find something to crow about every single day!"

208 Roper Road, Canton (Cherokee County), 678-319-0286, www.theartbarn.com

### Stems n Roots Garden

Lorri Mason is used to passersby commenting on her yard. "The thing I hear the most is, 'Wow! This is intense!'" she says. The comments are a source of pride for Mason, who raises chickens and bees and grows vegetables in sixty-four raised beds on her half-acre lot in Douglasville.

When Mason was growing up, her mother kept a garden to help put food on the table for her ten children. Mason decided to try her hand at growing vegetables when she was laid off from a corporate job in 2001. "It took a while to get a feel for the spacing, but once I did, I started growing a little bit of everything," she says.

Her initial efforts yielded a bumper crop, leading Mason to expand her backyard farm and start selling produce at the Piedmont Park Green Market. She grows everything from peaches and peanuts to greens and herbs. Most of the produce Mason grows is sold through the farmers' markets, but she also sells from her urban farm by appointment. Mason also teaches classes. "I want to show people that it's possible to grow a lot of food in their backyard," she says.

3370 Riley Road, Douglasville (Douglas County), 404-509-7137

## Archibald Smith Plantation House

Just outside of picturesque downtown Roswell, with its upscale boutiques and gluten-free cupcake shops, the Archibald Smith Plantation House is a step back in time. Built in 1838, it was home to a cotton farmer named Archibald Smith. The farmhouse and several outbuildings, including the slave quarters, cookhouse, barn, corncrib, and well, have been restored. The current plantation is much smaller than the original 300 acres that Smith tended, but it remains an important piece of the historic and agricultural heritage of Roswell.

935 Alpharetta Street, Roswell (Fulton County), 770-641-3978, www.archibaldsmithplantation.org

## Atlanta Botanical Garden

Since the first spade penetrated the soil in 1973, the thirty-acre award-winning Atlanta Botanical Garden has been regarded as an oasis filled with formal gardens and exotic plants. Adjacent to Piedmont Park, the site of the popular weekend Green Market, the garden staff took some inspiration from the growing urban food movement—and the White House garden—and added an edible garden in 2010. Each season, the garden is filled with something new—apple blossoms in the spring and colorful kale and wisps of asparagus in the fall—making it as beautiful as it is functional. "We wanted to show the aesthetic value of edibles," explains Amanda Campbell, manager of display gardens. "These plants have a lot of value as food, but they can look really beautiful, too."

## A Friend to Farmers

With a mission to promote "good food for all," Georgia Organics fosters connections between farmers, chefs, businesses, advocates, and consumers to promote local, organic agriculture. Over the past decade, Georgia Organics has worked to increase the number of organic and sustainable farmers in the state through mentorship programs, urban agriculture training programs, workshops, and an annual conference. In addition to legislative lobbying and other efforts to shape food policy in Georgia, the nonprofit organization has launched farm-to-school programs; sponsored Wholesome Wave, an organization that doubles each dollar spent at farmers' markets for those who receive federal or state nutrition benefits; and worked with the Atlanta Local Food Initiative to develop policies for farmers' markets in Atlanta. As part of their annual membership, farmers benefit from inclusion in the Local Food Guide and access to a Farmer Mentoring Program as well as a host of other resources, making the member-supported organization one of the top resources for Georgia farmers.

Unlike plantings in the Japanese garden, rose garden, and rock garden that even the most skilled horticulturalists could only aspire to, the edible garden is meant to serve as an inspiration. "It's one of our most popular gardens, hands down," Campbell says. "Being in an urban area, people are always curious to see what they can grow, especially in smaller spaces like containers."

Produce from the garden is used during weekend chef demonstrations and cooking classes. A significant amount of produce is also donated to local charities like the Atlanta Food Bank.

1345 Piedmont Avenue NE, Atlanta (Fulton County), 404-876-5859, www.atlantabotanicalgarden.org

## Atwood Community Gardens and Urban Farm

NEXT Steps Youth Entrepreneur Program operates an urban farm to teach students about careers in science, technology, engineering, and math while building leadership and management skills in a farm setting. The nonprofit launched a 3.5-acre training center in 2012 that includes an urban farm complete with vegetable beds, a chicken coop, and goat pens. Young entrepreneurs lead tours that include farm chores, educational and arts activities, and cooking demonstrations with ingredients from the garden. On Thursday evenings, the farm hosts a farmers' market to increase the availability of fresh local produce to residents of the local community.

The farm also supports sustainable food businesses launched by young entrepreneurs, including a vegan and organic catering company, a farmers' market management business, and natural foods retailers.

779 Atwood Street SW, Atlanta (Fulton County), 678-570-0398, www.nextstepsyep.org

## Habersham Gardens

It's not uncommon to have to park along a side street and walk several blocks to reach Habersham Gardens. Tucked into the Morningside neighborhood, the garden center lacks a parking lot, but that doesn't deter crowds. Walt and Deborah Harrison opened the garden center in 1995 (Walt has been running a successful landscaping company, Habersham Gardens Landscape Services, since 1978, but Deborah decided a retail nursery would be a nice complement to the business), and it's become one of the most popular places in Atlanta to purchase annuals, perennials, and trees. The increased interest in growing food has led to more shoppers coming into the garden center to find seeds, vegetable starts, and berry bushes. "In the last few years, edibles have become a lot more popular, medicinal herbs, too," says Walt. "People really like the idea of growing their own foods." Walt counts pawpaws, figs, blueberries, and medicinal herbs like hyssop as among the most popular edible plants and medicinal herbs sold at Habersham Gardens. He believes that customers count on the neighborhood garden center to provide "plants that are unique, that can't be found in the big box stores."

A robust calendar of events includes gardening workshops on a range of topics from container gardening and growing herbs to tending orchids. Habersham Gardens also promotes organic growing methods. Shelves are stocked with organic fertilizers, and the nursery even sells ladybugs to help manage garden pests.

Rembrandt and Gardener, two of the nursery's resident dogs, aren't much help with picking out vegetable starts or offering advice about cross pollinating persimmon trees, but both will eagerly accept belly rubs.

2067 Manchester Street NE, Atlanta (Fulton County), 404-873-2484, www.habershamgardens.com

## Patchwork City Farms

When the school bell rings at Brown Middle School, there is a good chance that Cecilia Gatungo and Jamila Norman are outside the classrooms, digging in the dirt. Their farm, Patchwork City Farms, is located on school grounds in what Gatungo describes as "the first commercial operation on the grounds of one of Atlanta's public schools."

Gatungo and Norman met at a neighborhood cleanup in 2008. While working on trash patrol, the women discovered a shared determination to make a difference in their historic West End neighborhood. "The area is considered a food desert," Gatungo says. "We decided that if there wasn't a local grocery store to provide [fresh, healthy food], we would grow it ourselves."

A series of fortunate events led the pair to lease a one-acre lot on the grounds of Brown Middle School. The "intensively planted" market garden is filled with dozens of varieties of fruits and vegetables, which are sold through the West End Farmers' and Artisans' Market, the East Atlanta Village Farmers' Market and the Grant Park Farmers' Market. Gatungo and Norman do some on-farm sales and lead tours, both by appointment. "Most people are amazed that there is such a resource in our neighborhood," says Gatungo.

765 Peeples Street, Atlanta (Fulton County), 404-665-7138

## Farmers Are a Hit in Hollywood

Filmmakers Christine Anthony and Owen Masterson had no idea that their first feature-length documentary would be so well received. *GROW!* follows a new generation of Georgia farmers, documenting the joys and challenges of working the land.

The film debuted at the annual Georgia Organics conference in March 2011 and went on to win several awards, including Best American Documentary at the 2011 Rome Film Festival, Best Documentary Short at the 2011 Asheville Cinema Festival, and Audience Choice at the 2011 Atlanta DocuFest.

"We made [the documentary] in part as a response to films like Food Inc., that showed how screwed up things are [and] leaned heavily on the problems without focusing on the solutions," says Anthony. "We wanted to show the positive side, show all of the ways you could farm sustainably and do it without owning land."

Anthony and Masterson, who live in Atlanta, spent an entire season with twelve farmers, all from Georgia farms, including Many Fold Farm, Hope Grows Farm, Jenny Jack Sun Farm, and Serenbe Farms. "We didn't plan it, but the timing was perfect," Anthony says. "The economy was bad and there was a generation starting to question old values and norms, who knew their hearts and passions were in agriculture. Every farmer in the movie knew they were part of a movement and felt really proud of their work."

## Scharko Farms

Tony and Linda Scharko bill themselves as "a couple of old hippies" growing produce at the only urban farm in Fairburn. It does seem like the couple is having a love-in with the land, using sustainable methods and biodynamic principles to grow vegetables, herbs, and cut flowers on their four-acre farm. During the growing season, Tony and Linda host sustainable gardening workshops and potluck suppers on the farm. The farm was established in 1968 and is one of the few remaining small family farms in the area. A visit to the roadside produce stand at the farm reveals what has kept the couple successfully working the land for more than four decades: passion for the simple pleasure of digging in the dirt.

240 East Campbellton Street, Fairburn (Fulton County), 770-964-9074

## Serenbe Farms

When Paige Witherington arrived at Serenbe Farms in 2006, the twenty-five-acre parcel of land in the Serenbe community was nothing more than a slab of red clay and granite. With the help of compost, cover crops, and crop rotation, Witherington, the farm manager, transformed the landscape into a thriving certified organic farm that grows 350 varieties of fruits, vegetables, herbs, and mushrooms. The farm also raises laying hens. "It was one of the worse possible pieces of farmland in the state. It's been so cool to see that you can take awful land and grow a lot of really pretty food on it," says Witherington.

A passionate advocate for organic agriculture, Witherington offers farm tours, manages a CSA, and hosts the Serenbe Farmers and Artists Market on Saturday mornings from May to November. Witherington estimates that at least 50 percent of the produce sold at the market is consumed within ten miles of the farm. "It's important to take time to form connections over food, to slow down and understand and appreciate where your food comes from," says Witherington.

8457 Atlanta Newnan Road, Chattahoochee Hills (Fulton County), 678-764-8273, www.serenbefarms.com

Paige Witherington manages Serenbe Farms, providing produce for a local CSA, a farmers' market, and area restaurants.

## Smith Family Farm

For a glimpse of historic farm life in the heart of the city, the Atlanta History Center has preserved the Smith Family Farm. In 1845, Robert H. Smith farmed more than 800 acres east of Atlanta. The farmhouse and open-hearth kitchen, both listed on the National Register of Historic Places, were relocated to the current site in the 1970s and turned into the centerpiece of a historic homestead.

Exploring the dairy, chicken coop, blacksmith shop, smokehouse, corncrib, and barn offers a glimpse of farming centuries ago, inspiring comments like, "Can you imagine running a farm with such crude equipment?" Even the grounds are historically accurate, featuring a slave garden as well as patches of corn and cotton. But the vegetable garden, overflowing with heirloom produce, looks much like backyard gardens popping up across the nation, proving that history does repeat itself.

130 West Paces Ferry Road NW, Atlanta (Fulton County), 404-814-4000, www.atlantahistorycenter.com

### Truly Living Well Farm

It's impossible to label Truly Living Well Farm. The eleven-acre farm in the heart of Atlanta is an urban farm with CSA subscriptions and a weekly farmers' market, but it's so much more, thanks to founder Rashid Nuri. "Agriculture is my calling, my mission, what God told me to do," says Nuri. "America is an urban society, and people have become so disconnected from their food. I want to reconnect people back to the soil."

With a background that includes a graduate degree in plant and soil science, managing agricultural programs in more than thirty countries, a decade with agribusiness giant Cargill, and a stint as the deputy administrator of the Farm Service Agency and Foreign Agricultural Service during the Clinton administration, Nuri has both the passion and the knowledge to meet his goal. He leased a plot of land in Atlanta's most famous African American neighborhood (the farm is around the corner from Ebenezer Baptist Church, where Martin Luther King preached), and crops are cultivated on the site of a dilapidated apartment complex where concrete foundations are still visible beneath some of the raised beds. Truly Living Well Farm has produced upwards of 10,000 pounds of produce annually since its inaugural season in 2006. The crops range from tomatoes and turnips to pawpaws and pineapples.

In addition to the farmers' market and CSA, organically grown produce from Truly Living Well Farm is sold to local farm-to-table restaurants like Empire State South and Restaurant Eugene. As a nod to Nuri's passion for education, the farm also serves as an outdoor classroom, teaching the community about sustainable urban agriculture through classes, internships, and summer camps. Along with giving helpful advice, Truly Living Well Farm also sells compost and plants to help new urban agrarians start their own gardens.

75 Hilliard Street NE, Atlanta (Fulton County), 404-520-8331, www.trulylivingwell.com

### Rancho Alegre

Pilar Quintero transitioned Rancho Alegre from an equestrian farm to an agritourism destination in 2007 because she wanted to expose kids to how their food was produced. "We want to show kids what a tomato looks like when it's still on the vine," she says. During field trips and tours, activities include milking goats, collecting eggs, and grooming horses as well as tours of the chicken coop, pig pasture, garden, and beehives. Although the farm is spread across twenty-one acres, Quintero has limited the amount of space dedicated to food production. "We want to show people that they can grow a lot of food in their backyards and that it's not rocket science," she says. "In the garden, the teachers and parents always have more questions than the kids because there is such a buzz about growing food and sustainable agriculture."

Realizing that the farm is in a food desert, Quintero opened a country store to sell honey, eggs, and raw milk from Rancho Alegre and other farms in the county to reinforce the connection between the farm and the food on the table. "More people want to know their farmer, know their food and we have a passion for sustainable agriculture that we want to share with people," Quintero says.

2225 Givens Road, Dacula (Gwinnett County), 770-339-3065, www.ranchoalegrefarm.com

## Pumpkin Patch at Yule Forest Highway 155

Allen and Susie Grant are the fourth generation to work the thirty-acre parcel of land on Highway 155. Although the couple still grows pumpkins (as well as blueberries in the spring and Christmas trees in the winter), the farm is as much an agricultural museum as a pumpkin patch. Susie Grant calls the farm "an agritourism and educational farm."

An outdoor classroom includes exhibits about life on the farm, Georgia crops, and famous farmers, while the science center building has reptiles. Grant believes that education needs to be fun, too, which means the farm has popular agritourism activities like a haunted house, a corn cannon, hayrides, and a small petting zoo. Of course, there's also a pumpkin patch.

13 Reagan Road, Stockbridge (Henry County), 770-954-9356, www.aboutyule.com

## Southern Belle Farm

Although Jake Carter grew up on Southern Belle Farm helping muck out stalls and feed cattle, the third-generation dairy-farmer-turned-cattle-rancher realized that his experience was unique. "We started noticing that kids in our area are two or three generations removed from the farm," he explains. "We wanted to help bring them back to the farm, to connect them with the source of their food and show them a good time."

The Carters decided to open their picture-perfect 200-acre farm to the public in 2005. It's still a working ranch, but on weekends, the pumpkin patch, corn maze, hayrides, petting zoo, and milking demonstrations make the main crop homegrown agricultural entertainment. The pig races are

The fall festivities and pastoral setting at Southern Belle Farm draws crowds from across the state.

one of the highlights of the weekend. The crowd cheers when "Boss Hog" releases four piglets with names like Miss Piggy and Kermit the Hog that speed across land and water to reach the finish line.

When Carter exclaims, "Opening up our farm and sharing what we do is our passion," there is no doubt he's sincere.

1767 Turner Church Road, McDonough (Henry County), 770-288-2582, www.southernbellefarm.com

## FARMERS' MARKETS

### Farmers Atlanta Road Market

To create a fellowship between local farmers and area residents, parishioners at St. Benedict's Episcopal Church started a farmers' market. Since 2009, Farmers Atlanta Road Market (FARM) hosts up to twenty farms and food producers selling items ranging from meat, eggs, and vegetables to homemade pasta, baked goods, and flowers. The founders decided to hold the market on Tuesday evenings between April and November hoping that the midweek schedule would help improve access to Georgia-grown, Georgia-made foods. In keeping with their mission to promote local foods, the market is only open to producers; resellers are not allowed.

2160 Cooper Lake Road, Smyrna (Cobb County), www.farmersatlantaroadmarket.org

## Get the Most from the Farmers' Market

There is no better place to shop for fresh, local produce than the farmers' market, but weaving through the morning crowds and checking out produce offered by dozens of vendors can feel a little overwhelming. Here are a few tips to make the most of the farmers' market:

*Arrive early*: The best selection of produce is available first thing in the morning. The market is also less crowded when it first opens, making it easier to talk to farmers.

*... or late*: The produce might be picked over, but the end of the market is also the best time to score a deal. Farmers don't want to pack up unsold produce and haul it back home.

*Ask questions*: Not sure how to cook kohlrabi? Want to make sure the peaches were picked at their peak? Don't be afraid to ask questions. Farmers want to talk about their produce.

*Be prepared*: Bring small bills so farmers won't have to make change, and remember to carry canvas bags to tote fresh produce. The lines move faster (and farmers are grateful) when shoppers think ahead.

*Look for local producers*: The best part of the farmers' market is buying fresh produce from local farmers. Some markets have loose rules that allow resellers to offer produce that was grown out of state (and, sometimes, out of the country). If the signage in their booths doesn't clearly identify the origin of the fruits, vegetables, dairy, meat, and eggs, ask.

## Marietta Square Farmers Market

On Saturdays and Sundays between April and November, up to sixty vendors set up tents on picturesque Marietta Square and welcome shoppers in search of fresh vegetables, grass-fed beef, free-range eggs, baked goods, and seedlings. The market, one of few open all weekend, attracts both farmers and backyard gardeners with excess produce. The market started with a few vendors who set up tents in a church parking lot in 2006. Since then, it's been voted one of the top ten markets in the Atlanta metro area and has a waiting list of vendors eager for market stalls to become available.

65 Church Street, Marietta (Cobb County),
www.mariettasquarefarmersmarket.net

## Dunwoody Green Market

When selecting its sellers, "green" is Dunwoody Green Market's middle name. All thirty of the market's vendors make or grow what they sell, and most of the produce vendors are either certified organic or Certified Naturally Grown. Visitors rave about the quality of Dunwoody's products—which range from produce and meats to honey, eggs, dairy, and prepared foods—and many vendors have won awards. In 2010, Goodness Gracious's hand-blended, baked granola—which uses 60 to 80 percent organic ingredients—won the "snack foods" category in the annual Flavor of Georgia contest. CalyRoad Creamery's soft goat cheese also took home top honors. Pine Street's bacon samples are another market favorite, as are the Red Queen Tarts, oozing with red plum, brown sugar, bourbon, and mixed-berry fillings. The market's website and Facebook page feature a multitude of mouthwatering recipes.

4681 Ashford Dunwoody Road, Dunwoody (DeKalb County),
www.dunwoodygreenmarket.com

## Decatur Farmers Market

The market is held on Wednesday evenings and Saturday mornings and features a rotating cast of farmers and food producers (the website shows an updated list of vendors before each Wednesday evening and Saturday morning market). While the vendors might change from week to week, the market insists that anyone selling at the market use organic and sustainable methods to grow or produce their products.

163 Clairemont Avenue, Decatur (DeKalb County), 404-377-0894,
www.decaturfarmersmarket.com

## East Atlanta Village Farmers Market

There is never a dull moment at the Thursday night market: hula hoop competitions, a dancing peach, and goat-milking demonstrations are commonplace. Several farms participate in the market, including Country Gardens Farm, Love Is Love Farm, and the Edgewood Farm Crew (all are Certified Naturally Grown or grown organically to meet market regulations). Most of the vendors at the weeknight market, which runs from April through December, sell prepared foods, including goat's milk cheese from Decimal Place Farm, breads from H&F Bread Co., and pesto from Hope's Gardens. The combination of farm-fresh foods and gourmet goodies makes it a great place to grab an evening nosh.

561 Flat Shoals Avenue, Atlanta (Fulton County),
www.farmeav.com

## Peachtree Road Farmers Market

On Saturday mornings between April and December, the faithful come to worship at the Cathedral of St. Phillip. Their altars are the booths overflowing with produce, meat, and cheese. Although the market has only been around since 2006, it has already become the largest producer-only market in the state and earned accolades as the best place to get produce by the *Atlanta Journal-Constitution.*

All of the farmers and ranchers who sell at the market must grow or raise their products while maintaining certified organic or Certified Naturally Grown status. Even the prepared food vendors face strict regulations to ensure their gourmet goodies use locally grown foods.

2744 Peachtree Road NW, Atlanta (Fulton County), 404-365-1000,
www.peachtreeroadfarmersmarket.com

## Atlanta State Farmers Market

Onions from Peru, star fruit from Indonesia, and avocados from California make the Atlanta State Farmers Market look more like an international grocer than a market for local growers. Look past the eighteen-wheelers and refrigerated trucks pulled up to the loading docks that double as market stalls (the market is a central distribution point for fresh produce) and there are local vendors. An entire section of the market is dedicated to produce grown by local farmers who are identified by "Georgia Grown" signs.

The market, also called the Georgia State Farmers Market and the Forest Park Farmers Market, is operated by the Georgia Department of Agriculture and, at 150 acres, is considered the largest market of its kind in the world. The market is open 24/7 to facilitate distribution, but most local vendors sell produce, meat, and eggs on weekends.

16 Forest Parkway, Forest Park (Fulton County), 404-675-1782, www.atlantaproducedealers.org

### Emory Farmers Market

On Tuesday afternoons, between lectures and intramural sports, faculty and students at Emory University shop for fresh produce, meat, honey, bread, and cheese at the Cox Hall Bridge. The weekly farmers' market is open to the entire community with a goal of providing healthy food choices in a convenient setting. Like all things collegial, the market offers educational opportunities, too. Faculty often give talks that coincide with market offerings: At the annual Yam Festival in October, a curator of African art from the university discussed the importance of yams to tribes in West Africa, and a partnership with Coca-Cola and the National Peanut Board during the Boiled Peanut Celebration highlighted the scientific reaction that occurs when peanuts are dropped into a bottle of Coke.

201 Dowman Drive, Atlanta (Fulton County), 404-727-6123, www.emory.edu/dining/emory_farmers_market.php

### Morningside Farmers' Market

It's worth setting the alarm on Saturday to be one of the first to arrive at the Morningside market. On any given Saturday, the scent of fresh herbs and artisan breads fill the air in the Virginia Highland neighborhood.

Established in the 1980s as a farmer cooperative, the small but thriving market has remained true to its roots and operates as the only market in Georgia where producers must be certified organic. Chef demonstrations have been a staple of the weekly market for more than twenty years; a brand new Shop with a Chef program expands on the concept by inviting a local chef to create a dish inspired by produce available in the market each week.

1393 North Highland Avenue, Atlanta (Fulton County), www.morningsidemarket.com

## Healing in the Garden

At Wesley Woods Hospital, an acute-care facility for senior citizens at Emory University, it's more common to find patients walking along garden paths or repotting perennials than engaged in rehab in the hospital's physical therapy department. Thanks to the Horticulture Therapy Program, founded in 1993, the hospital incorporated gardening activities into its rehabilitation program, allowing patients to heal in nature. To aid in rehabilitation exercises that include walking and working on range of motion and fine motor skills, the gardens include concrete floors for walker and wheelchair accessibility and standing-height planters. The gardens are also filled with heirloom plants that dementia patients may recognize from their childhoods. It's the only hospital in Atlanta with a registered horticultural therapist on staff to deliver programming.

## Piedmont Park Green Market

One of the prettiest parks in Atlanta is home to one of the most popular farmers' markets in The Big Peach. Voted one of the top five farmers' markets in Atlanta, the Piedmont Park Green Market is also one of the fastest growing, drawing upwards of forty vendors each week between May and December. Inside the Twelfth Street entrance, colorful booths flank paved trails that wind through the park. With products ranging from fresh produce and eggs to flowers and prepared foods, it's common to see shoppers stocking up on groceries as well as joggers stopping for a postrun snack. The park visitor center adjacent to the market features chef demonstrations, cooking classes, and canning workshops.

400 Park Drive NE, Atlanta (Fulton County), 404-875-7275,
www.piedmontpark.org/programs/green_market.html

## Sweet Auburn Curb Market

In the 1920s, Sweet Auburn Curb Market was the premier greenmarket in Atlanta. Back then, farmers traveled from across the region to sell fresh produce and livestock. The market has changed—several of the booths are vacant and resellers dominate the market floor selling exotic fruits and vegetables. "Local farmers are reluctant to have booths here because they don't think they can compete with resellers on pricing," explains vendor relations manager Anissa Harris. "We are offering incentives to get local farmers to come back to the market because we know it has potential."

Harris is committed to revitalizing the market, wooing new vendors like Country Produce and The Farm Stand and farm-to-table restaurants like Arepa Mia. To support the efforts of local farms, Harris also launched an on-site composting program. All of the food scraps collected from market vendors are composted, and the soil is used to grow fruits and vegetables at the Truly Living Well Farm in Atlanta. "We are working hard to make this one of the best markets in Atlanta," Harris says.

209 Edgewood Avenue SE, Atlanta (Fulton County), 404-659-1665, www.sweetauburncurbmarket.com

## Whistle Stop Farmer's Market

Named for the train tracks that run along the edge of the market in Thrasher Park, the Whistle Stop was voted one of the top five farmers' markets in Georgia. On Tuesday evenings from May through September, upwards of thirty-five vendors set up tents at the market near historic downtown Norcross to sell everything from produce, eggs, and milk to fresh bread, gourmet sauces, and all-natural dog treats. A packed calendar of special events includes cooking demonstrations, petting zoos, health screenings, and crafts activities for kids. A true community market, Whistle Stop has donated supplies to local community gardens and elementary schools and sponsored gardening classes and conferences.

1 Park Drive NW, Norcross (Gwinnett County), www.norcrossfarmersmarket.com

## FARM STANDS AND U-PICKS

### Gardner Farm

The Gardner family has been growing peaches in Henry County for five generations. At first, all of the fruit that passed through the packing shed was shipped to markets. When the orchard produced more fruit than the family needed to fill orders, the excess peaches were sold through a road-side stand. "A few bushels of peaches were set out by the road and people stopped to buy them," says Ansley Glenn.

Today, all of the peaches grown on the thirty-acre orchard are sold on the farm, either through the produce stand or U-pick. "All of the peaches are picked, hand-sorted and sold right here," Glenn says. "It's the freshest fruit you'll find."

Gardner Farm also grows blueberries and blackberries for U-pick, along with vegetables like tomatoes, peppers, squash, and zucchini that are sold at the farm stand, which is staffed by the Gardner family.

3192 Highway 42, Locust Grove (Henry County), 770-957-4912,
www.gardnerfarm.wordpress.com

## DAIRIES

### CalyRoad Creamery

All of the cheeses in the glass cases at CalyRoad Creamery are made with milk from local farms. Trained at the Vermont Institute of Artisan Cheese, cheesemonger Robin Schick combines skill and passion into ricotta, chèvre, feta, Halloumi, and aged goat cheese; her Camembert earned top honor in the Flavor of Georgia competition.

All of the cheeses are made on-site: Watch the artisan cheese-making process through a glass window between the shop and the manufacturing floor, and pull up a chair at the tasting table to sample the artisan cheeses. The shop also offers classes.

While the shop is the best place to stock up on CalyRoad Creamery cheeses, Schick also sells cheese at several farmers' markets, including the Sandy Springs Farmers Market, the Marietta Square Farmers Market, and the Dunwoody Green Market.

227 Hilderbrand Drive NE, Sandy Springs (Fulton County), 678-773-1629,
www.calyroadcreamery.com

## Using Software to Grow Salad

As a software engineer, Matt Liotta was more comfortable programming code than planting seeds. Growing up in Atlanta, he'd never flipped through a seed catalog, ordered compost, or fretted about plant starts. But in 2010, the techie geek became a farmer. With a high-tech twist, of course.

After selling his telecommunications company in 2008, Liotta took some time off to develop new business ideas. His latest venture, PodPonics, was a result of a trip to the supermarket. Walking through the produce aisle, he was shocked to find that most of the produce came from other countries. The solution to increasing local food production, he decided, was to apply his software engineering skills to farming. Liotta designed a computer system to control the light, temperature, water, and humidity in a recycled shipping container, turning the metal box into an urban farm. PodPonics produces five varieties of lettuce—Cherokee, red romaine, Tiede, Vulcan, and Tropicana—in eight decommissioned shipping containers. "I wanted to produce food where it was consumed," he says. "By controlling the lighting, humidity, and $CO_2$ levels with a software program, I can get the lettuce to be as fast growing as possible."

Each container has an output equivalent to 1.5 acres of farmland. PodPonics grows about five tons of lettuce annually for farm-to-table restaurants and specialty grocers. "I figured there would be some skepticism and worried that people wouldn't want to buy lettuce that was grown in a metal box but customers love it, they think it's really cool," says Liotta.

## AtlantaFresh Creamery

AtlantaFresh is one of the only artisan producers of Greek yogurt in the country. Each batch is handmade on-site with milk from Johnston Family Farm, a local dairy where the cows are pastured, grass-fed, and free of hormones and antibiotics. The fillings used in flavors like ginger peach and wildflower honey yogurts are made on-site using traditional recipes. Its yogurt is stocked at Whole Foods Markets and farmers' markets around Atlanta, but the best selection (and the lowest prices) are found at the Company Store. The real reason to skip the supermarket and go straight to the source: the samples. All of the yogurt flavors are available for taste testing, and the creamery routinely offers taste previews of its new flavors and products that are not yet available to the public. Tours of the creamery are available by appointment.

6679 Peachtree Industrial Boulevard, Suite M, Norcross (Gwinnett County), 678-240-4660, www.atlantafresh.com

## Many Fold Farm

At Many Fold Farm, choosing which tour to sign up for is a little like picking extracurricular activities at college: There are a lot of options, and each one sounds promising. Ross and Rebecca Williams, high-school-sweethearts-turned-sustainable-farmers, offer behind-the-scenes tours of the creamery, hands-on experiences with the sheep, pigs, and chickens, as well as a two-day package that includes participation in all aspects of cheese-making from milking to making—and tasting—cheese.

The couple raises sheep, using their milk to make farmstead cheeses. Instead of making common cheeses like feta, Gouda, and Gruyère in the creamery, they focus on producing small batches of Brebis, a creamy cheese used as pasta filling and the base for cheesecake; and Condor's Ruin, a dense, ash-ripened cheese named after the remains of a family dairy in the Chattahoochee Hills.

7850 Rico Road, Chattahoochee Hills (Fulton County), 770-463-0677, www.manyfoldfarm.com

## WINERIES

### Chateau Élan

A few miles off I-85, past strip malls and cookie-cutter neighborhoods, Chateau Élan offers a glimpse of the French countryside. The winery is the centerpiece of the 3,500-acre estate that includes a hotel, a spa, and golf courses. "We are our own destination," says Douglas Rollins, vice president of marketing.

Chateau Élan was the first vineyard in Georgia to grow vinifera grapes, according to Rollins, and started as a passion project for Dr. Dan Panoz, a pharmaceutical inventor who traded medications for muscadines. The winery grows Chardonnay, Sauvignon Blanc, Riesling, Cabernet, Chambourcin, Sangiovese, and Merlot grapes in one of the prettiest settings in the state.

Those who are curious about what it takes to turn twenty-five acres of grapevines into 25,000 cases of wine can sign up for a guided vineyard tour. The tours, offered on weekends, last an hour and include a glimpse of the vat room, cellar, barrel room, and bottling line as well as a private tasting and keepsake glass. During the week, guests are welcome to explore the grounds on a self-guided tour.

100 Rue Charlemagne, Braselton (Gwinnett County), 678-425-0900, www.chateauelan.com

## FESTIVALS AND EVENTS

### Pumpkin Festival

It might be a theme park complete with laser shows, train rides, and ropes courses, but in the fall, Stone Mountain Park adds traditional rural fun to its urban attractions. The annual Pumpkin Festival, held on weekends in October, started in 2002 and has grown to include scavenger hunts, a pumpkin-based game show, pie-eating contests, pumpkin crafts, and scarecrow decorating games; and the pumpkin patch is filled with pumpkins of all shapes and sizes.

1000 Robert East Lee Boulevard, Stone Mountain (DeKalb County), 770-498-5690, www.stonemountainpark.com

## Sheep Shearing Day

At the Antebellum Plantation and Farmyard, one of the exhibits at Stone Mountain Park, a collection of buildings dating between 1783 and 1875 offer a glimpse into the antebellum and agricultural heritage of Georgia. The farmyard is the most popular part of the exhibit thanks to the animals that call it home. It's a petting zoo, but animal trainers also work hard to teach kids about the animals, including the role of livestock on farms in the late eighteenth and early nineteenth centuries. "All of the potbellied pigs, goats, and sheep are heritage breeds that would have been on the farms at the time the plantations existed," explains public relations manager Jeanine Jones. "The farmyard is historically accurate, which makes it different from a lot of other [petting zoos]."

In May, the Farmyard hosts Sheep Shearing Day. A professional shearer gives all eight of the Southdown sheep their summer haircuts while explaining how it helps the sheep and the ways the wool can be used. "It was something we were doing every spring because the sheep needed it and we thought, this is something our guests would enjoy seeing," says Jones.

1000 Robert E. Lee Boulevard, Stone Mountain (DeKalb County), 770-498-5690, www.stonemountainpark.com

## Afternoon in the Country

Les Dames d'Escoffier International, an organization honoring women in the culinary and beverage industries, hosts Afternoon in the Country annually. The event brings together top chefs and mixologists who use ingredients from organic farms across the state to prepare farm-fresh foods. Renowned farm-to-table restaurants like Abattoir, Empire State South, JCT. Kitchen, and Miller Union serve up creative dishes in the gardens at the Inn at Serenbe, a historic farmhouse outside of Atlanta. Local farms like Brasstown Pork, Greenleaf Farms, Spring Mountain Chicken, White Oak Pastures, and Serenbe Farms also set up tables at the event to share their harvest. The event is a benefit for Georgia Organics.

Fulton County, www.ldeiatlanta.org

## Atlanta Food and Wine Festival

In 2006, Atlanta residents Dominique Love and Elizabeth Feichter were hired to design a campaign for a food and wine festival in Aspen. During one of many trips out West, the pair started talking about the need for a similar festival in Atlanta. Rather than just another festival, Love and Feichter envisioned an event that showcased the culinary traditions of the South. Their vision came to life in 2011. During the first annual Atlanta Food and Wine Festival, 100-plus chefs, mixologists, and growers came together for a weekend of cooking demonstrations, tasting seminars, and panel discussions. One of the highlights of the festival was the tasting tent. The event was wildly popular and has quickly become one of the premier culinary events in the state.

With so many events scheduled throughout the weekend, good planning—and a designated driver—are essential.

Midtown Atlanta (Fulton County), 404-474-7330,
www.atlfoodandwinefestival.com

## Attack of the Killer Tomato Festival

The chefs and mixologists who participate in the annual Attack of the Killer Tomato Festival are stars on the Atlanta culinary scene. For one night, the gastronomic superstars come together to benefit Georgia Organics. The event, which Ford Fry, chef/owner of JCT. Kitchen, introduced in 2009, pairs a chef with a local farmer to create a tomato dish. A panel of judges decides on winners in several categories, including best dish and best drink. Past participants include Tyler Williams of Abattoir and Ryan Smith of Empire State South.

Scoring a ticket to the popular event, hailed as "the single biggest experience in the state of Georgia that introduces consumers to sustainably produced local food and to the farmers who produce it," is a coup—but well worth the price of admission.

1198 Howell Mill Road, Atlanta (Fulton County), 404-355-2252,
www.killertomatofest.com

## Vineyard Fest

This annual event is the place to see and be seen in North Georgia. More than 1,500 people—many of whom could win "best dressed" awards—come to the sellout event. Led on the picturesque grounds of Chateau Élan, Vineyard Fest showcases the red, white, and muscadine wines produced at the winery. The festival also showcases wines from other Georgia vineyards. Winemakers set up booths in the winery and pour samples that complement the food and music. The "grape stomp" is the highlight of the weekend. Douglas Rollins, vice president of marketing, is always surprised at the number of women who are willing to kick off their designer shoes, hike up their skirts, and get grape juice between their toes.

100 Rue Charlemagne, Braselton (Gwinnett County), 678-425-0900, www.chateauelan.com

## Georgia State Fair

The pint-sized attendees at the Georgia State Fair race between rides and exhibits with speed and enthusiasm that almost rivals that of the NASCAR drivers who compete for the checkered flag during races. Most of the attractions at the fair are in keeping with the location at the Atlanta Motor Speedway: flashy and fast. Beyond the blinking lights and buzzers on the midway games and the twirling rides, a makeshift barnyard entices attendees with calves, goats, pigs, donkeys, and other farm animals that submit to enthusiastic embraces and offers of corn and hay. It's a rare chance to interact with livestock in the city. The Georgia State Fair is held twice a year, at the Atlanta Motor Speedway in the fall and at Central City Park in Macon in the spring.

1500 Tara Place, Hampton (Henry County), 912-373-6376, www.georgiastatefair.org

## Fall Festival at the Monastery of the Holy Spirit

In September, the monks at the Monastery of the Holy Spirit host a fall festival in their cloistered community. The daylong event introduces monastic life through exhibits at the Monastic Heritage Center, which includes a heritage barn, greenhouse, garden center, and bonsai nursery. The festival also celebrates the bounty of the season with hayrides, a petting zoo, and a marketplace featuring fudge, biscotti, and fruitcake made at the monastery as well as produce grown in the organic garden.

2625 Georgia Highway 212 SW, Conyers (Rockdale County), 770-483-8705, www.trappist.net

## SPECIALTY SHOPS

### Pine Street Market

Charcuterie from Pine Street Market is featured on the menus of several farm-to-table restaurants in Georgia, including Ecco, Leon's Full Service, and The Hil at Serenbe, and at the Peachtree Road Farmers Market and Dunwoody Green Market. Rusty Bowers, a graduate of the renowned Culinary Institute of America in Hyde Park, owns Pine Street Market and takes a nose-to-tail approach to making artisan meats. He purchases pastured Berkshire and Tamworth hogs from Gum Creek Farms in Roopville and turns the meat into award-winning coppa, prosciutto, salami, and, of course, hot dogs. He often incorporates other local ingredients into the meat; for example, using peppers to create roasted poblano sausage. Pine Street Market also works with Heritage Farms, White Oak Pastures, and other local farms. Their belief is that it's as important for consumers to know their butcher as it is to know their farmer. "A lot of people [who] come in will ask about the meat, things like where it came from and how it was prepared," notes store manager Kim Carothers. "They like knowing that they can look up the farm where we got the pork and talk to the butcher who prepared the cuts."

To encourage his customers to connect with the meat on their plates, Bowers hosts classes at Pine Street Market. Past offerings included sausage making and a "whole hog" class with Gum Creek Farms, an interactive workshop that focused on different cuts of pork and classic butchering techniques. "It's rare that our classes don't sell out," Carothers says. "It's something fun and different for people to do that gets them closer to their food."

4A Pine Street, Avondale Estates (DeKalb County), 404-296-9672, www.pinestreetmarket.com

## Deciphering Food Labels

The dizzying number of claims attached to our foods makes it difficult to know which labels to look for and, more importantly, which ones to trust. Here's the lowdown on a few popular labels.

*Grass-fed*: Currently, the USDA has no guidelines in place regulating the use of the term "grass-fed." Food producers are able to use the label without any proof that its claims are true. The American Grassfed Association is working to establish certification for grass-fed products.

*Cage-free*: There are no federal standards governing the use of this label. It's used to identify eggs laid by hens that are not confined to cages. But cage free doesn't always equal cruelty free. Even without cages, hens often live in very large flocks, and many never go outside.

*Animal Welfare Approved*: To use the label, farms and ranches must raise animals humanely from birth to slaughter. The certification requires animals to be raised outdoors on a pasture or range and with the highest standards of care.

*Free-range*: In order to use the label, which was approved by the USDA for poultry, birds must have access to open air and be free to roam for at least five minutes per day.

*Natural*: There is no regulation governing use of the word "natural" on products. Although the USDA requires that meat and poultry labeled "natural" do not contain artificial flavors, colors, preservatives, or synthetic ingredients, there is no verification system in place to ensure the term is being used properly.

## Sawicki's

If Lynne Sawicki isn't baking chocolate chip cookies from scratch or stocking the store with her homegrown produce, she can often be found offering recipe suggestions to customers. The passion and knowledge she brings to the shop have kept customers streaming in the doors since 2007. A proponent of supporting local farms, Sawicki cultivates relationships with local producers like White Oak Pastures, Sparkman's Dairy, and Riverview Farms to bring fresh-from-the-farm products to customers. Sawicki raises chickens and grows vegetables, providing the store with fresh eggs and produce.

In addition to serving as a neighborhood butcher shop and green market, Sawicki's also houses a bakery and deli, providing fresh breads and sweet treats, sandwiches, and farm-to-table meals to go.

250 West Ponce de Leon Avenue, Decatur (DeKalb County), 404-377-0992, www.sawickisfoods.com

## Bloomers Garden Center

Classes on vegetable garden preparation, planting vegetables with companion plants, vertical gardening, and composting help customers learn how to transform their yards into miniature farms. The educational workshops offered at the garden center, which Winkey and Pat Brinson purchased in 2005, are all part of a mission to ensure that novice vegetable gardeners are successful in their goal to grow their own food.

Bloomers Garden Center stocks more than just vegetable seeds and starts. Winkey and Pat also sell perennials like hostas, daylilies, and ferns that are grown on their farm, Triple Creek Flower Farm, in Carrollton.

8625 Banks Mill Road, Winston (Douglas County), 770-214-8333, www.bloomersgardencenter.net

## Boxcar Grocer

Alphonzo and Alison Cross wanted to make it easier for shoppers to skip big-box stores and find all of the foods on their shopping list in their neighborhood. The brother and sister entrepreneurs opened a corner market in the Castleberry Hill neighborhood in 2011. Their shelves are stocked with a carefully curated selection of gourmet foods and local produce from providers like AtlantaFresh Creamery, Truly Living Well Farm, Highland Bakery, Sweet Georgia Grains, Weeks Pure Raw Honey, and PodPonics. "The [big-box grocer] in the neighborhood closed and there was a lack of food accessibility that we wanted to fill," says Alphonzo. "In terms of focusing on local products, there is a lot of excitement about spurring the local economy by supporting local growers to keep the money in our community, and we wanted to capitalize on that."

To the regular selection of local foods, the Cross siblings added a pop-up market called Pop Food to the store. Alphonzo describes it as "a combination food court and farmers' market." The space is rented to vendors who sell prepared foods ranging from crepes and raw foods to international dishes. The space is also used for the monthly "vendor showcase" that highlights products from a different vendor one evening per month. In the store, farm tables, free WiFi, and fresh coffee from Café Campesino encourage shoppers to linger. "We've gotten a really good response from the community," Alphonzo says.

249 Peters Street SW, Atlanta (Fulton County), 404-883-3608, www.boxcargrocer.com

## Cacao Atlanta Chocolate Company

During a stint as a private chef on a boat in the Caribbean, Kristen Hard watched a group of women crushing cacao beans by hand. The experience intrigued her, and she decided to start experimenting with chocolate making. It's been more than a decade since she bought her first batch of cacao beans, and Hard has become one of the hottest chocolatiers in the nation.

Hard created a line of truffles for her first venture, K Chocolat, a wholesale chocolate business she founded in 2004. Continued experimentation in the kitchen led to new products and a growing desire to have a retail storefront. Cacao Atlanta opened in 2009 and was named one of the best chocolate shops in the world by *Travel and Leisure* magazine.

The chocolate Hard produces for Cacao is made from the cacao bean, a process that helped Hard to be dubbed the first "bean-to-bar" chocolate maker in the Southeast and the solo female bean-to-bar producer in the nation. To maintain the quality of her chocolates, Hard travels across the globe to source cacao beans directly from farmers. She also works with farms across Georgia to get ingredients for artisanal chocolates, making truffles scented with ginseng and honey and dark chocolate accented with the flavors of blackberries and beets.

312C North Highland Avenue, Atlanta (Fulton County), 404-221-9090, www.cacaoatlanta.com

## Farmer D Organics

Daron Joffe, better known as Farmer D, travels around the Southeast working with farmers, developers, and schools to amp up their landscapes with edibles. He's worked with Sir Richard Branson to create a farm-to-table experience at his spa, Natirar, and develops edible learning gardens for the Captain Planet Foundation. Winning the Pillars of the Earth Award for Entrepreneurial Spirit and being named the Biodynamic Rookie Farmer of the Year have made Farmer D a household name in Georgia. While most of his work involves big-budget design and installation projects, D still caters to small gardeners and farmers.

His garden center, Farmer D Organics, packs a lot of product into a small space. The signature raised-bed garden kits come with all of the goodies to plant a small edible garden, and items like seed bombs and slingshots make quirky gifts for environmentalists.

2154 Briarcliff Road NE, Atlanta (Fulton County), 404-325-0128, www.farmerd.com

## Roswell Provisions

If Laura Ingalls had designed a general store for Walnut Grove, it would look like Roswell Provisions. The store, with its exposed brick walls, wrought-iron fixtures, antique cabinets, and jars of penny candy, is a modern take on pioneer chic, and the selection of foods is just as local as it was when Ma and Pa were doing the shopping.

Lorry Kemp teamed up with husband and wife Cyril Blacha and Kelly Smith-Blacha to open the general store in 2011. There are imported items like olive oil and wine, but the focus is on showcasing local products. Roswell Provisions carries flavored butter, salsa, honey, eggs, cheese, wine, and fresh fruits and vegetables all grown or produced within a few miles of the store.

955 Canton Street, Roswell (Fulton County), 678-682-8669, www.roswellprovisions.com

## Savi Urban Market

Located in the Inman Park neighborhood, Savi Urban Market helps customers fill their reusable bags with locally grown and raised fresh fruits, vegetables, meat, and dairy products, as well as baked goods and an impressive selection of specialty foods and wines. Paul Nair opened the market in 2009 to provide an alternative to supermarket chains while offering natural foods to the masses. Sweet Grass Dairy, Dillwood Farms, Udderly Cool Dairy, AtlantaFresh Creamery, and other local producers are represented in the market.

287 Elizabeth Street NE, Atlanta (Fulton County), 404-523-3131,
www.saviurbanmarket.com

## Sevananda Natural Foods Co-op

The natural foods co-op in Little Five Points partners with local farmers to provide members with farm-fresh produce. The co-op was started in 1974 when a group of like-minded community members came together to create a member-owned cooperative that supported local farms. Although the co-op does stock products from outside Fulton County, about 25 percent of the fruits, vegetables, and herbs come from growers whose farms are within 200 miles of the store. Most of the products in the store are organic. Like all food co-ops, Sevananda also sells other natural foods, beauty products, and vitamins and supplements. The staff is knowledgeable about the products and the growers. The co-op also offers classes on raw foods and vegetarian cooking.

467 Moreland Avenue NE, Atlanta (Fulton County), 404-681-2831,
www.sevananda.coop

## Star Provisions

If the butcher, baker, and candlestick maker jumped out of their nursery rhyme and started a business together, this would be it. Named for the slaughterhouse that occupied the building in the 1930s, Star Provisions houses a butcher, cheese shop, bakery, produce market, and boutique.

Anne Quatrano and Clifford Harrison, chefs and owners of Bacchanalia, a popular farm-to-table restaurant in the same building, opened Star Provisions in 1999 because diners kept asking where they could find the same ingredients used in the restaurant. "The focus is on local, artisan producers," explains cheese monger Tim Gaddis. "We also have popular imports and hard-to-find gourmet items."

Star Provisions is the place to stock up on fresh produce from Woodland Gardens and Summerland Farms, cheese from CalyRoad Creamery and Sweet Grass Dairy, and grass-fed beef, free-range chicken, and pork from Georgia producers. For customers who can't wait until they get home to taste cheese, bread, and other gourmet items sold in the shop, a farmhouse table in the center of the shop offers a place to indulge. Not hungry? Just swoon over the copper cookware and farmhouse-inspired decor items.

1198 Howell Mill Road NW, Atlanta (Fulton County), 404-365-0410, www.starprovisions.com

## The Spotted Trotter

Even with GPS, it's hard not to wonder if the directions to The Spotted Trotter are wrong. As a European-style butcher shop and charcuterie that specializes in locally raised meats, its location in a nondescript strip mall in the heart of a residential neighborhood seems odd. Despite its unusual location, The Spotted Trotter, named after the colloquialism for pig, attracts legions of fans. One of the biggest reasons the restaurants at the Ritz Carlton, Hyatt Regency, and 4th and Swift count on retail manager Scott Stroud to provide beef and pork for their menus is the commitment to sourcing top-quality meat. "Someone from the business has been to each of the farms we work with," Stroud explains. "It would be impossible to have that connection if we were getting [cuts] from Oregon."

The offerings change each week, but the USDA-inspected butcher shop always features sustainably and humanely raised products. "Since we know the farmers and deal with them directly, if someone is looking for an unusual cut of meat, we can track it down and bring it in," says Stroud. "Most butcher shops won't do that for their customers, but we want to support our customers and the farmers in our community just like our community has supported us."

1610 Hosea L. Williams Drive NE, Atlanta (Fulton County), 404-254-4958, thespottedtrotter.com

## Bleu House Market

It's no coincidence that the Bleu House Market and Bleu House Café are side by side. The Adams family owns the houses, and homemade lunches are served in both, but there is a difference between the cute cottages: In the Bleu House Market, managed by Amy Adams (her parents, John and Maureen, run the café), the soups, sandwiches, and desserts share space with boutique items and locally grown produce. The shop stocks specialty items like black lava sea salt and cookbooks as well as fresh fruits and vegetables from Hayden Grove Farm and Phoenix Gardens and yogurt from AtlantaFresh Creamery. The market offers the perfect blend of farm-fresh, family-owned, and funky.

62 College Street NW, Norcross (Gwinnett County), 678-527-6278, www.bleuhousemarket.com

# FARM-TO-TABLE RESTAURANTS

## Freight Kitchen & Tap

When L&N Railroad built the Woodstock Train Depot in 1912, there is a good chance that some of the freight delivered through the depot included boxcars filled with produce. Fresh fruits and vegetables are still delivered through the depot; but instead of traveling thousands of miles in a boxcar, the produce is delivered by local farmers and unloaded from the backs of pickup trucks and into the kitchen. The farm-to-table focus makes Freight Kitchen & Tap a popular spot to grab a bite in downtown Woodstock. With the help of farms like Sweetwater Growers, Buckeye Creek Farm, Mountain Valley Farms, and Rockin S Farm, chef Kyle Shankman prepares southern staples like chicken and waffles with peaches, honey, and pecans; pecan-crusted salmon; and ratatouille with spinach, okra, peppers, eggplant, tomatoes, and edamame.

Freight Kitchen & Tap also has a good selection of local libations, including beers from Burnt Hickory Brewing, Monday Night Brewing, and Red Brick Co. and spirits from Thirteenth Colony Distillery, the first legal distillery in the state. Sadly, there are no Georgia wines on the menu.

Housed in the only building in Woodstock listed on the National Register of Historic Places, Freight retains its historic charm.

251 East Main Street, Woodstock (Cherokee County), 770-924-0144, www.freightkitchen.com. $

## Chicken and the Egg

It doesn't matter which came first, the chicken or the egg, as long as both are farm fresh and prepared to perfection, which is the approach this Marietta restaurant takes with all of its dishes.

The strip mall setting might not be appealing, but the interior is as appetizing as the dishes. Servers wearing jeans and chambray shirts—a look that should be called farmhand chic—move between weathered wooden tables, delivering "modern farmstead fare" like fried green tomatoes, grilled peaches, sweet tea–brined pork chops, fried chicken, and mac and cheese. Executive chef Joseph Ramaglia believes in "keeping the preparation simple and letting the food speak for itself." There is no question that the oversized portions are screaming, "Eat me!"

800 Whitlock Avenue, Suite 124, Marietta (Cobb County), 678-388-8813, www.chickandtheegg.com. $

## Muss & Turner's

Mussman and Turner met while working at an Atlanta restaurant and became fast friends. Over dinner and drinks, the pair decided to go into business together. When Muss & Turner's opened in 2002, Chris Hall became a regular diner and, eventually, a partner.

The trio—Mussman and Hall are chefs while Turner handles business operations—focuses their efforts on making great food in a casual environment. Inspired by the farm-fresh foods available from White Oak Pastures, Serenbe Farms, Sweet Grass Dairy, and Riverview Farms, Hall prepares dishes like Berkshire pork chops with grit cakes and apple cider–braised local greens and risotto with butternut squash, mushrooms, and truffled dwarf peaches to showcase classic Georgia flavors.

"Most people make a list of their meals for the week, go to the supermarket with a list, and buy all of the things on the list. My approach to food is the exact opposite," says Chris Hall. "I have no idea what I'm going to cook most days; I take the best [ingredients] available and write my menu around them. It's a paradigm shift in how we think about food, and it's just the right way to cook."

1675 Cumberland Parkway SE, Smyrna (Cobb County), 770-434-1114, www.mussandturners.com. $$

## Cakes & Ale

During a stint in the kitchen at California's renowned farm-to-table restaurant Chez Panisse, chef Billy Allin learned about the importance of using fresh, local ingredients to create dishes that keep diners coming back for more. It worked. Under Allin, Cakes & Ale earned a spot on the 10 Best New Restaurants list from *Bon Appetit* magazine in 2012.

Allin grows produce for the restaurant in his backyard garden, providing some of the ingredients for dishes like braised rabbit loin with onions, carrots, and beets, and a salad with dandelions, apples, scallions, turnips, and shaved Thomasville tomme cheese with fresh baked bread. The restaurant also hosts periodic—and incredibly popular—Sunday suppers, served family-style, using the season's bounty.

155 Sycamore Street, Decatur (DeKalb County), 404-377-7994, www.cakesandalerestaurant.com. $$$

## No. 246

All of the recipes on the menu at No. 246 come from Italy, but the ingredients used in dishes like ravioli with goat cheese and tomatoes and agnolotti with sweet corn, wild mushrooms, tarragon, and ricotta were grown in Georgia. A combination of farm-fresh fare and wood-fired cooking techniques allow chef Drew Belline to create seasonal specialties that have helped the restaurant earn a reputation as a top pick in Decatur. The best seats in the house are at the Chef's Counter. Diners can reserve a spot next to Belline's workstation and feast on a five-course prix fixe menu while chatting about local foods and Italian cooking techniques with Chef Belline.

129 East Ponce de Leon Avenue, Decatur (DeKalb County), 678-399-8246, www.no246.com. $$

## Revolution Doughnuts

Doughnuts will never be considered health food, but Maria Moore Riggs is making fried dough a little more nutritious—and a lot more delicious—by using ingredients from local farms. All of the handcrafted doughnuts at Revolution are made with organic ingredients, local milk, and fresh fruit. "Getting to know local producers and using their products just made sense," says Moore Riggs. "Instead of opening a bucket of blueberry frosting made with artificial colors and flavors, the glaze on our blueberry doughnuts is made from fresh blueberries."

Moore Riggs started selling doughnuts at the Decatur Farmers Market in 2009. With the help of funding from Kickstarter, she opened the doors to a brick-and-mortar shop in downtown Decatur on National Doughnut Day in 2012. She sources as many ingredients locally as she can, using fruit from Mercier Orchards for her apple fritters and bacon for the salted caramel and bacon doughnuts from the Spotted Trotter; all of the milk used to make the fried dough is supplied by Sparkman's Dairy. "Most people don't come here because we're using local products; they come here because the doughnuts are really delicious," Moore Riggs says. "But they get the extra benefit of knowing that we're supporting local farms."

908 West College Avenue, Decatur (DeKalb County), 678-927-9920, revolutiondoughnuts.com. $

## Sprig

Until Sprig opened in 2010, it was nearly impossible to order dinner in Decatur from a restaurant that supported local farmers. Hailed as the first "scratch kitchen" in town, executive chef Britt Cloud whips up southern foods made with ingredients that were grown and raised in the South. Diners curious about where their food came from can look for a list of farmers on a blackboard behind the bar. Often at least some of the produce was picked from the small vegetable garden next to the restaurant. Owners Anthony and Jennifer Tiberia decided to plant a small plot to showcase their commitment to local fare and provide Cloud with instant access to his favorite herbs and common ingredients like tomatoes and peppers. In an effort to make sure the entire menu reflected local foods, the couple also sought out beer from Georgia breweries like Terrapin and Wild Heaven to feature on their beverage menu.

2860 Lavista Road, Decatur (DeKalb County), 404-248-9700, www.sprigrestaurant.com. $

## 4th and Swift

When veteran chef Jay Swift opened a restaurant in Old Fourth Ward in 2009, he wanted to create a menu that reflected the neighborhood: classic and southern. The restaurant is located in the former Southern Dairies building, so it seemed fitting to create a menu focused on local foods. "Cooking with local ingredients isn't some new thing; it's an old thing that has been brought back," Swift says. "I wanted to cook modern southern food, and to do that, I had to seek out good southern ingredients."

## Iconic Onion

Vidalia onions are featured on restaurant menus across Georgia in dishes ranging from salads to desserts—and the Vidalia Onion Committee and Georgia Department of Agriculture want chefs to shout it from the rooftops (or at least add an icon to their menus to give the sweet onion a little recognition). In 2012, the groups introduced a logo, the outline of an onion surrounding the letters VO, for chefs to use on their menus.

As part of the new logo program, which organizers tout as formal recognition of an "internationally renowned agricultural treasure," restaurateurs must agree to label only genuine Vidalia onions with the logo. According to Wendy Brannen, executive director of the Vidalia Onion Committee, the logo is important because it identifies Vidalia onions as agricultural products that are unique to the region, separating them from onions grown in other parts of the country and the world. The label started appearing on restaurant menus in 2012.

Swift partnered with local farmers to source ingredients for traditional dishes like heirloom tomato salad, sweet corn and ricotta ravioli, and seasonal vegetable assortments. Instead of complicated preparations, Swift lets the flavors of the foods speak for themselves. "Nothing good happens to food between the time it leaves the farm or ranch and gets to the table," he says. "By buying local, we can eliminate some of the degradation that happens when [food] sits on the truck for several hours or several days. Local food is just better food."

621 North Avenue NE, Atlanta (Fulton County), 678-904-0160, www.4thandswift.com. $$$

## 5 Seasons Brewing

With three locations in Metro Atlanta, chef/owner Dave Larkworthy might use more local produce than any other chef in the region. "Between the three locations, we have sixty to ninety specials a day plus the regular menu, and 90 percent of the meat and produce we use is organic and comes from local farms," Larkworthy says. "I have no idea how many pounds that adds up to, but it's significant, especially because each restaurant seats at least 300 people."

Larkworthy developed a passion for local, organic foods while working in kitchens with his father, chef John Larkworthy, and has been committed to featuring local ingredients on menus since he opened his first restaurant at age twenty-three. When he opened 5 Seasons Brewing in 2001 (adding additional locations in 2006 and 2009), Larkworthy knew he wanted to serve unpretentious food and beer with an emphasis on local and organic ingredients. "It was selfish, really," he says. "I figured the more I bought from local farms, the more the farmers would be able to grow and the cheaper [the ingredients] would be and the more I would be able to buy—and that is exactly what has happened."

Through partnerships with growers like Cane Creek Farm, Gaia Gardens, Moore Farms, and Crystal Organic Farms, Larkworthy sources ingredients for classic dishes like seasonal soups, farm greens, sweet tea–brined fried chicken with squash casserole, and Georgia organic grass-fed beef burgers. When it comes to working with 5 Seasons Brewing, the farmers are excited about more than the boost to their bottom lines. Farmers use the spent grains from the brewery for compost for their fields. Several of the beers made in the brewery, including Georgia Peach Wheat, Pumpkin Ale, and Watermelon Wheat, incorporate locally grown fruits.

3655 Old Milton Parkway, Alpharetta (Fulton County), 770-521-5551, www.5seasonsbrewing.com. $$

## Atlanta Food Truck Park

Although the Atlanta Food Truck Park was designed to provide a permanent location for food trucks to serve daily noshes to the masses, the mobile offerings have expanded far beyond tacos and cupcakes. It's turned into a mix of farm stands, gourmet goodies, and artisan products, all sold from shops on wheels. Wally B's sells local honey; both Joyful Noise Farm and Barbara and Ginny's Eggs and Produce are stocked with pastured chicken and free-range eggs; pickles and sauces are available from Jamaican Hots; and during harvest season, peaches and apples are available at Farm2Market. The Atlanta Food Truck Park hosts regular vendors and a rotating bevy of trucks that make appearances on a whim.

1850 Howell Mill Road, Atlanta (Fulton County), www.atlantafoodtruckpark.com. $

## Bacchanalia

It's no surprise that Bacchanalia has been voted one of the top ten restaurants in Atlanta for more than a decade. Chefs and owners Anne Quatrano and Clifford Harrison are involved in all aspects of a meal, from farm to table. The couple produces fruits, vegetables, nuts, and eggs for the restaurant on their organic farm, Summerland Farms, and transforms them into sumptuous suppers in the restaurant kitchen, providing a unique connection to the dishes served in the former meatpacking plant.

Instead of creating a signature menu with rotating specials, Quatrano and Harrison prepare a five-course prix fixe menu that changes with the harvest. Each evening, diners are treated to a menu with two appetizers, an entree, a cheese course, and dessert. The cuisine is creative—glazed veal sweetbreads with chestnuts and apples, squab breast with sweet corn and pickled blueberries, muscadine sorbet topped with scuppernong marshmallows and peanuts—and, to the delight of locavores, most of the ingredients not grown on Summerland Farms are sourced from other local producers. When the chefs extend their reach outside the Georgia border, their provenance is listed on the menu. Even the servers are involved in producing the foods that are offered, pitching in on the farm outside of their restaurant shifts.

1198 Howell Mill Road, Atlanta (Fulton County), 404-365-0410, www.starprovisions.com/bacchanalia.html. $$$

## Bantam + Biddy

Bantam + Biddy is fast food with a local twist. Top Atlanta chefs Shaun Doty and Lance Gummere wanted to share their appreciation for local, pastured poultry, organic vegetables, and regional sides with the masses. The restaurant has all of the staples of a casual dining spot: chicken sandwiches, half chicken and sides, and chicken pitas. But Doty and Gummere (who raises Ameraucana and Rhode Island Red chickens in a backyard coop) wanted to add upscale twists like gluten-free bread, beer mustard, and wasakaka (roasted chicken with garlic sauce). The location in Ansley

Mall helps Doty and Gummere achieve their goal of sharing farm-to-table food at reasonable prices with Atlanta.

1544 Piedmont Road NE, Suite 301, Atlanta (Fulton County), 404-907-3469, www.bantamandbiddy.com. $

## BOCADO

*Creative Loafing* called the burger at BOCADO one of "100 Dishes to Eat in Atlanta Before You Die." It's one of several "best of" accolades that have drawn diners to the Midtown restaurant since it opened in 2010. Regular patrons might argue that the Georgia peaches with pickled blueberries, pistachio and arugula pesto, and cured duck salami should have made the list.

The stark space with industrial fixtures and exposed brick walls doesn't seem like the kind of place where farmers would hang out, but the volume of fresh produce coming through the kitchen from local farms proves otherwise.

887 Howell Mill Road, Atlanta (Fulton County), 404-815-1399, www.bocadoatlanta.com. $$

### Briza

Executive chef Janine Falvo worked in some of the best farm-to-table restaurants in the nation, serving seasonal food at Parcel 104 and Carneros Bistro and Wine Bar before taking her passion for farm-fresh fare to Briza. In the kitchen of the Midtown restaurant, the former *Top Chef* contestant whips up southern-inspired dishes like short ribs with Vidalia onion puree, sweet potato fries, and pork chops with succotash and okra. Even the cocktails have farm-to-table flair: the West Peach Tea is made with local mint, lavender, and honey.

866 West Peachtree Street NW, Atlanta (Fulton County), 678-412-2402, www.brizarestaurant.com. $$$

### Ecco

At Ecco, the magic may happen in the kitchen but the inspiration starts on the rooftop. The Midtown restaurant planted a rooftop garden in 2008 to supply executive chef Craig Richards and sous-chef Justin Jordan with instant access to tomatoes, squash, peppers, cucumbers, and fresh herbs to supplement the meat and produce they order from local farms.

Jordan believes Ecco is the only restaurant in Atlanta growing produce on the roof. Diners are curious about the connection between the rooftop

When sous-chef Justin Jordan needs ingredients for farm-to-table meals at Ecco, he climbs up to the restaurant's rooftop to harvest fresh herbs and vegetables from the on-site garden.

garden and menu items like piquillo peppers and braised beef, wood-fired pizzas topped with house-made pesto, and spaghetti al torchio with heirloom tomatoes, basil, and pecorino. Their questions give servers an opportunity to explain their farm-to-fork philosophy. "There are so many farms in our backyard that it makes sense to serve only the freshest produce," Jordan says.

Ecco is also the first certified green restaurant in the state. In addition to reducing its food miles with a rooftop garden and local suppliers, the restaurant composts its food waste and captures rainwater in barrels to irrigate the garden. "We create waste and use energy, so why not try to put some of it back?" Jordan says.

40 Seventh Street NE, Atlanta (Fulton County), 404-347-9555, www.ecco-atlanta.com. $$

## Empire State South

Tucked into the shadow of high-rise buildings in the heart of Midtown Atlanta, the patio of Empire State South resembles the porch of a Wild West ranch. Candles flicker in mason jars on the wooden tables, and servers wearing jeans and plaid shirts deliver farm-fresh fare to the table, while diners take their turns on the bocce court.

Chef/partner Hugh Acheson, a six-time nominee for and 2012 winner of the James Beard Foundation's Best Chef: Southeast award and author of *A New Turn in the South: Southern Flavors Reinvented for Your Kitchen*, created a menu that highlights the best foods and farms in the South. Together with executive chef Ryan Smith, Acheson serves up heirloom grits, collard greens, and local seafood.

999 Peachtree Street NE, Atlanta (Fulton County), 404-541-1105, www.empirestatesouth.com. $$$

## Farm Burger

On the surface, Farm Burger is a just another burger joint. The menu is filled with meat-on-a-bun combinations like the Farm Burger, beef topped with white cheddar and caramelized onions, and a chicken burger with smoked gouda, barbecue sauce, coleslaw, and onions. A closer look reveals that this is not an average fast-food restaurant: Most of the ingredients for the burgers, from the grass-fed beef and pasture-raised chicken to the vine-ripe tomatoes and feta that are served in the Buckhead restaurant, come from local farms. Even the beers are from local breweries.

Owners Jason Mann and George Cooke juggle the restaurant with farming operations: Both are also owners/founders of Moonshine Meats, a ranch that raises grass-fed beef, pastured pork, and heritage poultry; and Full Moon Farms, a co-op of small, sustainable farms providing ingredients for regional restaurants. Their goal is to redefine fast food, one burger at a time.

3365 Piedmont Road, Atlanta (Fulton County), 404-816-0603, www.farmburger.net. $

## The Feed Store

True to its name, the Feed Store served as a retail outlet for farm feed and supplies in the 1920s. Ada Estelle Smith Harris ran the business, called J. D. Smith Grain, a staple in the College Park neighborhood. The building is listed on the National Register of Historic Places. Harris's granddaughter, Celita Bullard, reopened the business as a farm-to-table restaurant in 2003. Since then, the restaurant has become known for creative fare like baked beans with Coca-Cola (a surprising take on local ingredients) and other classic southern dishes, including fried chicken and shrimp and grits.

3841 Main Street, College Park (Fulton County), 404-209-7979, www.thefeedstorerestaurant.com. $$$

## Floataway Café

Anne Quatrano and Clifford Harrison, chefs/owners of award-winning Bacchanalia, have also earned "best of" nods for the dishes served up at Floataway Café. Located in a hard-to-find (but worth the search) renovated warehouse, the restaurant serves seasonal dishes with Italian and Mediterranean influences. Even the drink menu changes with the seasons. In the spring, the Prosecco with pureed strawberries is a favorite.

1123 Zonolite Road NE, Atlanta (Fulton County), 404-892-1414, www.starprovisions.com/floatawaycafe.html. $$

## Greenwood's on Green Street

The clapboard house on Green Street stands out in the historic Roswell neighborhood, not just for the peace sign dangling from a post in the boulevard or the old pickup truck with sedum bursting from its bed or the legions of diners waiting for a table. It's the food that helped make the restaurant a neighborhood institution. Bill Greenwood has been serving up southern favorites like fried chicken, pork chops, and soul food sides like black-eyed peas and collard greens using locally grown produce and organic meat, grains, and dairy since 1986.

1087 Green Street, Roswell (Fulton County), 770-992-5383, www.greenwoodsongreenstreet.com. $$

## H. Harper Station

The name H. Harper Station has significance for restaurateur Jerry Slater: it honors his grandfather, Harold Harper, who was a railroad engineer (and the building, with its long, narrow shape, resembles a historic train depot). The menu establishes a strong sense of place, featuring ingredients from local farms like Gum Creek Farms, Sweet Grass Dairy, and Gaia Gardens in menu items like roasted winter squash with arugula, maple pecans, and pickled raisins; grilled pork loin with honey garlic glaze; hoppin' John with Sea Island red peas, and other southern dishes.

904 Memorial Drive, Atlanta (Fulton County), 678-732-0416, www.hharperstation.com. $$

## Happy Belly Curbside Kitchen

Terry and Dawn Hall might pull into parking lots and office parks all over Atlanta, open a window on the side of their bright-green truck and start taking orders, but the couple, who started Happy Belly in 2012, don't think of their business as a food truck. Instead, Dawn calls it a curbside kitchen. To be sure, the menu is far more extensive than most food trucks offer, and, unlike food trucks that focus on a certain type of cuisine—think taco truck or cupcake truck—Happy Belly prepares dishes worthy of an up-scale farm-to-table restaurant. Most of the dishes prepared in the curbside kitchen, including the signature kale Waldorf salad with green apples, pecans, and blue cheese and pear barbecue pulled pork on cornbread, are made with seasonal, organic ingredients from local farms. The menu, just like the location, is constantly changing to reflect the availability of local meat and produce. It's "farm-to-street" fare for the masses.

Fulton County, 404-719-3257, www.happybellytruck.com. $

## The Hil

The Hil takes the idea of a neighborhood restaurant to a new level. As part of the small Serenbe neighborhood, it attracts legions of regulars who vie for a spot in the dining room to see what's on the menu. Although the dishes change with the seasons, most of the fruits and vegetables featured in dishes like margherita pizza and Berkshire pork ribs with okra stew are grown just a few steps from the kitchen at Serenbe Farms. During farm visits, chef Hilary White collaborates with farm manager Paige Witherington to select produce and eggs for simple, farm-fresh dishes.

9110 Selborne Lane, Palmetto (Fulton County), 770-463-6040, www.the-hil.com. $$

## Holeman and Finch Public House

Linton Hopkins competed on *Iron Chef*, was named Best New Chef by *Food and Wine* magazine in 2009, and won the James Beard Foundation's award for Best Chef: Southeast in 2012. To Georgia farmers, though, he is best known as the chef with a relentless devotion to local foods. Along with his wife, Gina, Hopkins is one of the founders of the popular Peachtree Road Farmers Market, helping growers connect with their communities. He also champions local ingredients in the dishes he creates for Holeman and Finch Public House as evidenced by the Farm section on the menu. Dishes like skillet fried corn, squash gratin, and caramel peaches with seasonal vegetables emphasize seasonal ingredients. The farm-fresh focus extends throughout the menu, featuring foods from growers like Riverview Farms, Dillwood Farms, and Hidden Springs Farm.

2277 Peachtree Road NE, Atlanta (Fulton County), 404-948-1175, www.holeman-finch.com. $$

## Holy Taco

When it comes to creating dishes for his Mexican fusion menu, chef Robert Phalen relies on southern farmers. Phalen sources most of the potatoes, rice, peppers, tomatoes, goat, beef, and seafood from sustainable farms and fisheries like White Oak Pastures, Walker Farms, and Rise 'N Shine Farms. The successful combination of international flavor and local ingredients have led to accolades for Phalen, who grew up on a farm and graduated from Johnson and Wales University in Charleston. *Creative Loafing* bestowed Holy Taco with the Best Mexican Food honor in 2009 and wrote, "[It's] some of the coolest, most interesting food around."

1314 Glenwood Avenue, Atlanta (Fulton County), 404-320-6177, www.holy-taco.com. $$

## JCT. Kitchen

JCT. Kitchen serves up southern favorites like fried chicken, shrimp and grits, and chicken and dumplings using ingredients from local producers. Ford Fry, executive chef and owner, partners with local producers like Sweetgrass Dairy, Riverview Farms, and Elliott Shimley Veal to create a seasonal menu.

All of the elements of the restaurant, from the design—a farm table in the center of the dining room doubles as a serving station and flatware wrapped in blue and white dishtowels—to the name—"JCT." denotes a railroad junction and is a nod to the tracks behind the restaurant that once transported livestock from farms to the local packing plant—hint at the commitment to farmstead fare.

1198 Howell Mill Road, Atlanta (Fulton County), 404-355-2252, www.jctkitchen.com. $$

## King of Pops

A backpacking adventure, a pink slip, and a love of fruit popsicles led Steven Carse out of a cubicle and onto the streets. Carse, who was laid off from a job in finance in 2009, decided to take advantage of the time off to re-create the *paletas*, popsicles made from fresh fruit, he discovered during a trip to Central America with his brother, Nick. He perfected the recipe, purchased a pushcart, and started hawking popsicles on a street corner in Atlanta. The King of Pops was a huge success. Since the first popsicle was sold in 2010, Carse has purchased several more carts, pedaling popsicles all over Atlanta, Athens, and Charleston, South Carolina. Using ingredients from the farmers' market, Carse develops popsicle flavors that change with the seasons. Patrons will happily hand over $2.50 in exchange for a fresh fruit popsicle in flavors like Georgia peach and basil, fig and honey, raspberry lime, watermelon mint, and blackberry mojito.

Fulton County, www.kingofpops.net. $

## Leon's Full Service

Prohibition might be over, but that hasn't stopped local speakeasy, Leon's Full Service, from drawing crowds. A seasonal cocktail menu highlights local ingredients (The Wasp combines Georgia peach honey with Redemption Rye and Rebel & Rose is a mix of Old Tom Gin and crème de peche from Pearson Farm, lemon, lavender, and vanilla), and several of the beers come from local breweries, including Terrapin Brewing Company and Sweetwater Brewing Company. At the service-station-turned-neighborhood-pub, chef Eric Ottensmeyer also takes a "think local" approach to food, creating casual pub fare with an upscale twist. The burger is made with grass-fed beef from White Oak Pastures, and the pub fries are served with a choice of fourteen homemade sauces, like goat cheese fondue and smoked tomato mayonnaise, that feature local ingredients.

131 East Ponce de Leon Avenue, Decatur (Fulton County), 404-687-0500, www.leonsfullservice.com. $$

## Local Three Kitchen and Bar

Chris Hall, Todd Mussman, and Ryan Turner are the local three, chefs/owners who are serious about a commitment to supporting local farms. Their motto, "Local is a priority and seasonal makes sense," is reflected in their food. Dishes like vegetable stew with squash, fennel, and carrots in Parmesan broth and herbed chicken schnitzel with mac and cheese and apple and cabbage slaw are crowd favorites. "We never set out to be a southern restaurant, but when you cook local, those influences impact the menu," says Chris Hall. "We aspire to be a local restaurant, and that means working with local farms. Why wouldn't you source ingredients from your backyard instead of shipping them in from California?"

While Hall is a passionate supporter of local farms, sourcing ingredients from Gum Creek Farm, Crystal Organic Farm, Love Is Love Farm, and Serenbe Farms, and one of the cofounders of the Farmers Atlanta Road Market, he doesn't boast about his commitment. Most of the time, he doesn't even list the names of the farms on the menu, which is not a sign of disrespect, as Hall points out: "If I listed all of the farmers we work with, the menu would look like the Yellow Pages." Rest assured, all of the meals Hall prepares are farm fresh.

3290 Northside Parkway NW, Atlanta (Fulton County), 404-968-2700, www.localthree.com. $$

## Miller Union

Before stepping into the kitchen at Miller Union, Steven Satterfield studied architecture and toured in an indie rock band. The self-taught chef fell in love with food and changed careers. While working under renowned Atlanta chefs Anne Quatrano and Scott Peacock, Satterfield learned to cook with fresh, seasonal ingredients, which got him thinking, "How can I do this all the time instead of just when there are specials?"

At the helm of Miller Union, named for its former role as Miller Union Stockyards, where farmers sold horses in the 1800s, Satterfield uses seasonal ingredients to make dishes like grilled pork loin with griddled grits, apple chutney, and Vidalia onions and black bass filet with spinach-arugula puree and potato cakes. All of the ingredients are sourced from local producers like Love Is Love Farm, Crystal Organics, White Oak Pastures, and the Turnip Truck. The "put ups" are one of the highlights of the menu. Served with sourdough bread, preserves like peach bourbon butter, beet marmalades, and classic chowchow are true southern staples. "It's honest, approachable food," he says. "We get great ingredients so we don't have to do a lot to make them shine."

During quarterly Harvest Dinners, Satterfield creates a three-course prix fixe menu featuring ingredients from local farms. The suppers are served family style at farmhouse tables. "The idea of sitting down at the dinner table and passing plates is very southern," he says. "We want our food to bring people together."

999 Brady Avenue NW, Atlanta (Fulton County), 678-733-8550, www.millerunion.com. $$$

## Murphy's

There wasn't much happening in Virginia Highlands when Murphy's opened its doors in the 1980s. Over the past three decades, the neighborhood has gone from up-and-coming to hip and happening, but the restaurant, known for its brunch menu, has retained its original focus on comfort foods made from local ingredients. Executive chef Ian Winslade uses seasonal ingredients from regional farms whenever possible, creating celebrated dishes like eggs Virginia Highland, crab cake Benedict, and Georgia white shrimp and grits. Winslade shows his affection for local foods through special events like cooking demonstrations at the Atlanta Botanical Garden, where he prepares meals using ingredients from their edible garden, and donating a portion of the proceeds from certain meals to programs like Schoolyard Sprouts, a program that helps establish gardens at local elementary schools. The restaurant also hosts a Sunday Supper Series featuring a prix fixe family-style meal made with seasonal ingredients from sustainable farms.

997 Virginia Avenue NE, Atlanta (Fulton County), 404-872-0904, www.murphysvh.com. $$

## ONE. Midtown Kitchen

The combination of seasonal dishes and a fabulous setting with unparalleled views of Piedmont Park and downtown Atlanta has made ONE. Midtown Kitchen a neighborhood favorite since it opened in 2002. All of the meals are prepared in an open kitchen—a seat at the bar offers the best views—and everything from the pasta and mozzarella to the tomato sauce is made in-house. But it's not just the farm-fresh meals that have earned chef Drew Van Leuvan legions of fans. The craft cocktails at ONE. like Grow a Pear, made with fresh pears, lemon, vodka, and star anise, incorporate fresh juices, homemade syrups, and garnishes fresh from the farm.

559 Dutch Valley Road, Atlanta (Fulton County), 404-892-4111, www.onemidtownkitchen.com. $$

## Parish: Foods & Goods

As its name suggests, Parish is part restaurant and part market, but it's 100 percent focused on local, artisanal foods. Executive chef Edward Russell creates dishes like Sapelo Island clams and Georgia trout, all served in a dining room in the historic Terminal Building. The menu changes nightly to reflect the season's harvest. Special events like the Farmers' Market Menu offer Russell another opportunity to showcase local ingredients. The restaurant, the site of a former pipe factory, retains many of its original architectural elements, including exposed brick, crown molding, and tin ceilings that are complemented with modern touches like Murano glass chandeliers. On the lower level of the Terminal Building, Parish Market is stocked with wine, cheese, bread, and pastries with an emphasis on local producers. The market also serves prepared foods like soups, salads, and sandwiches for takeout or for a nosh at the communal tables.

240 North Highland Avenue, Atlanta (Fulton County), 404-681-4434, www.parishatl.com. $$

## The Porter Beer Bar

A pub in the Little Five Points neighborhood, the Porter Beer Bar is best known for its beer selections. But it's not just the 800 microbrews and imports that have drawn crowds since the restaurant opened in 2008. The husband and wife owners Nick Rutherford and Molly Gunn partner with local farmers to source ingredients for their pub grub. Some of the produce used in the restaurant comes from the couple's small urban garden dubbed "The Farm," where they grow vegetables like tomatoes, squash, and lettuce in raised beds.

"Fine dining restaurants led the charge toward local, seasonal food," Gunn says. "We both come from a fine dining background [the couple met while working for a five-star restaurant in Buckhead], and we wanted to take the same concept and apply it to a more casual restaurant."

The only limitation in creating a menu, according to Gunn, is that "the food has to go well with beer." In addition to a regular menu of burgers, fish and chips, and sauerkraut and beer brats, Rutherford prepares daily specials like chicken fennel ravioli and pork rillette, and he uses local ingredients as much as possible. "It takes talent to execute [dishes] based on what farmers bring in the door," Gunn says. "But it makes for better-tasting food."

1156 Euclid Avenue, Atlanta (Fulton County), 404-223-0393, www.theporterbeerbar.com. $

## Restaurant Eugene

Although Restaurant Eugene was named one of the top forty restaurants in the nation by Gayot.com, and executive chef Linton Hopkins is a four-time nominee and the 2012 winner of the James Beard Foundation's Best Chef: Southeast award, the true stars at this restaurant in the South Buckhead neighborhood are the farmers.

As one of the founding partners of the Peachtree Road Farmers Market, Hopkins believes in supporting local farmers and sources ingredients from dozens of local producers, including Flat Creek Lodge, Decimal Place Farm, Indian Ridge Farms, Greenleaf Farms, and Woodland Gardens. All of the bread used in the restaurant comes from the bakery Hopkins owns, H&F Bread Company. He was one of the first Atlanta chefs to list his purveyors on the menu.

Hopkins is a passionate advocate for preserving the history of the region, especially its culinary traditions. The menu at Restaurant Eugene changes daily to reflect the availability of fresh produce, and almost everything, including the condiments, is made from scratch.

2277 Peachtree Road NE, Atlanta (Fulton County), 404-355-0321, www.restauranteugene.com. $$$

## The Shed at Glenwood

At The Shed at Glenwood, it's impossible to be bored with the menu. Chef Todd Richards tweaks the offerings daily to reflect the availability of fresh produce, meat, and seafood. Just in case new combinations of daily sliders (miniature burgers with seasonal fillings like fried green tomatoes and goat cheese, sausage with tomatoes and cucumbers, or brisket), small plates, and mains aren't enough to keep diners interested, Richards introduced monthly themed lunches in 2012. The lunches, held on one Friday afternoon per month, showcase a menu designed around specific themes, including Thanksgiving. Diners are also encouraged to make reservations for the Chef's Counter. The four-course prix fixe menu is available every evening and offers the opportunity for up to six people to enjoy supper at a counter overlooking Richards's kitchen workstation.

475 Bill Kennedy Way SE, Atlanta (Fulton County), 404-835-4363, www.theshedatglenwood.com. $$

## Sun In My Belly

Alison Lueker was one of the first chefs in Atlanta to champion the local food movement. Located in the Kirkwood District, the restaurant serves pimento cheese omelets, challah French toast, meatloaf, and fried green tomatoes—all made with ingredients sourced from local farms.

The restaurant is located in an old hardware store in the middle of a residential neighborhood, and the atmosphere is as traditional as the menu: butcher paper covers the tables, drinks are served in mason jars, and cookbooks spill off of the shelves.

2161 College Avenue NE, Atlanta (Fulton County), 404-370-1088, www.suninmybelly.com. $$

## Table & Main

At Table & Main, words like "fresh," "artisan," and "local" come up over and over. The lingo overheard at the farm-to-table restaurant isn't surprising given that chef/partner Ted Lahey sources most of his ingredients from farms, creameries, bakeries, and breweries in Georgia. From the hush puppies and Brunswick stew to the hog 'n waffle, all of the dishes Lahey creates are pure southern.

Lahey, a graduate of the culinary program at Johnson and Wales University, is no stranger to cooking with farm-fresh ingredients. He worked at celebrated farm-to-table restaurants like Five & Ten and South City Kitchen before joining Table & Main, where he puts his own spin on local fare.

1028 Canton Street, Roswell (Fulton County), 678-869-5178, www.tableandmain.com. $$

## Terrace at the Ellis Hotel

The cliché that most hotels in the downtown business district serve stale Danishes and overripe fruit for breakfast does not apply to Terrace. When Scott Blackerby took over as executive chef in 2011, he implemented a menu filled with farm-to-table fare and banished mass-produced breakfast pastries in favor of roasted vegetable Benedict, farm-fresh egg sandwiches, and locally milled grits. "We started asking, What can we do to keep our carbon footprint down?" explains Blackerby. "Incorporating more local, seasonal ingredients into the menu was the obvious solution; there are a lot of local farmers here, so we never run out of options."

The historic hotel opened its doors in 1913 and is listed on the National Register of Historic Places. As a nod to its past, Blackerby makes preserves much like the original hoteliers would have. At first, most of the diners were hotel guests, but when word spread that Terrace served farm-fresh foods on its fabulous outdoor patio, locals began lining up for breakfast, lunch, and dinner.

As the local food movement grew, the Ellis Hotel decided to launch a Farm-to-Table Package, inviting guests to spend the morning at the farmers' market with Blackerby, sampling seasonal ingredients and choosing the makings of a five-course evening meal. "People are interested in how their food is grown," he says. "We take them from the farm stand to the table."

176 Peachtree Street NE, Atlanta (Fulton County), 678-651-2770, www.ellishotel.com/terrace. $$

## Watershed on Peachtree

With Emily Saliers of the Indigo Girls as part owner, Watershed had instant appeal. In 2012, chef Joe Truex took over the kitchen and Watershed moved from a converted gas station in Decatur to a spot at the base of a condo high-rise between the Buckhead and Midtown neighborhoods. The neutral palette and crafty touches—canning jars as light fixtures, lithographs of quilts covering the walls—make the restaurant look like a spread from a Martha Stewart magazine. A new location and change in the kitchen didn't change the soul of Watershed, though. It is, as it always was, a restaurant serving creative dishes made with ingredients from local farms. As a nod to the restaurant's moniker, Truex serves up seafood dishes like Sapelo Island clams, baked flounder with Gulf Coast shrimp and sautéed spinach, and triggerfish, alongside southern favorites like pork chops and fried chicken.

1820 Peachtree Road, Atlanta (Fulton County), 404-809-3561, www.watershedrestaurant.com. $$

## Woodfire Grill

Thanks to executive chef Kevin Gillespie's second-place finish on the Food Network's *Top Chef*, Woodfire Grill became known as "the toughest reservation in town." It might have been hopes of catching a glimpse of Gillespie that drew diners into the restaurant, but the food kept them coming back. In 2012, Gillespie announced that he was leaving Woodfire Grill and former chef de cuisine E. J. Hodgkinson was taking over as executive chef. Despite a change in leadership, Woodfire Grill remains committed to serving seasonal dishes and supporting local farms.

The best way to experience the culinary creativity is through the tasting menu. Offered as a five- or seven-course meal, it features seasonal dishes inspired by foods sourced from local producers, including Dillwood Farms, Whippoorwill Hollow Organic Farm, Ashland Farms, Jenny Jack Sun Farm, and White Oak Pastures.

1782 Cheshire Bridge Road, Atlanta (Fulton County), 404-347-9055, www.woodfiregrill.com. $$$

## Yeah! Burger

Yeah! Burger is fast food with a conscience. When Shaun Doty opened the restaurant in 2010, he wanted to make casual foods from artisan products while supporting local producers whenever possible. The gourmet burgers are made with grass-fed beef or bison, natural chicken, or organic veggie patties, sandwiched between buns baked with organic flour by a local bakery. Even the toppings—organic ketchup, hydroponic lettuce, nitrate-free bacon, and cage-free fried eggs—also have a farm-to-table focus. "We focus on sourcing ingredients from small Georgia farms," says executive chef Cristy Norton.

It's not just the food that makes Yeah! Burger stand out, though. The restaurant takes its social and environmental responsibilities to heart, too. It was voted the number 1 place to work by the *Atlanta Journal-Constitution* and eschews the traditional trappings of a burger joint in favor of greener alternatives: Instead of plastic cups and utensils, the restaurant uses biodegradable dinnerware; there is no dumpster outside the back door because all of the food scraps are composted; and regular meat and produce deliveries mean that the restaurant has no need for a freezer. Despite all of the extras, the prices are still lower than most casual dining restaurants. "There are a lot more people who want to know where their food comes from," Norton explains. "In the last 10 years, [farm-to-fork] has been focused on fine dining. We have a niche market that brings the concept to everyday foods."

1168 Howell Mill Road, Suite E, Atlanta (Fulton County), 404-496-4393, www.yeahburger.com. $

# LODGING

## The Inn at Serenbe

What started out as a weekend home blossomed into one of the most popular farm stays in the Southeast. When Steve and Marie Nygren purchased a farmhouse on sixty acres in 1991, their plan was to use the property as a weekend escape from the hustle and bustle of Atlanta. As they began spending more and more time on the farm—often with family and friends filling the guestrooms in the farmhouse—the couple decided to open an inn on the farm. Marie Nygren chose the name "Serenbe" to reflect what she hoped the inn would provide—a place to be serene. Over the years, Serenbe has grown to include 1,000 acres of farmland and pastures with more than 100 farm animals, including rabbits, goats, chickens, pigs, horses, and donkeys.

Five cottages offer plush accommodations complete with luxe linens, fireplaces, spa bathrooms, and screened porches. The farmhouse once occupied by the Nygren family has been remodeled to include seven guestrooms.

The Farmhouse restaurant features recipes made with fresh ingredients harvested at Serenbe Farms, a five-acre certified organic farm on-site.

10950 Hutcheson Ferry Road, Palmetto (Fulton County), 770-463-2610, www.serenbeinn.com. $$–$$$$

## RECIPES

### Strawberry Lavender Jam

*In the summer, chef Scott Blackerby has a local farmer deliver flats of fresh strawberries to the Ellis Hotel. He features the perfectly ripe berries on the breakfast menu as toppings for waffles or serves strawberries with yogurt, but he also sets some aside to make his trademark strawberry lavender jam. The spread is a guest favorite at the breakfast table at Terrace, the on-site restaurant.*

MAKES 2½ CUPS

| | |
|---|---|
| 4 | cups strawberries (about 1 pound), hulled |
| 1 | cup sugar |
| ½ | cup light agave nectar |
| 2 | teaspoons dried lavender flowers |
| 1 | packet Fruit Jell Freezer Jam Pectin |
| 2 | (10-ounce) jam jars, ready to use |

In a large bowl, crush the strawberries and sugar with a potato masher until small pieces remain and the mixture is quite liquid. Set aside.

Bring the agave nectar and lavender to a quick simmer over medium-high heat. Remove from the heat and let cool for 5 minutes. Add the pectin and stir until combined. Fold into the strawberries.

Ladle the jam into the clean jars, leaving a ½-inch space at the top. Seal on the caps and let sit for 30 minutes.

Store in the freezer until ready to use or transfer to the fridge and eat!

## Light Georgia Pecan Pie with Honey Pecan Topping

*Georgia is the largest pecan producer in the nation, and the Georgia Pecan Commission has earned a reputation for supporting pecan growers and coming up with delicious recipes to turn just-picked pecans into flavorful dishes. This recipe for pecan pie is a commission favorite.*

MAKES 1 9-INCH PIE

FOR THE PIE:

| | |
|---|---|
| 2 | large eggs |
| ¼ | cup sugar |
| 1 | cup light corn syrup |
| 2 | tablespoons all-purpose flour |
| 1 | tablespoon vanilla extract |
| 1 | cup chopped Georgia pecans |
| 1 | (9-inch) unbaked pie shell |

FOR THE TOPPING:

| | |
|---|---|
| 3 | tablespoons light brown sugar |
| 1 | tablespoon butter |
| 3 | tablespoons honey |
| 1 | cup Georgia pecan halves |

TO PREPARE THE PIE:

Preheat the oven to 375 degrees. Using an electric mixer, beat together the eggs, sugar, corn syrup, flour, and vanilla until creamy. Stir in the pecans.

Pour the filling into the pie shell and bake for 40–50 minutes (adding the topping during the last 5 minutes of baking) or until the filling is set.

TO PREPARE THE TOPPING:

In a small pot, combine the brown sugar, butter, and honey. Cook over low heat, stirring, until the mixture comes to a boil. Stir in the pecans and remove from the heat.

Remove the pie from the oven and spread the topping evenly over the top. Return to the oven and broil until the topping is bubbly and golden brown.

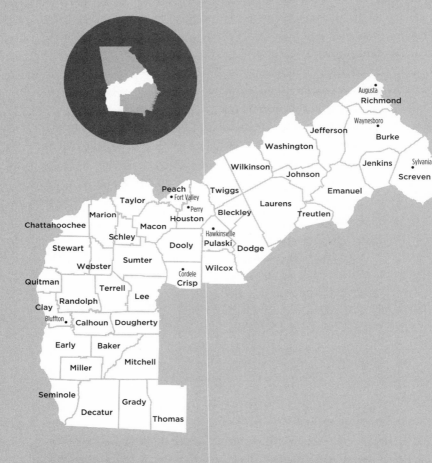

Augusta
Richmond

Waynesboro
Jefferson
Burke

Washington
Jenkins
Sylvania

Wilkinson
Johnson
Screven

Peach
Fort Valley
Taylor
Twiggs
Emanuel

Perry
Laurens
Marion
Houston
Bleckley
Treutlen

Chattahoochee
Schley
Macon

Stewart
Dooly
Hawkinsville

Webster
Sumter
Pulaski
Dodge

Wilcox

Quitman
Cordele
Crisp

Clay
Terrell
Lee

Randolph

Bluffton
Calhoun
Dougherty

Early
Baker

Miller
Mitchell

Seminole
Grady

Decatur
Thomas

# Upper Coastal Plain

Agriculture is the primary industry in the Upper Coastal Plain, which spreads across central and southwestern Georgia, stretching from South Carolina to Alabama to the Florida line. The expansive swaths of land are home to cotton and tobacco farms, sprawling sustainable ranches, and Centennial Farms, land that has been owned—and worked—by the same families for generations. The region also boasts some of the largest pecan and peach orchards and peanut crops in the state. The distances between agritourism destinations might be long in this region, but the pastoral landscapes are stunning, and there is always a peach-packing shed or road-side stand selling fresh fruit if you need an excuse to pull off the road.

## FARMS

### Sand Hills Adventure Farm

Growing up, Brett Gunn remembers his grandfather growing cotton and raising cattle on the farm. Childhood memories of spending time on the farm got Gunn thinking about inviting others to share his love of the land. He started Sand Hills Adventure Farm in 2012. Although the farm, which has been in the family for more than a century, is no longer a working farm, activities like hayrides, hay mazes, a petting zoo, a corncrib, and a pumpkin patch offer a nod to its agricultural heritage.

3951 Noah Station Road, Keysville (Burke County), 706-925-2615, www.sandhillsga.com

At White Oak Pastures, chickens spend their days taking dust baths and pecking for bugs in the pastures.

### White Oak Pastures

Will Harris received an American Treasures Award from the MADE: In America foundation for his success in raising organic beef. White Oak Pastures is the largest certified organic farm in Georgia and has been certified humane by organizations like Animal Welfare Approved and Global Animal Partnership. Dr. Temple Grandin designed the on-site abattoir, which is one of just two on-farm USDA-inspected grass-fed beef plants in the nation. It's a different way of farming from the industrial agriculture Harris practiced in the past. The farm focuses on humane treatment of animals, environmental stewardship, and the local food movement. "Nature abhors a monoculture," explains fifth-generation farmer Jenni Harris. "We got really good at selling grass-fed beef and decided to diversify."

In 2011, the farm added chickens, sheep, hogs, guinea fowl, ducks, and rabbits. The animals are free to roam and engage in their natural behaviors; the hogs root, chickens scratch in the dirt, and rabbits nibble on clover. Harris rotates the animals between pastures to maintain the health of the farm. The farm also added a four-acre vegetable garden and started a CSA as well as an on-site store stocked with meat and produce from the farm. Originally, Jenni thought the farm "wouldn't attract a lot of foot traffic because we're in a very rural area; [now] the area is famous for White Oak Pastures."

In addition to a CSA, a farm store, and tours of the farm, White Oak Pastures opened Pasture to Plate, an on-farm restaurant, in 2012. It's open for breakfast and lunch. During special farm dinners, celebrated local chefs prepare meals with ingredients from the farm. "We really like to be connected to the consumer," Jenni says.

22775 Georgia Highway 27, Bluffton (Clay County), 229-641-2081, www.whiteoakpastures.com

## Kackleberry Farm

Lisa and Mitch Vaughn are teachers who bring their passion for education to the farm. "We thought about starting a pumpkin patch but figured people wouldn't drive all the way out here just for a pumpkin patch, so we started a pumpkin patch and a corn maze, and it's grown from there," says Lisa.

In fact, the couple turned their farm into an expansive outdoor classroom, engaging visitors in agricultural education. It started with a pumpkin patch and corn maze in 2007, and activities have expanded to include hayrides, pig races, a petting zoo, gem mining, pedal cart races, and jumping pillows. "It's become a destination," says Lisa. "People will come and spend six or seven hours here!"

Mitch teaches students with special needs and wanted to incorporate as many sensory activities as possible, encouraging visitors to experience the farm through sight, touch, sound, and smell.

1025 Verdree Road, Louisville (Jefferson County), 706-830-4968, www.kackleberryfarm.com

## Lane Southern Orchards

Mention agritourism in Georgia and the first question is, "Have you been to Lane?" Lane is Lane Southern Orchards, a 6,000-acre peach and pecan orchard hailed as one of the premier agritourism destinations in the state. The original farm, Diamond Fruit Farm, was established in 1908, and a packing shed was added in 1990. All of the fruit grown in the orchards was shipped to supermarkets across the nation. During business meetings, peach lovers and curious passersby knocked on the door of the sales office to request tours or try to buy peaches. Recognizing the demand, the Lane family decided to change their business model. They set up a picnic table in the parking lot and sold peaches to the public. "It just grew from there," says CEO Mark Sanchez.

Lane Southern Orchards has developed a reputation as one of the most successful agritourism destinations in Georgia.

The packing shed is still the heart of the operation. More than twenty-five million peaches are graded, packed, and shipped every season, and a catwalk built over the assembly line offers an up-close view of the process, which runs from May to August. On a farm tour, a trolley travels through the orchards while the driver explains the history of the farm and the process of harvesting pecans and thirty varieties of peaches. Of course, there are plenty of opportunities for taste testing.

The gourmet shop and bakery are filled with peach and pecan products, including preserves, pies, bread, and homemade ice cream. Staffers wearing "Who's Your Farmer?" T-shirts offer samples of local products, including wine and peaches. During the summer months, be prepared to wait for a taste: More than 300,000 visitors come through the doors every year to experience the locally grown goodness. "We were told it would never work because we're too far off the interstate," Sanchez says. "I guess we proved that theory wrong!"

All of the products available in the 70,000-square-foot retail shop are also sold through the Lane Southern Orchards mail-order business.

Although Lane Southern Orchards is most well known for its peaches, the farm also operates a U-pick strawberry patch in the spring and a fall festival with a pumpkin patch and corn maze.

50 Lane Road, Fort Valley (Peach County), 478-825-3592, www.lanesouthernorchards.com

## Pearson Farm

At Pearson Farm, growing peaches and pecans is all about math: 2,300 acres of pecans + 1,400 acres of peaches = 100 years of success for farmer Al Pearson. The family started growing peaches in the 1890s. Most of the peaches are shipped to supermarkets and restaurants or sold through a thriving mail-order business, but the farm store is stocked with more than thirty varieties of peaches and fifteen varieties of pecans plucked from the orchards and sold directly to the public. During harvest season, the farm offers tours of the historic packing shed and serves countless scoops of homemade peach ice cream. In addition to the hum of the machinery in the packing shed and the slurping sounds of customers enjoying fresh peaches, it's not uncommon to hear rock music blaring from the orchards or see scarecrows standing at attention between the trees, both tactics Al Pearson and his son, Lawton, use to scare off wild hogs, deer, and other pests who want to feast on their Georgia-grown crops.

5575 Zenith Mill Road, Crawford (Peach County), 478-827-0750, www.pearsonfarm.com

## Bricko Farms/Kricket Krap

In Richmond County, Bill Bricker is known as "The Connoisseur of Manure." The moniker is hard earned. Since 1977, Bricker, owner of Bricko Farms, has been raising crickets and using the manure to enhance compost. It takes 400,000 crickets about thirty days to make one pound of droppings. "It's like wine, you don't rush it," says John Bricker, the second-generation manure connoisseur. "You have to be patient with the process."

Bill Bricker, who grew up on a small farm, had no idea synthetic fertilizers existed until he attended college at Virginia Tech in the 1970s. He still prefers gardening naturally and tests all of the compost he produces in an on-site garden. The protein-rich compost, dubbed Kricket Krap, is sold on-site in bags or by the truckload, making Bricko Farms a popular spot during planting season. As Bill Bricker says, "It's good crap."

824 Sand Bar Ferry Road, Augusta (Richmond County), 706-722-0661, www.bricko.com

## Old Freeman Family Farm

When Old Freeman Family Farm celebrated its 100th birthday in 1993, Danny and Becky Anderson decided to celebrate by having the farm certified as a Centennial Farm. It's one of just 401 farms in Georgia to receive the designation, which recognizes farms that have preserved the agricultural history of the state. The family has done their best to preserve the historic homestead, maintaining the 1863 farmhouse and re-creating some of the buildings that used to be on the farm, including a cotton gin, smokehouse, and mule barn. "We wanted to play on the history of the farm and turn it back to the way it used to be," says Becky Anderson. Crops like cotton, sugarcane, and peanuts are still grown on the land.

Although the farm offers agritourism activities like a pumpkin patch, corn maze, barrel train, and petting farm, the focus is on providing an educational experience by showcasing traditional farming activities. On fall weekends, there are cane-grinding exhibits and peanut threshing and hay baling using antique equipment. A small farm market in the barn is filled with fresh produce and preserves. "It's a special place," Anderson says.

644 Scarboro Highway, Sylvania (Screven County),
www.andersonfreemanfarm.com

## Wade Plantation

Towering pecan trees dominate the landscape at the 24,000-acre plantation. During October, almost a million pounds of nuts are harvested and packaged as products ranging from roasted pecans and caramel pecans to pecan coffee. A small retail shop on the plantation sells pecans in November and December, but most are shipped through a mail-order business that has been operating since 1923. Customers from all over the world order pecans from Wade Plantation. "Unlike other big pecan producers, we do everything in small batches to protect the quality of the product," explains retail operations manager Kathy Dixon.

The entire process of harvesting, sorting, cleaning, sizing, and packaging pecans is showcased during tours of the processing facility. Aside from tours (offered by appointment) and the retail sales operation, the plantation is not open to the public. The current owners, Morris Communications Company, publishers of *Augusta Magazine* and *Savannah Magazine*, maintain the plantation as a private hunting lodge.

752 Oglethorpe Trail, Sylvania (Screven County), 800-414-7941,
www.wadepecans.com

## Don't Pick the Pecans

With 88 million pounds of pecans produced annually in Georgia, it's common to drive past orchards where tree branches are laden with pecans and fallen nuts cover the ground. But think twice before hopping out of the car for a taste. According to Georgia law, it's illegal to pick pecans on private land—even if the tree branches extend over public roads and the nuts have fallen to the ground. Stealing more than $500 worth of agricultural products is a felony in Georgia. The 2010 Georgia Code was designed to protect pecan growers from thieves who steal their nuts and sell them to wholesalers for a tidy profit. In 2012, the retail price for a pound of pecans, about thirty nuts, sold for up to $12. (In 2009, the same pound of nuts sold for less than $7 per pound.) During pecan season, which runs from October to January, it's not uncommon for farmers to watch their nuts disappear. As prices increased, so did pecan thefts. Although there are no official numbers, some growers estimate losses totaling tens of thousands of dollars across Georgia. To combat the losses, some growers have installed fences or put up security systems while others have hired security guards to patrol the orchards. It hasn't stopped thieves from filling buckets with the premium nuts—a problem most growers blame on the economy.

Mark's Melon Patch has been growing fresh produce and selling it at a roadside farm stand for more than twenty-five years.

## Mark's Melon Patch

Mark Daniel started growing watermelons in high school and selling them from the bed of a pickup truck on the side of the road to earn money. Two decades later, Mark's Melon Patch is still a go-to destination for watermelons, but the original five-acre patch has grown into a seventy-acre farm where Daniel grows fruits and vegetables, ranging from honeydews and cantaloupe to sweet corn and peanuts, and sells them alongside other Georgia-made, Georgia-grown products. And watermelons are still one of the most popular items at the roadside farm stand. The fields hidden behind the stand are the place to be in the fall, when Mark's Melon Patch transforms into Mark's Pumpkin Patch. Families pick pumpkins from the pumpkin patch, shoot corn cannons, climb aboard a tractor-pulled wagon for a ride around the farm and navigate through hay mazes. "There are women sitting under trees picking peanuts off of the vines and generations of families spending time together on the farm," says farm stand manager Dean Jackson. "It's a real southern moment, like stepping back in time."

8580 Albany Highway, Dawson (Terrell County), 229-698-4750, www.marksmelonpatch.com

# FARMERS' MARKETS

## Cordele State Farmers Market

Cordele is hailed as the watermelon capital of the world, and the market is a major distribution point for national and international shipping. During watermelon season, which lasts from June to August, more than 200 million pounds of watermelons are shipped from the market. The sheer number of watermelon growers in Crisp County makes the market one of the best places to find locally grown watermelons. But there is more to the market than melons. When watermelon season is at its peak, dozens of vendors set up booths to sell fresh produce; the number of vendors dwindles significantly after watermelon season.

1901 U.S. Highway 41, Cordele (Crisp County), 229-276-2335


# FARM STANDS AND U-PICKS

## Byne Blueberry Farms

It's not an accident that there are no signs leading to Byne Blueberry Farms or that the fields of blueberries look more like an industrial operation than a U-pick farm: A full 90 percent of the blueberries grown on the farm are shipped to retail markets like Whole Foods and Earth Fare. In June and July, the farm is open for U-pick. Since the farm is the oldest certified blueberry farm in the Southeast, the berries are in high demand. "As people became more interested in organic [produce], there was an increased demand for U-pick, so we decided to give it a shot," says Dick Byne.

Byne started growing blueberries in 1980 after considering various crops for the twenty-acre farm. He decided against cotton and soybeans because "the prices were decimated" and settled on blueberries because there were no other farms in the area growing the crop. It was a risk that paid off: Byne Blueberry Farm runs a successful commercial operation, demand for U-pick organic blueberries is at an all-time high, and the farm's value-added products like blueberry salsa and chocolate blueberries have won Flavor of Georgia awards.

537 Jones Avenue, Waynesboro (Burke County), 706-554-6244,
www.byneblueberries.com

## Garden Fresh Farm

According to Stephen Feitshans, U-picks shouldn't be limited to berries, peaches, and apples. In 2011, he transitioned twenty-five acres of his family farm into a U-pick veggie patch. "Most of the food you buy tasted much better when it came out of the field . . . [but] by the time it was picked and shipped, it lost a lot of its flavor," he says.

Instead of filling plastic bags in the produce aisle and settling for less-than-perfect produce, on Garden Fresh Farm you can fill a five-gallon bucket with all of the just-picked potatoes, butter beans, okra, peppers, tomatillos, tomatoes, cucumbers, butternut squash, zucchini, and peas it will hold—for $10. "It's a tremendous savings, and that is a huge draw to the farm," Feitshans says. "But it's not the biggest draw. You know how some people are crazy about wine? The people that come here are crazy about peas, about fresh produce."

78A Mossy Creek Drive, Perry (Houston County), 478-396-2665

## Barbour Farms

Between April and September, the farm stand on Highway 49 does brisk business selling Georgia-grown produce. Bill Barbour grows 650 acres of peaches and 800 acres of pecans in Peach County, shipping most of the crops to supermarkets; he started the roadside stand to have a direct connection with shoppers. Barbour also supports area farmers by selling their produce at the stand. The business is second nature to Barbour, who started working in a packinghouse in Fort Valley when he was just eight years old.

235 Georgia Highway 49, Byron (Peach County), 478-956-2112

## Hardy Farms Peanuts

Peanuts grow underground, like carrots. It's a fact that always surprises people, according to Brad Hardy, vice president of sales and marketing at Hardy Farms Peanuts. He points to 600 acres of green tops popping out of the dirt behind the processing plant. Between July and November every year, Hardy Farms Peanuts harvests four million pounds of peanuts, and one-quarter of their crop is turned into boiled peanuts. The thirty roadside stands licensed by Hardy Farms and spread across middle Georgia are the best places to find the sought-after boiled peanuts. "If you pass a roadside stand selling boiled peanuts, chances are good the peanuts came from Hardy Farms," says Hardy. "The stands are almost like fast-food restaurants

Cousins Brad Hardy and Ken Hardy operate a peanut empire that includes more than thirty roadside stands all over Georgia. All of the peanuts are grown, boiled, and packaged on their Hawkinsville property.

but for peanuts. One of the reasons they are so successful is because people in the South are used to buying boiled peanuts at roadside stands."

Hardy Farms started selling boiled peanuts in the 1990s. At the time, customers were coming to the processing plant with bags and buckets to purchase peanuts. There was no question that boiled peanuts, which are soaked in the shell and cooked for twenty minutes, were popular, so the Hardy family decided to capitalize on the market. The roadside stand out-side the processing plant is one of their first—and most popular—loca-tions. The rustic stand won't win any design awards, but the unmistakable smell of peanuts cooking is enticing enough to make fans overlook the aesthetics.

Hardy Farms won a Keeper of the Flame award from the Southern Foodways Alliance for their commitment to preserving a treasured south-ern food.

1659 Eastman Highway, Hawkinsville (Pulaski County), 478-783-3044, www.hardyfarmspeanuts.com

## Jacobs Produce

Between April and October, the fields at Jacobs Produce are filled with colorful crops ranging from strawberries, blackberries, and peaches to tomatoes, butterbeans, and sweet corn. Linda and Herbert Jacobs started the U-pick farm in 1992 to offer fresh, local strawberries. The popularity of the strawberry patch inspired the couple to grow other crops, and it wasn't long before their grandchildren inspired the addition of goats, chickens, cows, and donkeys to the farm. "Kids would come out and ask us to pet them, so we started letting school tours come to the farm," recalls Linda.

2695 Scarboro Highway, Rocky Ford (Screven County), 912-754-7257

## Taylor Orchards

The largest commercial peach orchard in Georgia spans 3,600 acres with peach trees in four counties but still manages to retain the feel of a small roadside farm stand. Patsy Wainwright, the daughter-in-law of founder Walter Wainwright, has the same motto as the postal service during peach season: Neither rain nor sleet nor dark of night will keep her from manning the peach stand. While Miss Patsy sells bags of Empress, Harvester, Red Globe, and Flame Prince or the twenty-six other varieties of peaches grown in the orchard and offers tips for how to store, cook, or preserve the fresh fruit, the packing shed hums behind her. More than eighteen million pounds of peaches run through the shed between May and August. Most of the peaches are shipped to chain grocers and farmers' markets across the Southeast, but Miss Patsy sells boxes of fresh peaches on-site. Her southern charm is as sweet as the peaches, which has kept customers coming back for generations. "We produce the fresh Georgia peaches that Georgia is famous for," says Miss Patsy. "It's an experience to come here and see the shed running to get an idea of the process of getting peaches from the field to market."

The roadside stand closes in August, but a small store carries jams, jellies, bread, and ice cream all year.

1665 East Fall Line Freeway, Reynolds (Taylor County), 478-847-4186,
www.taylororchards.com

### Southern Swiss Dairy

When Jimmy and Ginny Franks started Southern Swiss Dairy in 1992, all of their milk was picked up in tanks and shipped offsite. In 2010, the couple built a processing plant and invited customers to the farm to purchase everything from 2 percent and skim milk to eggnog and homemade ice cream. It's added a new dimension to their business and garnered a lot of loyal followers. "There are customers who drive sixty miles to get our buttermilk," says Ginny Franks. "One of the reasons they like our buttermilk—all of our milk—is because it's local and they know where it's coming from."

Both Jimmy and Ginny come from farming families and are used to long days and hard labor that come with raising cattle and producing milk. Opening a farm store has allowed the couple to share their love of farming and fresh milk. For customers, the benefits are in the bottle. Within twenty-four hours of milking, the milk is bottled and available for sale in the farm store; it can take weeks for milk to reach supermarket shelves, according to Franks. In addition to buttermilk, the dairy bottles whole milk, skim milk, 2 percent milk, heavy cream, and half-and-half, as well as butter, homemade ice cream, and, seasonally, eggnog.

Unlike other dairies that raise Holsteins for milk, Southern Swiss raises brown Swiss cows, a breed Franks refers to as "moody, temperamental, and headstrong." The milk, she believes, is more full-bodied than milk from other breeds, including Holsteins—and judging by the number of customers who shop at the farm store, she must be right.

279 Rosier Road, Waynesboro (Burke County), 706-339-1739,
www.southernswissdairy.com

## Do Dogs Drink Milk?

If the labels on milk sold at some Georgia farms are to be believed, dogs and cats are drinking a lot of milk.

According to the U.S. Food and Drug Administration, Georgia is one of twenty-six states banning the sale of raw milk for human consumption. To sell raw milk, which is unpasteurized, farms must label the milk "pet milk" and include a warning that it is not for human consumption. Proponents of raw milk believe that it is richer, creamier, and healthier than pasteurized milk. The state of Georgia tried to have all raw milk dyed black to discourage human consumption; residents rallied against the attempt, defeating the proposed policy in 2007.

In 2010, Georgia State Representative Doug McKillip (D-Athens) introduced the Dairy Consumer Choice Act to amend Article 7, Chapter 2, of Title 26 of the Official Code of Georgia Annotated to allow the sale of raw milk for human consumption. At press time, the bill was still in the House.

### Sweet Grass Dairy

With cheeses like Georgia Gouda, Asher blue, Thomasville Tomme, a Camembert-style cheese known as Green Hill, and Heat, a semisoft cheese spiced with chili peppers and chipotles on the menu, it's hard to choose a favorite. The best option: order the cheese board. "Making cheese is a science, but it's also very artful," says Mat Willey, communications director for Sweet Grass Dairy. "That comes through in our cheese."

Cheeses from Sweet Grass Dairy are distributed in forty states and featured on countless local menus, but the option to order all of their cheeses in a downtown shop operated by cheesemongers and dairy farmers Jeremy and Jessica Little is relatively new. The couple joined the family dairy in 2002 and learned to make handcrafted cheese with milk from grass-fed cattle. After mastering the process and increasing production to

3,500 pounds of cheese per week, they decided to expand their efforts into the retail market. Cheese is the main staple at the marketplace, but other products—olives, jellies, pasta, bread, wine, and beer—mostly from local producers, are also served. "There is much more interest in locally produced products, [so] opening a retail space made sense," says Willey. "People know they could go to the farm if they wanted to, but this is a different option, something that isn't found anywhere else."

106 North Broad Street, Thomasville (Thomas County), 229-228-6704, www.sweetgrassdairy.com

## AQUACULTURE

### Owen and Williams Fish Hatchery

Paul Williams, wearing khakis and a tan fishing vest, looks like he stepped out of the pages of an L.L. Bean catalog. Instead of a rod and reel, he carries a net and maneuvers between artificial ponds as he explains the process of raising catfish, bluegill, bass, and carp. "A lot of people have never seen a fish hatchery before," he says.

During tours (by appointment) Williams stops at different tanks to show the difference between catfish eggs, hatchlings, and full-grown catfish. The hatchery has been operating for more than three decades, producing annually three million fish that are shipped to ponds around the world. "We put fish in the pond at Augusta National [Golf Club]," Williams beams.

20 Fish Farm Road, Hawkinsville (Pulaski County), 478-892-3144, www.owenandwilliams.com

# CHOOSE-AND-CUT CHRISTMAS TREES

## Beall's Christmas Tree Farm

At Beall's Christmas Tree Farm, finding the perfect Christmas tree is an adventure. After picking up a saw at the office, visitors are sent out to explore all seventeen acres of the farm, which are covered with swaths of trees in all shapes, sizes, and shades, from Leyland cypress, Murray cypress, and eastern red cedars to Silver Dusts and Castlewellan Golds. After choosing and cutting a tree, visitors return to the office where the Beall family, who have owned and operated the farm since 1981, help shake the trees, drill holes in the bottom, wrap them for transport, and strap them onto cars. Sam and Katherine Beall manage the farm, while their three children act as "elves," handing out candy canes and spreading holiday cheer.

1533 Highway 80 East, East Dublin (Laurens County), 478-689-6447, www.beallchristmastreefarm.gacta.com

## Busy Elves Christmas Tree Farm

Busy Elves Christmas Tree Farm puts its focus squarely on the customer. When Jody Putnal retired from the insurance business in 1983, he established the farm as a way to connect with people and provide them with a memorable Christmas tree–buying experience. He also instills strong communication and leadership skills in the young "elves" he hires, so they can help customers find that special tree, then cut, wrap, and load it. Visitors can cut their own trees, choosing from a selection of Blue Ice junipers, Carolina Sapphires, and Nailar blues among others. Busy Elves Christmas Tree Farm also stocks precut trees like Virginia pines and Fraser firs. The farm sells wreaths, bows, and hot refreshments and also features a petting zoo, complete with alpacas, rabbits, pigs, doves, and ducks.

102 U.S. Highway 82, Leesburg (Lee County), 229-883-3933

# VINEYARDS AND DISTILLERIES

## Still Pond Vineyard

Muscadine wines sold across Georgia are made from grapes grown at Still Pond Vineyard. The farm started as a commercial grape-growing operation: Charles Cowart grew 180 acres of vines and sold the fruit to supermarkets and wineries. In 1991, his son, Charlie, took over the farming and looked for opportunities to make it more profitable. He built a processing facility to crush and press grapes for wineries. "A light bulb went off," he recalls. "I thought, if someone could teach us to make wine, we could use this place twelve months of the year instead of six weeks during harvest time."

With the support of other winemakers in the region, Still Pond Vineyard released its first wines in 2003. All of the eighteen wines produced in the winery, several of which have won national and international awards, are named for the region, including Confederate Peach, Plantation Red, Crimson Clover, and Farmhouse White. "We wanted to keep the wines as connected to the area as possible," Charlie says.

Even the name Still Pond has regional significance. During the Civil War, a moonshine still where Confederate soldiers produced peach brandy was hidden in the brush near the pond on the farm. Using the grapes his father grows, winemaker Charlie Cowart takes a more legal approach to producing alcohol on the land. "The nice thing about being a small winery is that we can take our time because we don't have production deadlines," he says. "We care about the process and want to do it right."

1575 Still Pond Road, Arlington (Calhoun County), 229-792-6382, www.stillpond.com

## Cane River Vineyard

Bob Evans and Jennifer Cox know that a small plot of land a mile off of the interstate is an odd location for a vineyard. But the location is exactly what has made Cane River Vineyard popular. Since the couple started serving thirteen varieties of red, white, and fruit wines made from muscadine grapes in 2010, travelers on I-75 have pulled off of the highway for a break and a sip. "We want to keep things small," says Cox. "The winery will never be a huge commercial enterprise; it was designed to be a relaxing, fun stop that brings a southern touch to the interstate."

Cane River Vineyard might be small, but its wines are making a big splash: Several of their wines are award winning, including Peach County Peach, which won a silver medal at the Finger Lakes International Wine Competition. The vineyard was also voted the best place in the county to take a date.

144 Cane River Drive, Byron (Peach County), 478-956-3767

### Richland Distilling Company

Erik Vonk loves rum. After working for a multinational staffing agency for decades, Vonk moved from California to Georgia in 1992 and became fascinated with the idea of growing sugar cane to make rum. It took more than a decade to perfect the process and navigate miles of red tape before Richland Distilling Company released its first batch of rum in 2012. "It was much more difficult than I thought," Vonk admits.

One of the biggest hurdles was figuring out how to produce rum in a dry county. Vonk originally planned to manufacture rum on his farm in Stewart County, where he grows thirty-five acres of sugar cane. He pointed to Jack Daniels Distillery, operated in a dry county in Tennessee, as a possible precedent, but the county wouldn't budge. In order to obtain all of the required licenses and permits to legally produce rum, Vonk had to open the distillery in downtown Richland, which allows the production, distribution, and sale of alcohol. With all of the pieces in place, he got down to business.

Richland Distilling Company makes artisan rum from cane juice. It's a rare process (most distillers use molasses) that, according to Vonk, produces rum that "is much more flavorful and much more aromatic."

Despite the effort required to open a distillery, Vonk has no plans to mass produce Richland Rum. Instead, he limits production to 20,000 bottles per year. "If we produce more than that, it starts to become an industrial operation and loses its artisan quality," he says. The distillery is open to the public for tours, and a tasting room in downtown Richland pours samples.

333 Broad Street, Richland (Stewart County), 229-321-0678, www.richlandrum.com

## Thirteenth Colony Distilleries

On a whim, Alton Darby and Kent Cost decided to make moonshine as gifts. The local sheriff heard about it and suggested the pair, real estate developers from Columbus, research the legal ramifications of making alcohol without the proper permits. Instead of setting up an underground still, they obtained the required licenses to make distilled liquor. Their first product, Plantation Vodka, which has been awarded multiple gold medals in national competitions, hit the market in 2009. "It speaks to Southwest Georgia and the quail plantations in the region," explains Lindsay Cotton, director of marketing for the distillery. The distillery also produces gin and corn whisky, all made from corn grown in nearby Leslie, Georgia.

Graham Anderson, director of stillroom operations, distills up to 300 gallons of alcohol annually. "I'm not too much farther ahead than the guys making alcohol in the woods," he says. "It's as close to the traditional process as we can be."

Tours of the distillery showcase the process from grinding the corn to pouring the alcohol into barrels to distill. It's a process Arthur describes as "farm to bar."

305 North Dudley Street, Americus (Sumter County), 229-924-3310, www.13colony.net

## FESTIVALS AND EVENTS

### Watermelon Days Festival

In Cordele, billed as the Watermelon Capital of the World, the competition is on to see who can spit a watermelon seed the farthest. Held annually in June, Watermelon Days Festival, started in 1949, celebrates Georgia's status as the nation's leading supplier of the oversized fruit. Festival-goers can indulge in slices of the sweet treat as well as other sweet snacks, such as red velvet funnel cake and fried Oreos. Those craving competition can participate in the watermelon-eating contest, watermelon-decorating contest, or—for those with a strong arm—the watermelon-chucking contest. But nothing gets the competitive juices flowing more than the famous watermelon seed–spitting contest. Even Watermelon Capital beauty pageant winners are required to whet their whistles and spit. So far, the record distance is sixty-four feet.

902 North 7th Street, Cordele (Crisp County), 229-273-1668, www.cordelecrispga.com

## Georgia National Fair

Every October, the Georgia National Fairgrounds and Agricenter turns into an agricultural wonderland, where it's possible to visit exhibits and tour educational displays depicting all aspects of agriculture during the eleven-day event, which attracts close to 500,000 attendees.

Most of the exhibits are hands-on, giving visitors an opportunity to see, touch, and taste commodities and livestock. Meet dozens of breeds of rabbits and understand how their fiber is spun into yarn; learn how cotton, the leading cash crop in Georgia, is grown and turned into everyday objects like clothing and blankets; meet experts from the University of Georgia's Horticulture Department who showcase local agricultural products like fruits, vegetables, nuts, and wine; and watch baby chicks hatching and bees working in their hives. One of the most popular exhibits is the dairy barn where cows and goats are milked and samples of fresh milk are gulped down by eager taste-testers. The event also honors the history of agriculture in the state through exhibits on Centennial Farms and displays of antique tractors and farming equipment.

Like all good agricultural fairs, the Georgia National Fair has an award-winning livestock program. Members of Georgia 4-H clubs and Future Farmers of America compete in several categories, hoping to take home blue ribbons for their agricultural projects. One of the exhibits offers information about the criteria judges use to evaluate the efforts of participants and gives visitors an opportunity to use the knowledge to award ribbons to display projects.

401 Larry Walker Parkway, Perry (Houston County), 478-987-3247, www.gnfa.com

## Georgia Peach Festival

Although sales of Georgia's official fruit have slipped to third in the nation, the peach still ranks high in the hearts of Georgians everywhere, especially in the county that bears its name. It's in Peach County that over half of Georgia's peaches are cultivated, and it's here that the fuzzy fruit is celebrated each June during an eight-day festival in the sister cities of Byron and Fort Valley. Started in 1986, the Georgia Peach Festival features concerts, kids activities, fireworks, arts and crafts, and a Miss Georgia Peach beauty pageant. But the crowning glory of the festival is not the parade of beauty queens; it's the unveiling of the world's largest peach cobbler. The colossal cobbler, which takes ten hours to bake, is made with 90 pounds of butter, 150 pounds of sugar, and 75 gallons of peaches. Visitors from as far away as Michigan line up for hours just to get a bite.

201 Oakland Heights Parkway, Fort Valley (Peach County), 478-825-4002, www.gapeachfestival.com

## Plains Peanut Festival

The town of Plains in western Georgia is proud of its two most famous exports: its peanut crop and its one-time peanut farmer, President Jimmy Carter. The Plains Peanut Festival, started in 1996, honors both. The one-day celebration in September features an array of peanuts in all of their crunchy glory: boiled and roasted and ground for peanut butter ice cream. The festival also showcases a variety of arts and crafts vendors and plenty of kids' activities, from train rides and horseback riding to a petting zoo. But the day's highlight is an appearance by President Jimmy Carter himself. Crowds from as far as the Midwest line up to get books autographed by the former president—who was raised in Plains and still maintains a residence there—or hear him tout the health benefits of "goobers."

Various venues in Plains (Sumter County), 229-824-5373, www.plainsgeorgia.com/peanut_festival.html

## SPECIALTY SHOPS

### Stripling's General Store

Road trippers driving along the Georgia Highway 300 between Georgia and Florida often stop into Stripling's in search of a bathroom. If the restrooms get customers in the door, the butcher shop, private-label barbecue sauce, salsa, and seasonings keep them in the aisles. The general store started out as a small on-farm butcher shop called Stripling's Sausage Kitchen in 1978 and has grown to become a full-fledged grocer known for its farm-to-fork pork and sausage products.

The Hardin family raises hogs in nearby Moultrie and processes the pork in an on-site USDA-certified processing plant. "We raise and process the hogs and sell them in the store; we are truly farm-to-fork," says Lisa Hardin. "We're really proud of the fact that we have control of our products from beginning to end."

Mild, medium, and hot sausage, fresh and smoked sausage, and beef jerky and other gourmet pork products from Stripling's are shipped all over the globe via their mail-order business. Through the United Service Organization (USO), Stripling's started Jerky for the Troops to send their pork jerky to soldiers serving overseas who wanted a taste of home.

2289 Georgia Highway 300 South, Cordele (Crisp County), 229-535-6561, www.striplings.com

### The Orchards at Atwell Pecan

Atwell Pecan has been processing pecans in Jefferson County since 1935. Of the five million pounds of nuts that go through the processing plant every year, 90 percent are Georgia grown. In 2007, with demand for pecan candies at an all time high, the family-owned business run by Jerry and Susan Dowdy and their daughter, Sue-Anna Dowdy Maley, added a retail shop, The Orchards, to their existing mail-order business, which ships products ranging from a single bag of nuts to $200 gift baskets. Raw pecans are the most popular items in the bright boutique, but candy cases filled with chocolate-covered pecans, almond bark, pecan pralines, and other sweet treats tempt the taste buds. All of the sweets, which Maley calls "the best candy in the South, made from the finest chocolate," are made on-site.

705 South Main Street, Wrens (Jefferson County), 800-548-NUTS, www.theorchardsgourmet.com

## Fresh Food: There's an App for That

A host of fresh food apps are available for smart phones, putting local food resources at your fingertips. Here are a few worth downloading:

*Label Lookup*: A free iPhone app created by the National Resources Defense Council to help users decipher labeling claims. The app provides definitions for over 200 labels, from antibacterial and biodegradable to Eco-Safe, shedding light on product claims and helping users make purchasing decisions. A dedicated food section includes definitions for labels like free-range, Certified Humane, and Food Alliance Certified. Users can search based on product, label, or rating.

*Eat Local*: Released by the National Resources Defense Council in 2012, this free download includes nationwide listings of farmers' markets, searchable by zip code. Each market listing features the address and a list of its offerings. The app also lists seasonal recipes to help you make the most of fresh, local ingredients.

*Locavore*: Rated the best iOS app for foodies by *Time* magazine, this free iPhone app uses your GPS location to find nearby farms and farmers' markets. Click on one of the colored pins for the address, contact information, and list of available items. The app also includes listings of produce currently in season as well as a "coming in season soon" list with timelines of when new crops will appear at local markets.

## M&T Meats

When hog farmers Alvin Mathis Jr. and Fred Thompson started M&T Meats in 1963, the pair processed two hogs per week and sold the sausage from a small wooden shed. In 2009, M&T Meats unveiled a brand-new store with a full-service butcher shop with meat cases stocked with pork products like sausage, pork loin, and rib roasts as well as chicken, beef, and seafood, with an emphasis on products from Georgia farms. All of the hogs are processed in an on-site abattoir. "When we built a $2 million building in the middle of nowhere Georgia, people thought we were crazy," explains second-generation owner Phil Mathis. "We knew that people would be willing to drive to the country to get fresh meat, and we're proud of that."

Mathis, a hog farmer, took over the business from his father and grandfather in 1993. He's added an on-site smokehouse and takes great care to bring new products to market, like pork loin stuffed with jalapeño cheese sausage. The effort has helped Mathis grow the business into a nationally recognized brand with customers that include John Travolta, Morgan Freeman, and Burt Reynolds. "They order gift boxes every Christmas," Mathis says.

230 Lower River Road, Hawkinsville (Pulaski County), 478-892-9810, www.mtmeatco.com

## Merritt Pecan Company and General Store

Richard and Tammy Merritt have been growing and processing pecans since 1980. Most of the nuts are shipped to wholesale customers or sold through a mail-order business. A general store at the processing plant stocks all of the pecan brittle, candy-coated pecans, honey-roasted pecans, chocolate-covered pecans, and plain (shelled) pecans available through the mail-order catalog, no postage required. The small shop carries other Georgia-grown products, including wine, honey, and peaches.

4051 Georgia Highway 520, Weston (Webster County), 800-762-9152, www.merritt-pecan.com

# FARM-TO-TABLE RESTAURANTS

## New Moon Café

When the phone rings at this downtown Augusta café, chances are good it's an inquiry about the featured dishes on the Local Lover menu. Owner Christine Tomasetti-Allewelt introduced the new menu to emphasize the abundance of quality foods produced locally. Depending on the season, the menu incorporates shrimp, grits, buttermilk, and fresh produce from local farms.

1002 Broad Street, Augusta (Richmond County), 706-823-2008, www.newmoondowntown.com. $

## Frog Hollow Tavern

"When you go into the kitchen, there are bushels of peaches and baskets of tomatoes, not boxes of produce from [other countries]," explains the bartender, Gwen. The focus on fresh foods is the reason Frog Hollow Tavern is the most recommended farm-to-table restaurant in Augusta. Chef Sean Wight designs the menu around produce and meat from local producers like Split Creek Farm, Border Springs Farm, Oaklyn Plantation, Sweet Grass Dairy, and Anson Mills. Dishes like wild-caught shrimp and grits, braised Berkshire pork shoulder with smoked Gouda mac and cheese and braised collards, and tomato salad with feta cheese and Georgia olive oil change seasonally to reflect the local bounty.

1282 Broad Street, Augusta (Richmond County), 706-364-6906, www.froghollowtavern.com. $$

## Café Campesino

In the summers, hot and humid conditions might make South Georgia feel like the tropics, but the conditions still aren't right for growing coffee. So, since sourcing coffee beans from local farmers isn't an option, Café Campesino imports beans from farmer cooperatives in countries like Indonesia, Peru, Bolivia, and Ethiopia. All of the beans are fair trade and organic. "We have a direct relationship with farmer cooperatives," explains sales manager Nema Etheridge. "Our goal is to support organic agriculture and treat the farmers fairly, and the cooperatives help us do that."

All of the beans are roasted in the on-site roastery in Americus. Roaster Nancy Aparicio grinds the raw beans into single-origin and blended coffees like Sumatra Viennese Roast, Georgia Organics Special Blend Medium Roast, and Justice Blend Full City Roast. The coffee is sold by the cup or by the pound in a café adjacent to the roastery. On Friday mornings, "cuppings" are held in the café. Similar to wine tastings, the events are an opportunity to sample different gourmet coffees, making observations about their smell and taste. "Coffee has more flavor profiles than wine," says Etheridge. "It's like any agricultural product that is affected by climate and soil. Cupping brings us back to the farm because we can taste the impact of those elements."

Tours of the roastery are also offered by appointment.

725 Spring Street, Americus (Sumter County), 229-924-2468, www.cafecampesino.com. $

## LODGING

### Quail Country Plantation
In 1992, Paschal and Kay Brooks took over the hunting preserve that her parents started more than four decades ago. The plantation, which started at 360 acres and has grown to include 1,480 acres, is open for guided quail hunts from October to March. Although Quail Country is still best known as a hunting preserve, Kay and Paschal have expanded beyond the annual hunts. "It's evolved and it's a blessing," Kay says.

The couple added a tribe of goats, stocked the fish pond with bass and bream for fishing, and tweaked the menu to feature southern favorites like butterbeans, catfish, and peach cobbler made from Georgia-grown ingredients. Guests can bring in quail from their hunts or their catch from the stocked pond and have it prepared for supper. "We have become really well known for our food," Kay says. "If our guests are hungry, it's their own fault because we feed 'em good southern food and a lot of it!"

1134 Quail Country Road, Arlington (Early County), 229-308-8039, www.quailcountry.com. $$$

## Dublin Farms Bed and Breakfast

Europeans Maria Runggaldier and Heinz Krassnig loved the concept of agritourism, which was introduced in Italy to help struggling farmers supplement their incomes. The couple wanted to bring a touch of the Old Country to the South with their on-farm bed and breakfast. The landscape of the thirty-acre farm, with its rolling hills and lush landscapes, reminded the couple of European *agritourismo*.

At the working farm where horses and donkeys graze in the pastures, a renovated farmhouse with four private guestrooms is available for overnight stays. Guests are treated to continental breakfasts on the terrace and meals at Ristorante da Maria, where Runggaldier, who attended culinary school in Italy, prepares traditional Italian meals like *bruschette* with grilled eggplant, mozzarella, tomatoes, olive oil, and fresh herbs and *arrosto di pollo farcito con verdure* (roasted chicken with vegetables) made with locally grown ingredients.

875 James Currie Road, Dublin (Laurens County), 478-275-8766, www.dublinfarm.com. $

## Koinonia Farm

Koinonia Farm is an intentional Christian community that was founded in 1942. The residents live on-site and share duties, including farming and food preparation. In addition to growing produce, meat, and eggs, residents tend to an expansive pecan orchard. The pecans are harvested and processed on-site and then packaged and sold at the farm store. The products range from raw pecans and cinnamon-spiced pecans to pecan pies, pecan bark, and pecan brittle. All of the proceeds from the sale of pecan products help support the community. The farm welcomes overnight guests, who are encouraged to work alongside residents on the farm or in the pecan-processing plant. For those who prefer not to put in a shift on the farm, tours are offered several times a week. At noon, the dining hall serves communal meals made from ingredients grown in the farm. For a small donation, anyone can break bread with Koinonia residents. "People are hungering for things that are real, seeking a deeper connection to their communities, land, and food," says Koinonia resident Kat Mournighan. "This isn't a traditional farm with an everyday agritourism experience; we offer something different."

1324 Georgia Highway 49 South, Americus (Sumter County), 229-924-0391, www.koinoniapartners.org. $

## RECIPES

### Apple Crudo

*Sean Wight, chef at Frog Hollow Tavern in Augusta, doesn't believe a commitment to farm-to-table dining ends with the entrees. Or that fruit needs to be saved for dessert. Wight uses a seasonal trifecta of apples, fresh greens, and Vidalia onions to create a starter that gets diners excited.*

SERVES 2

|   |   |
|---|---|
| 1 | large Fuji apple |
|   | Thinly sliced country ham (about 2–3 ounces) |
| ¼ | cup good-quality blue cheese |
|   | (Wight likes Flat Creek Lodge in Swainsboro) |
| 2 | ounces Vidalia onion salad dressing |
|   | Baby mixed greens or arugula |
|   | Zest of 1 lemon, 1 lime, and 1 orange |
|   | Good local honey |
|   | Salt and freshly ground black pepper to taste |

Core and thinly slice the apple. Arrange the apple slices on a serving plate in layers. Sprinkle the ham and blue cheese over the apple. Toss the greens and fruit zest with the dressing and gently place on top of blue cheese and ham. Drizzle with the honey and season with salt and pepper.

## Brown Sugar Bacon Popcorn

*There is nothing wrong with chocolate-covered pecans or pecan pralines, but Sue-Anna Dowdy Maley knows that sometimes the best snack combines sweets and salt. To satisfy the cravings of shoppers at The Orchards at Atwell Pecan, she created a recipe with the sweet taste of Georgia-grown pecans with the salty bite of bacon.*

MAKES ABOUT 4 QUARTS

| | |
|---|---|
| ½ | cup unpopped popcorn |
| 3 | tablespoons pecan oil |
| ⅓ | pound bacon (about 5 slices thick-cut bacon), cut into 1-inch pieces |
| 1 | cup chopped pecans |
| 1½ | teaspoons salt |
| ¾ | cup light brown sugar, packed |
| 1 | stick unsalted butter |

Pop the popcorn in the oil and set aside. Cook the bacon until crispy; remove to paper towels and reserve the drippings. In the same skillet, toast the pecans and ½ teaspoon of the salt. Return the bacon to the skillet and add the brown sugar and butter. Cook over low heat until the sugar is melted. In a large bowl, toss the popcorn and remaining salt with the bacon-sugar mixture. Spread the popcorn on a baking sheet lined with waxed paper to cool before serving.

# Lower Coastal Plain

Running from South Carolina to Florida, the Lower Coastal Plain encompasses the Atlantic coast of Georgia, including Savannah and the Sea Islands. The area is best known as a shipping port, and, thanks to its location on the shores of the Atlantic Ocean, it's a popular destination for aquaculture activities like shrimping and fishing (and restaurant menus featuring fresh catch). Savannah boasts creative urban farming initiatives, farmers' markets, and farm-to-table restaurants, while more remote parts of the region have agritourism offerings ranging from island escapes with agricultural emphasis, remote state farms where park rangers double as farmers, and farms growing and raising some of the most unusual crops in the state, including buffalo, olives, and patented pumpkins. The Lower Coastal Plain is what Georgia residents refer to as "below the gnat line," which means swarms of small bugs are ubiquitous in the summer, especially on farms.

## FARMS

### Thompson Farms

Happy pigs come from Dixie, Georgia. Andrew Thompson raises Berkshire hogs on 350 acres, giving each one room to roam across the pastures and plenty of mud for afternoon soaks. Thompson Farms earned top ratings from Whole Foods. It's the only pork producer in the country to earn the coveted Five-Step Animal Welfare Rating Standard from the natural foods retailer for their ethical treatment of animals, which requires that animals born on the farm spend their entire lives there. In 2011, Thompson Farms

A sow nurses her piglets in the sunshine at Thompson Farms.

built a USDA-certified processing facility on-site to meet the rating standard that requires the pigs to be processed on the farm.

The on-site smokehouse and retail store draws visitors to the farm, but the chance to visit the pigs is the real reason to make the trip to rural Dixie. "We get calls from people saying, 'Are you open? We want to come out and buy pork and visit the pigs,'" says Andrew Thompson. "We believe in transparency, so anyone who wants to come by to see the pigs is welcome to." All of the pork products, from jerky and chops to sausage and bacon, are smoked on-site using peach wood and sold under the Dixie Smokehouse label.

2538 Dixie Road, Dixie (Brooks County), 229-263-9074,
www.thompsonfarms.com

### Pebble Hill Grove

Most of the pecans grown in Georgia are treated with pesticides, fungicides, and chemical fertilizers, and the twenty-seven-acre pecan orchard at Pebble Hill Grove was no exception. Frank and Teresa Bibin purchased the farm in 1994 and used conventional methods to grow the nuts. Concerned about the impact of the chemicals on the environment and their health, the couple decided to pursue organic alternatives. In 1996, they installed bat houses hoping that they would provide insect control. It worked. With the help of Bat Conservation International, Pebble Hill Grove has established several bat colonies and has become a refuge for thousands of bats. Their success using bats for insect control inspired Frank and Teresa to trade fungicides for beneficial microbes and chemical fertilizer for cover crops, allowing them to become a certified organic pecan orchard. In addition to selling pecans at the farm (by appointment), Frank and Teresa offer organic elephant garlic and pomegranates. To help backyard gardeners and farmers who want to control insects naturally, the couple also sells bat houses.

9047 Moultrie Highway, Quitman (Brooks County), 229-775-3347, www.pebblehillgrove.com

## Bethesda Academy

The students at Bethesda Academy learn reading, writing, arithmetic, and crop rotation. A five-acre garden on school grounds is a learning laboratory for the sixth- to twelfth-grade boys who study environmental science and entrepreneurship while growing fresh fruits and vegetables in garden beds and a greenhouse and raising chickens and goats on the private school campus.

A grant from the Natural Resource and Conservation Service helps fund the garden, and Georgia Organics teaches students about organic farming techniques. The students run a farmers' market on school grounds on Tuesday and Thursday afternoons and operate a booth at the Forsyth Farmers Market.

9250 Ferguson Avenue, Savannah (Chatham County), 912-351-2055, http://www.bethesdaacademy.org/academics/work-experience/ bethesda-farm-gardens

## Hunter Cattle

Concerned about the source of their food, Del and Debra Ferguson decided to purchase a farm to raise their own cattle, pigs, chickens, and produce. Their children, Kristan and Anthony, also moved to the farm with their families. "We were butchering our own cattle and our friends started asking about buying meat and telling their friends about our meat," Kristan recalls. Despite the demand, the family was not prepared to add a retail element to the farm. Instead, their focus was on building custom homes around Statesboro. All of that changed when the housing market crashed.

"We had houses that weren't selling, and we were about to lose the farm," says Kristan. "We decided we needed to pay for the farm with the farm. My mom had this crazy idea to open Moo Ma's Farm Store to sell what we produced."

In 2009, Hunter Cattle Company increased its production, selling meat and eggs produced on the farm as well as produce, milk, butter, honey, and specialty products from other farms. "We're all about supporting local farms because we aren't competing with each other, we're competing with Walmart," she says. It's also become a popular stop for educational tours, parties, and special events. In fact, the demand to spend time on the farm led the family to put their home-building skills to use and transform a former tobacco barn into farm accommodations. The Tobacco Loft and The Roost opened in 2012. "We never dreamed of having this huge farm. Everything we have done is because of demand," Kristan says.

934 Driggers Road, Brooklet (Bulloch County), 912-823-2333, www.huntercattle.com

### General Coffee State Park

In Nicholls, the state park is the best place to buy heritage-breed chickens, goats, eggs, fresh herbs, and cane syrup. The park operates a ten-acre farm complete with goats, chickens, turkeys, donkeys, sheep, pigs, horses, and mules. In addition to selling produce, fiber, and eggs, the park also breeds the animals and sells their offspring to local farms. Seeds from the heritage garden are sold in the park office. Horseshoes and other farm tools are made in the on-site blacksmith shop, and mules are used to grind the sugar cane, which is boiled down into syrup on-site. "We're one of the only parks in Georgia that has historic farming equipment and keeps it in use," explains assistant park manager Jason Carter.

The park also hosts sheep-shearing and spinning demonstrations and Taste of the Farm programs that feature tours and samples of produce from the Heritage Garden. Several historic buildings are located on the park grounds, including the Meeks log cabin, which dates back to 1840 and features exhibits that depict traditional farm life. The Meeks log cabin is the oldest standing structure in the county. "The park isn't near a major metropolis, so it doesn't get used as much as other state parks," says Carter. "It's a shame because it's a really neat place."

46 John Coffee Road, Nicholls (Coffee County), 912-384-7082, www.gastateparks.org/GeneralCoffee

## Understanding Organic

In supermarkets and natural food stores, products from iceberg lettuce to ice cream are emblazoned with the green-and-white "USDA Organic" label, while vendors at farmers' markets promote produce as "organically grown" on their signs. Despite the shared use of the word "organic," there is a difference between the claims.

In 2002, the United States Department of Agriculture (USDA) established the National Organic Program to set a national standard that certifies agricultural products. In order to display the USDA Organic seal, a product must contain at least 95 percent organic ingredients. The certification guarantees that crops are grown without pesticides, chemical fertilizers, and other synthetic ingredients; to be certified organic, products like meat and milk must come from animals that have not been given antibiotics or growth hormones. Government-approved certifiers inspect farms to make sure organic standards are being followed. The USDA also allows the use of a "made with organic ingredients" label, which means at least 70 percent of the ingredients in a product are organic. By law, farms promoting their products as "organically grown" must also follow the USDA organic program guidelines, although many farmers use the term without the blessing of the USDA.

## Red Brick Farm

When Caroline Ables talks about leaving her teaching job to turn ten acres of the farm she operates with her partner, Lamar Merritt, into a U-pick and agritourism destination, her passion is unmistakable. "There was nowhere to bring the [schoolchildren] to pick strawberries locally and I really wanted them to have an experience on a farm," she recalls.

Ables talked Merritt, a row crop farmer who grows cotton and peanuts, into turning a portion of their farm into a U-pick. The couple planted strawberries, tomatoes, cabbage, collards, and other veggies and hung a sign at the road. Families started showing up in carloads eager to pick fresh produce in their community. Merritt has even gone out to the tomato patch in his pajamas to offer late-night pickers a flashlight.

"It's really important to us to promote eating fresh, buying local, and knowing your farmer," Ables says. An educator at heart, Ables also invited teachers to bring their classes to the farm, combining an education program with farm activities. Red Brick Farm is the only operating farm in Coffee County offering field trips. In the fall, the farm operates a pumpkin patch, corn maze, corn pit, and train ride.

Ables is also a talented cook. With the help of her mom, a cattle rancher who lives next door, she makes jellies, sauces, salsa, and pickled okra, all sold from a farm store on her screened-in porch. Merritt contributes cane syrup and boiled peanuts (his jalapeño nuts have a great kick). "We have so many people who come out here to pick produce and say, 'I remember doing this when I was a kid,'" Ables says. "We want to give the next generation those same experiences on the farm."

225 Lake Demie Lane, Douglas (Coffee County), 912-381-4667

## Calathora Farms

"Calathora," Gaelic for fruitful rest, defines how the Morton family approaches farming: productive but not frantic. Three generations live on the farm, growing fruits and vegetables, raising pastured chicken, cattle, goats, and sheep, and producing honey, in harmony with nature and each other. All of their animals and crops are raised naturally; no chemicals, hormones, or GMO seed or feed are used on the farm. Tours are scheduled by appointment.

1299 Georgia Highway 111, Moultrie (Colquitt County), 229-890-1889, www.calathora.com

Georgia Certified Farmers' Markets sell fruits, vegetables, herbs, meat, and eggs that were grown or raised in Georgia.

### Heritage Organic Farm

Heritage Organic Farm was the first farm in Georgia to receive its organic program certification from the U.S. Department of Agriculture. Even before the USDA granted Shirley Daughtry official certification in 1991, she was using organic techniques like crop rotation, cover cropping, and beneficial insects to grow fruits and vegetables on her twenty-acre farm. A commitment to organic farming helped Daughtry earn the Land Steward of the Year award from Georgia Organics in 2006. But she's not farming for accolades. Instead, Daughtry wants to share farm-fresh produce with the masses. The bulk of the fruits and vegetables grown on Heritage Organic Farm are sold through a CSA program; Daughtry also sells at local farmers' markets. When excess produce is available during harvest, signs are posted along the roadside inviting customers to purchase produce from the farm. Daughtry hosts annual events like Heritage Farm Day when the farm is open to visitors for U-pick, produce sales, and tours.

485 Scuffletown Road, Guyton (Effingham County), 912-728-3708, www.heritageorganicfarm.com

## Madrac Farms

Melissa Reagan became fascinated with the idea of starting a pumpkin patch after a visit to Nebraska in 2010. "My cousin convinced me to go to the pumpkin patch," she recalls. "I thought it wasn't going to be any fun, but I had the best time!"

Back in Georgia, she convinced her husband, Guerry, a master electrician, that growing pumpkins would be a great learning experience for their daughters, Rachel and Madelyn. As Melissa quickly discovered, starting a pumpkin patch in Georgia was harder than it sounded. "Pumpkins don't grow here," she explains. "At most of the pumpkin patches in the Southeast, the pumpkins are brought in from the Midwest and the Northeast. For us to grow pumpkins, we would have to plant them in April and harvest them in July—and who wants a pumpkin in July?"

Research led her to the University of Georgia, where there were trials of a hybrid pumpkin called Orange Bulldog that was adapted to grow in the Southeast. She purchased seeds and waited. In 2011, a crop of Orange Bulldog pumpkins was available at Madrac Farms, along with several other varieties of pumpkins and fresh produce, turning the teaching garden into a full-fledged agritourism destination. Melissa also added a petting farm with goats, chickens, and pigs to help visitors make the connection between the farm and their food. "We want people to come to the farm to learn something and have fun at the same time," she says.

580 Ralph Rahn Road, Rincon (Effingham County), 912-704-7651, www.madracfarms.com

## Gilliard Farms

Gilliard Farms has the distinction of being the first African American–owned organic Centennial Farm in the state. Jupiter Gilliard acquired the land in 1874 to raise livestock and grow vegetables for his family. In 2011, Matthew Raiford returned to Georgia from Washington, D.C., to work the land that his forefathers farmed, which still belonged to his family but had fallen fallow. "I came back to Georgia to save the family farm," he says.

Raiford operates the farm with his sister, Althea Raiford. The pair are committed to growing fruits and vegetables using organic methods; a flock of free-range hens are also being raised on the farm. "Our goal is to get to the point where the farm sustains itself," Raiford explains.

Once the gardens and orchard are established and the hens are at peak production, Raiford, a chef on Little St. Simons Island, will provide farm-fresh produce to his restaurant and other area eateries. Eager to show off their progress in reestablishing the family farm and honoring their agricultural heritage, the brother and sister farming team welcome visitors by appointment.

163 Florines Way, Brunswick (Glynn County), 912-342-2742, www.gilliardfarms.com

## Gayla's Grits

Gayla Shaw got into the grits business by accident. Her husband, Kevin, is a row crop farmer who cultivates hundreds of acres of corn along with cotton, peanuts, and wheat. Grinding some of the corn into grits for their family seemed like fun. Gayla started experimenting with making stone-ground grits in 1997 and discovered that the homemade southern staple was a favorite at the dinner table (especially when she prepared the grits with mozzarella cheese and sour cream). Gayla and Kevin had the recipe printed on bags and gave the grits to their families and friends for Christmas. Soon, the holiday tradition became a successful business. Gayla's Grits are sold through mail order and at shops across Georgia, including Whisk Organic Market, Steel Magnolias, and The Junction. A growing interest in agritourism led the couple to start offering tours of the mill (by appointment) to demonstrate the process of taking corn from the fields and turning it into grits for the table.

126 East Highway 122, Lakeland (Lanier County), 229-316-3382, www.gaylasgrits.com

## Georgia Olive Farms

When Jason Shaw, Sam Shaw, and Kevin Shaw tell people about their farm, Georgia Olive Farms, they are always asked the same question: "You can grow olives in Georgia?" Georgia might not be the first place that comes to mind for olive production, but brothers Jason and Sam and their cousin Kevin want to change that. The trio, an insurance agent, banker, and row crop farmer, started growing the exotic fruits in Lakeland in 2009. "We saw what California had done with olive production in the last decade and felt like we were in a strategic [geographic] location to do something similar," explains Kevin.

## Farm-Fresh Freeway

In 2012, the state of Georgia introduced the newest tourism trail, the Georgia Grown Trail. The route travels through 175 miles of South Georgia from Nashville to Bluffton, passing through nine counties—Baker, Berrien, Calhoun, Clay, Clinch, Colquitt, Cook, Lanier, and Mitchell—on Highway 37, passing some of the most popular agritourism destinations in the state, including Georgia Olive Farms, Horse Creek Winery, Sparkman's Cream Valley, Lauri Jo's Southern Style Canning, and White Oak Pastures. Signs along the route highlight destinations like dairies, wineries, farms, farmers' markets, and farm-to-table restaurants.

Their combined skills in farming, sales, and finance prepared the trio to tackle the challenge of growing a new crop and introducing artisan olive oil to the public. In 2011, Georgia Olive Farms produced seventy-five gallons of olive oil. The first batch was bottled and labeled by hand. It sold out within twenty-four hours. To accommodate the demand for Georgia olive oil, the farm supplements their harvest with olive oil from other producers to create a chef's blend. Georgia Olive Farms sells its extra virgin olive oil at local organic markets, gourmet shops, and restaurants.

The planned purchase of a mill will allow the farm to process olive oil on-site. In the meantime, Georgia Olive Farms is managing the orchard and hosting tours and tastings in an effort to make Georgia olive oil a household name. "We've learned a lot along the way," Kevin says. "The biggest lesson has been that we can produce a good-quality olive oil in Georgia. It's been well received, and we're really excited about the future."

347 North Highway 221, Lakeland (Lanier County),
www.georgiaolivefarms.com

## Seabrook Village

Laura Devendorf was inspired to action when she learned of plans to tear down a one-room schoolhouse that dates back to 1865. She relocated the school and turned it into the first building of a new African American living history museum that showcases life for black farmers in the early 1900s.

During tours, Miss Florence Roberts shows visitors how to turn cream into butter by shaking a mason jar, how to grind corn into grits and meal and sugarcane into syrup, and how to use a pea sheller. "Kids need to know where their food comes from and the process it took to get it to the table," she says.

Since the establishment of Seabrook Village in 1991, the museum has grown to include eight turn-of-the-century buildings and historic artifacts that were donated by collectors and members of the community. The Springfield Legacy Foundation, a nonprofit organization started by Devendorf to preserve the environmental, historical, and cultural treasures of the region, provides funding to support the museum. "There is so much more here than kids could ever learn in a book," Florence says. "We are saving the cultural heritage that was so important here, showing [visitors] how people lived and ate and what they grew here."

425 West Oglethorpe Highway, Hinesville (Liberty County), 912-368-3580

## Georgia Buffalo

Troy Bivens bought fifty acres of land between I-95 and U.S. Highway 17 with the intention of developing it. The real estate market crashed, causing him to rethink plans to build warehouses on the property. Inspired by an uncle who raises buffalo in Minnesota, Bivens cleared the land and relocated a small herd to the brand-new pastures in 2011, transitioning from real estate developer to rancher.

Georgia Buffalo has grown to include a grass-fed herd of twenty-five animals—a number Bivens hopes to grow to 200 by 2015. Bivens and his partner, Sherry DiSimone, are looking for additional land to expand their ranch to meet the demand for buffalo meat at restaurants like Local 11Ten, Alligator Soul, and Sea Island resort.

Although bison is becoming popular on restaurant menus, the site of the herd still attracts stares. "Here in the South, we have to educate people about [buffalo]," says Bivens. "We're the only buffalo ranch in Southeast

Georgia Buffalo is one of a handful of buffalo ranches in the Southeast. The sight of buffalo grazing in pastures has drawn a lot of attention.

Georgia, so it's an unusual sight; people pull over on the side of the road all the time to check out the herd." Curiosity about the buffalo led Bivens and DiSimone to start offering tours. Visitors can board the "buffalo buggy" to go out into the pasture for an up-close look at the animals. In the farm store, coolers are filled with cuts of fresh bison meat.

11495 US Highway 17, Townsend (McIntosh County), 855-242-2833, www.georgiabuffalo.com

### Calhoun Produce
When the farm store at Calhoun Produce opens in the mornings, the freezer is packed with ziploc bags of shelled butterbeans. Within hours, the butterbeans are sold out and the phone is ringing off the hook with requests for more. "Our customers want to blanch and put up butterbeans just like their parents and grandparents used to do," says Shelia Rice. "It's a southern thing!"

A giant strawberry outside of Calhoun Produce lets passersby know where to find farm-fresh berries.

Rice's parents, Gerald and Joyce Calhoun, started the farm in 1992. The bulk of the produce grown on the farm is shipped to supermarkets across the Southeast, but the family keeps enough butterbeans stocked in the farm store to meet local demand. Almost.

Butterbeans might be the main crop, but Calhoun Produce does a lot more than grow the popular legume. Produce grown on the farm is shipped to supermarkets like Whole Foods and Food Lion and sold at local farmers' markets and at the farm stand. The on-farm store also carries private-label jams, jellies, and other specialty products. For visitors who want to do more than grab produce and go, the farm operates U-pick strawberry and blueberry patches in the spring and a pumpkin patch, corn maze, and fields of sunflowers for cutting in the fall. Calhoun Produce donates strawberries to the community strawberry cook-off in the spring; all of the recipes from the cook-off are kept at the farm store to provide inspiration to shoppers. "We started out small and built up the activities gradually," says Rice. "The best thing about agritourism is seeing how happy families are when they come to the farm."

5075 Hawpond Road, Ashburn (Turner County), 229-273-1892, www.calhounproduce.com

## Red Earth Farm

All of the animals at Red Earth Farm are named after activists: The pastures are home to cows named Che (Guevara), Howard (Zinn), and Geronimo; a Sannan goat named Ingrid (Betancourt); and a chicken named Rosa (Parks), a quiet statement about their progressive views. All of the animals are pasture raised and organic.

Janisse Ray, environmental activist and author of books like *Ecology of a Cracker Childhood* and *Wild Card Quilt*, and her husband, Raven Waters, have been growing their own food for more than two decades. Access to family land allowed the couple to grow a garden and raise animals, but their desire to operate sustainably was at odds with the collective ideals about agriculture. To pursue their goal of an organic farm, the couple purchased land in 2008.

Although their primary reason for farming is to produce food for their family, Janisse and Raven also sell some of their grass-fed beef, pastured pork, organic vegetables, heirloom seeds, hand-milled soap, and homemade soda at the Statesboro Farmers Market and during special events on the farm. "It's a mini alternative Wal-Mart," jokes Janisse.

Raven leads workshops on farming and homesteading topics ranging from organic gardening and raising chickens to home brewing and cheesemaking. To ensure the workshops are accessible, the fees are based on a sliding scale and scholarships are available. "We are trying to grow the community and promote sustainability and healthy food," Janisse says. "Our mission is to show people how to live engaged with the land, eating foods they produce themselves while having a high quality of life and a high fun quotient."

895 Catherine T. Sanders Road, Reidsville (Tattnall County), 912-557-1053, www.redearthfarm.weebly.com

## Georgia Museum of Agriculture

Visiting the Georgia Museum of Agriculture at Abraham Baldwin Agricultural College feels a little like stepping onto the set of a Wild West movie (minus the shootouts on Main Street). Designed to replicate agricultural life from the 1800s, the ninety-six-acre living history museum boasts dozens of historic buildings, including a cotton mill, a turpentine shed, a blacksmith shop, barns, and farmhouses. There are fields of cotton that are plowed by the mules Cotton and George, row crops like corn and peanuts, and several produce gardens, as well as livestock typical of an nineteenth-century farm: turkeys, sheep, guinea hens, and cows. The Tift House, which was built in 1887 for Captain H. H. Tift, the founder of Tifton, showcases how wealthy landowners lived.

The college came up with the idea to create a historic village and agriculture museum in 1974. Since its inception, the Georgia Museum of Agriculture has been important to the fabric of the (largely rural) community. Most weekends, costumed interpreters offer demonstrations, sharing the history of the buildings and describing life in the 1800s. During annual special events, the museum runs cotton-ginning demonstrations, grinds sugarcane, produces turpentine, and churns butter. "We want to help keep these traditions alive," says Garrett Boone, assistant director of marketing for the museum. "These are the kinds of activities that were part of life for the people who grew up here."

During the week, the museum is open for self-guided tours.

1392 Whiddon Mill Road, Tifton (Tift County), 229-391-5200,
www.abac.edu/museum

## Buckhorn Creek Ranch

Growing up, Steve Coleman watched a news program about a farmer who opened his farm to the public and thought, What a neat thing to do! Coleman knew farming was a hard life. His grandfather, Moses Coleman Sr., worked in the fields as one of the first Vidalia onion growers in the region. Watching him planting and harvesting onions from morning until nightfall didn't deter Coleman. In 1987, he achieved the dream that was sparked during the news report he watched in the second grade, opening Buckhorn Creek Ranch with two buffalo. "I thought the buffalo were neat and thought other people would, too," he recalls.

As Coleman's fascination with exotics grew, so did his collection. The farm has grown to include elk, wild boars, antelope, fallow deer, and a camel. The 250-acre farm serves as a wildlife preserve and educational center. "It's a good opportunity for visitors to get up close with the animals," he says. "On the wagon rides, we stop and feed them, which everyone loves."

Coleman hasn't totally abandoned his farming roots. There are mules, cattle, sheep, ducks, turkeys, horses, and other farm animals at Buckhorn Creek Ranch, as well as free-range chickens. He also grows vegetables in "Mr. Steve's Garden" and stocks a farm stand with watermelons, honeydew melons, squash, cucumbers, Serrano peppers, and his specialty, heirloom tomatoes. "The adults and the kids love to visit the garden," he says. "They get to try the different vegetables, and we pick some and feed it to the animals. It's part of the experience."

1944 Georgia Highway 135, Vidalia (Toombs County), 912-583-2737,
www.buckhorncreekranch.net

## Vidalia Onion Museum

Few vegetables are so popular that entire museums are created in their honor, but the Vidalia onion is not an ordinary vegetable. "You can promote it all day long, but it won't matter until a chef gets in there and cuts it and eats it," says Bob Stafford, director of the Vidalia Onion Business Council. "It's the taste that counts." Planted in low-sulfur volcanic soil that is found in just twenty counties in Georgia, the onions have a sweet, mild taste. Since the museum opened in 2011, visitors from more than forty countries have walked through the doors eager to learn more about the eponymous Georgia onion.

Yumion, the colorful mascot who greets visitors, might give the impression that the museum takes a lighthearted look at the Vidalia onion, but inside it's serious business. Exhibits explain the science behind growing Vidalias the economic impact and provide recipes featuring the sweet onions; a multimedia exhibit shows off various pop culture references, including a clip of *Who Wants to Be a Millionaire* during which "Where do Vidalia onions come from?" was the $25,000 question. Outside, a small plot of onions has been hailed as "The World's Smallest Licensed Vidalia Onion Field." As Stafford explains, "Fraud used to be a serious problem; growers were putting their onions in Vidalia bags and selling them as the real thing. We put a stop to that; we have a good product, and we protect it."

100 Vidalia Sweet Onion Drive, Vidalia (Toombs County), 912-537-1918,
www.vidaliaonion.org

## What is a Vidalia Onion, Anyway?

The Vidalia onion is no ordinary onion. Farmers started growing the sweet onions in the 1930s. Recognizing that their onions looked the same as—but tasted much different from—other onions at the supermarket, Georgia growers banded together to protect their unique product. In 1986, the Georgia State legislature granted legal status to the Vidalia onion; federal protection was granted in 1989. According to the ruling, Vidalia onions can be grown only in twenty counties in Georgia (where the soil has the low sulfur content needed to produce their sweet flavor): Candler, Emanuel, Bulloch, Truetlen, Wheeler, Montgomery, Evans, Tattnall, Toombs, Telfair, Jeff Davis, Appling, Bacon, and portions of Jenkins, Screven, Laurens, Dodge, Pierce, Wayne, and Long. Current production of Vidalia onions is limited to 100 farmers on 1,200 acres of farmland. The name "Vidalia" has been trademarked by the Georgia Department of Agriculture, and the Vidalia onion has the honor of being the state vegetable of Georgia. Although Vidalia onions are grown only in Georgia, the sweet vegetables are in high demand, and farmers ship their crops across the United States and Canada.

Three generations of the Poppell family help out on the farm. Photograph by Amos Moses, courtesy of Tanya Poppell.

## Poppell Farms

During the fall, cars with tags from Georgia, Florida, Tennessee, South Carolina, and Illinois fill the parking area at Poppell Farms. It's the pumpkin patch and corn maze that draws them in and the southern hospitality that keeps them coming back.

The idea to create an agritourism destination came to Genell and Tanya Poppell in 1996. A customer purchased a truckload of pumpkins to sell at a fall festival in another state, and the couple, part-time farmers who worked other jobs and managed 400 acres of produce, decided a fall event could work on their farm, too. The pumpkin patch and corn maze were a hit.

Poppell Farms has expanded its offerings since their inaugural season. Every October, upwards of 20,000 visitors come to the farm for the corn maze, hayrides, pumpkin patch, petting farm, pony rides, and jumping pillow. Seeing families enjoying the farm gives the couple great pleasure. "We love our jobs, especially seeing the excitement when kids who have never been to a farm or touched a farm animal get to do those things for the first time," says Tanya Poppell. "We want to help families create memories," says Genell Poppell.

1765 Hyma Poppell Loop, Odum (Wayne County), 912-586-6380, www.poppellfarms.com

## Statesboro Mainstreet Farmers Market

The support of the Downtown Development Authority helped the farmers' market grow from a handful of vendors in 2007 to a thriving market with more than forty farmers and craftspeople from across the county. A dedicated group of board members worked with farmers to extend their seasons and provided grants for market promotion, helping to create one of the best farmers' markets in the region.

Held in picturesque downtown Statesboro, the market offers a smorgasbord of farm-fresh products, from the rainbow carrots Relinda Walker grows at Walker Organic Farms (arguably the best on the planet) and Freeman's Mill stone-ground grits and cornmeal to grass-fed beef from Hunter Cattle Company and artisan cheeses from Sweet Grass Dairy. "The farmers' market has really helped bring attention to the concept of farm-to-table in our region," explains Barry Turner of the Downtown Development Authority. The market runs from April to November.

2 East Main Street, Statesboro (Bulloch County), 912-489-1869, www.visitstatesboroga.com

## Forsyth Farmers Market

Although Forsyth Park is the most iconic park in historic Savannah, just five vendors signed up to participate in the first season of the Forsyth Farmers Market in 2008. Fast-forward to the present, and the market has fifty approved vendors selling everything from buffalo meat and plantation rice to cheese and peaches on Saturday mornings. It's a producers-only market, which means all of the vendors must grow or raise their own products; resellers are not allowed. Market manager Ben Baxter also ensures that all of the vendors fit with the market's mission. "We want to promote healthy eating in our community," he says. "We're different from other farmers' markets because we focus on fresh, local and healthy foods; it's not a carnival atmosphere, there are no cupcakes here."

Bull Street and Park Avenue, Savannah (Chatham County), www.forsythfarmersmarket.com

## Farmers on the Move

You don't have to wake up early on Saturday mornings to buy locally grown foods. Thanks to Farm a la Carte, farmers can bring fresh produce to you. A spinoff of the food truck concept, mobile farmers' markets are catching on in Georgia.

Revival Foods launched Farm a la Carte in 2012. The farmer-founded, farmer-run mobile market stocks fresh produce, meat, eggs, nuts, cheeses, jams, jellies, and sauces—all produced by farmers in South Georgia, including LJ Woods Farm, Bethesda Gardens, Flat Creek Lodge, and Walker Organic Farms—helping farmer-founder Bradley Taylor make local food more accessible in Savannah.

The truck, a retrofitted cargo trailer designed by students from Savannah College of Art and Design, pulls up at organic restaurants, schools, and parking lots throughout Savannah on Tuesdays and Wednesdays and parks at the Forsyth Farmers Market on Saturdays. Scheduled stops are posted on its website and Facebook each week.

"Not everyone goes to the farmers' market and buys a week's worth of food," says Taylor. "We wanted to address the need for midweek access to farm-fresh food and make it convenient for people to find locally grown products." Shoppers can place online orders and pick them up from the mobile market or treat Farm a la Carte as a roving supermarket, stopping by to pick up dinner fixings or an afternoon snack. "Like a small grocery store, we offer the convenience of retail with the soulful, funky feel of a farmer-run venture," Taylor says.

Riverview Farms in Ranger, Georgia, also operates a mobile market, Farm Mobile, to bring farm-fresh foods to residents of Gordon County; and the Fulton County Cooperative Extension has two mobile units rolling through the streets as part of the Fulton Fresh Mobile Farmer's Market program that started in 2011.

## Downtown Swainsboro Farmers Market

When the market launched in 2010, just eight vendors set up booths in the town square. Though it got off to a slow start, a determined group of farmers and a supportive downtown development commission helped the Little Market That Could become a staple in the community. "There was a real demand for it, and we decided to jump in with both feet," says Lynn Brinson, director of downtown development. "The community got behind it, and it's been a big success. It really livens up the town."

The Friday evening market, held between April and October, has doubled in size, attracting a diverse array of vendors from certified organic growers to dairies and bakeries. All of the vendors are local growers and producers.

215 West Main Street, Swainsboro (Emanuel County), 478-237-7025, swainsborofarmersmarket.wordpress.com

## FARM STANDS AND U-PICKS

### Roberts Taste of the Farm

At first glance, the roadside store appears to be a rural grocer, a place to stock up on canned soup, peanut butter, paper towels, and charcoal for grilling. But listening to the phone ring off the hook with requests for butterbeans and tomatoes, it becomes clear that the mass-produced products are just a small fraction of the offerings.

Steve and Elaine Roberts opened the store in 2011 to sell produce and grass-fed beef produced on their farm. Elaine struggles to keep the produce case full, selling out of peas, butterbeans, tomatoes, corn, squash, cucumbers, and peppers within hours of stocking the store. "We wanted to make it more convenient for people to buy from us without having to come out to the farm," explains Elaine Roberts. "Most of our business is from people who called the farm to order produce and want to pick it up in the store."

The store also welcomes walk-in customers who are eager to purchase produce without having to drive to the farm.

1750 East Marion Avenue, Nashville (Berrien County), 229-543-0021, www.robertstasteofthefarm.com

## Southern Grace Farms

Tobacco used to be a cash crop for seventh-generation farmers Steve and Tim McMillan. In the 1990s, when demand for tobacco was in sharp decline, the brothers knew it was time to come up with a different plan. The alternative? Berries. "We started with a few acres and it grew from there," says Steve's wife, Laura McMillan.

Southern Grace Farm now grows sixty acres of blackberries and strawberries that are shipped to supermarkets across the Southeast. The rise of agritourism inspired them to designate a few acres for U-pick. Once the concept caught on, the McMillans added blueberries, peaches, nectarines, and plums, turning the former tobacco farm into acres of edibles.

The brothers also grow peanuts and mill them into peanut flour. An uncommon product, it's sold through specialty grocers and on their website. "You can use peanut flour to make almost anything you would make with regular flour," explains Laura McMillan. "You're just swapping a starchy flour for a protein flour."

Overall, McMillan believes the experiment has been a success. "We're proud to say, 'We grew this,'" Laura says.

11946 Enigma Nashville Road, Enigma (Berrien County), 229-533-8585, www.southerngracefarms.com

## Bar C 'Mater Patch

A smaller farm provided bigger opportunities for Kurt Childers. "We scaled back our operation so that we could have a more direct relationship with our customer," he says. A third-generation farmer, Childers focused on commercial vegetable production until 2012, when he downsized his farm from 1,200 acres of owned and leased land to 200 acres. Instead of growing vegetables for supermarkets, he planted fields of sweet corn, peas, okra, butterbeans, bell peppers, and tomatoes, turning the farm into a U-pick veggie patch. "We wanted to get produce into the hands of our customers when it was as fresh as possible," Childers says. "It doesn't get much fresher than when you pick it yourself."

The U-pick operation runs from June to August. Bar C 'Mater Patch provides the vegetables, and customers provide the manpower, filling five-gallon buckets with enough produce to fill their tables and put up for the winter.

2054 Yates Road, Barney (Brooks County), 229-561-3466

## Ottawa Farms

Chatham County might be known for its Vidalia onions, but Pete Waller is doing his part to promote it as a prime strawberry- growing region. A third-generation farmer whose family has farmed the 700-acre parcel since the 1800s, Waller is president of the Georgia Strawberry Growers Association and grows some of the best berries around. From March to May, the strawberry patch at Ottawa Farms is open for U-pick (in June, the blackberries are ripe, and blueberries are ready to be picked in June and July). The farm also hosts its Strawberry Festival in April. The annual event features live music, pig races, pony rides, and a tractor show and sells fresh strawberries and homemade strawberry ice cream.

702 Bloomingdale Road, Bloomingdale (Chatham County), 912-748-3035, www.ottawafarms.com

## DC Durrence Farm

"We grew tobacco, and when the crop stopped making sense, we had to find another way to make a living," explains Danny Durrence. He transitioned fifteen acres of his farm into a U-pick patch, replacing tobacco with watermelons, strawberries, sweet corn, broccoli, beans, squash, and tomatoes. He also raises pigs, cattle, and chickens. The farm stand operates on the honor system, which surprises out-of-town customers. "A guy from New York stopped by and laughed at the payment box," Durrence says. "He said, 'If we did this [in New York], everything would be gone.'"

Opening the farm up to customers has required Durrence to become an educator as well as a farmer. "Most urban people have no clue where their food comes from, [and] sometimes they're not even sure if it was grown in the U.S.," he says. "When they come here, they know exactly where it was grown and when it was picked."

14381 Highway 301, Glennville (Tattnall County), 904-591-9119

## M&M Fruits and Vegetables

The plywood signs nailed to tree trunks along Highway 31 promise melons, strawberries, corn, and peanuts. Morris and Margie Selph have operated roadside produce stands for more than four decades. The couple moved to this location in 1999 to provide fresh, local produce to regular customers and passersby in search of a snack. A few times a week, Morris travels to local farms across the county to pick up produce, loading his pickup truck with whatever is in season. "What we've got, you can't go into Walmart to find, and that keeps people coming back," he says.

661 Highway 31, Helena (Telfair County), 912-568-1561

## Rutland Farms

After multiple expansions, Rutland Farms grew from a 36-acre homestead in 1916 to an expansive 4,500-acre farm operated by father and son farmers, Greg and Ryan Rutland. The bulk of the land is covered in row crops like peanuts, cotton, and tobacco. In 1998, the Rutlands planted a patch of strawberries, put up an honor box, and invited passersby to pick the fruit. "It was really popular and we found out really quickly that there were a lot of people who wanted to stop by the farm to buy produce," Ryan says.

The success of the small U-pick operation led Ryan, a fifth-generation farmer with a degree in agribusiness from the University of Georgia, to develop plans for adding a retail component to their commercial farm. In 2011, a 4,000-square-foot retail market opened on the farm, turning a business plan Ryan created in college into a reality. The Market at Rutland Farms is stocked with twenty-two varieties of fruits and vegetables grown on the farm. To provide a true taste of Georgia, the market also carries produce, nuts, and specialty products from other regional providers. In the spring, Rutland Farms still opens its strawberry fields for U-pick; blueberries and blackberries are also available for picking. "This is something that I've always dreamed of doing, and it's been pretty cool to see it come to fruition," Ryan says.

5597 Union Road, Tifton (Tift County), 229-821-0289,
www.rutlandfarms.com

### Berry Good Farms

Sampling is encouraged on this U-pick farm—and judging by the number of berry pickers whose lips are stained with fruit juice, the policy is very popular. In the spring and summer, when the blueberries, blackberries, and peaches are ripe, Berry Good Farms opens for U-pick. After the little ones have had their fill of berries and tire of helping, visiting with the goats, sheep, and chickens will keep them occupied.

At U-picks all over Georgia, the berries are ripe for picking.

930 William Gibbs Road, Tifton (Tift County), 229-821-0746, www.yourberrygoodfarms.com

## DAIRIES

### Dreaming Cow Creamery

Janelle and Kyle Wehner might call their thick, cream-top yogurt "New Zealand style" but it's made in South Georgia. Even the milk used to make flavors like maple ginger, vanilla agave, and honey pear comes from the family dairy (the same dairy that Kyle's sister, Jessica, and brother-in-law, Jeremy, use in the award-winning cheeses they produce under the Sweet Grass Dairy label). The yogurts are non-homogenized and contain no refined sugars, but they are chock full of local products, including honey from the Savannah Bee Company. "We are working on turning the business into a nationally recognizable brand," says Kyle. During an annual tour of the yogurt-making facility in the fall, learn what it takes to transform milk from a grass-fed Jersey herd into thick, flavorful yogurt.

940 Magnolia Church Road, Pavo (Brooks County), 229-859-2677, www.dreamingcow.com

## Sparkman's Cream Valley

The herd of jersey cows at Sparkman's Cream Valley produces 4,000 gallons of milk per day. "Jersey cows produce milk with a higher solid content ratio that gives better texture and flavor," explains Steve Hargrove, sales manager. Cattle from the closed herd have been producing milk for the Sparkman family since 1967. For decades, the Dairy Farmers Association picked up the excess milk, mixed it with milk from dairy farms across the country, and sold it to supermarkets. "We wanted to sell our milk to consumers, not to an association," Hargrove says.

Five years ago, the family opened a farm store to sell their products directly to the public. To allow customers to see the process, there is a viewing window between the store and the processing facility. The coolers are stocked with products ranging from low-fat milk and chocolate milk to drinkable yogurt, all produced on-site. Their next project: Turning the milk into ice cream.

Hargrove attributes the popularity of the projects to the cattle mooing in the pasture outside the store. "It's all about the cows," he says. "Without a healthy herd, it's impossible to have a good product."

1263 Rossman Dairy Road, Moultrie (Colquitt County), 229-941-4082, www.sparkmanscreamvalley.com

## AQUACULTURE

### Lady Jane Shrimp Boat

Captain Larry Credle used to operate *Lady Jane* as a commercial shrimping vessel, part of a fleet of boats trawling the Atlantic for wild Georgia shrimp. Changing fishing regulations led Captain Larry to reconsider his commercial shrimping career. He retrofitted his vessel, turning the *Lady Jane* into the only shrimp trawler on the East Coast licensed by the United States Coast Guard to carry passengers. "When I was fourteen, I was out on a fishing trawler with my dad and I said, 'You know dad, people would pay to come out here and watch us do this,'" recalls Credle, a fourth-generation commercial fisherman. "He said, 'Son, you're crazy!' I wish he was alive now to see how successful we've been."

Credle has been running educational charters since 2005. His floating classroom is berthed in Brunswick and takes passengers into inland waterways where the crew tosses nets into the open water to catch shrimp. A marine biologist is onboard to share information about the horseshoe crabs, jellyfish, sea turtles, and puffer fish that come up in the nets along with the shrimp. "Every time the net comes up, the catch is entirely different," Credle says. "It's so interesting to see all of the different creatures."

Information about the catch is logged and shared with the University of Georgia and the Georgia Department of Natural Resources, who use it for research purposes, and the sea creatures are tossed back into the ocean—except for the shrimp, which are sorted from other catch and set aside for a shrimp boil.

During tours, Captain Larry shares stories from the sea and explains the lifecycle of shrimp and the process for catching them, along with details about marine life and the fate of commercial shrimping fleets.

1200 Glynn Avenue, Brunswick (Glynn County), 912-265-5711, www.shrimpcruise.com

## VINEYARDS AND WINERIES

### Horse Creek Winery

In the 1980s, Ed Perry decided to phase out of cattle farming and explore new agricultural opportunities. After experimenting with strawberries and watermelons, he decided to plant muscadine vines—but he never planned to make wine. He sold grapes to national supermarket chains, shipping his Georgia-grown produce across the country.

"We always had leftover grapes that went to waste, and I started asking, What can I do with this?" Perry recalls. Turning the leftover grapes into wine was the obvious choice. Still, Perry had no plans to become a winemaker. Instead, he shipped grapes to wineries in Georgia and Florida. When a winemaker commented that his grapes made exceptional wines, Perry decided to produce his own vintages. It's been a successful experiment. All of the eighteen wines made at Horse Creek Winery have medaled in national and international competitions; several wines, including Winnersville White, Miss Blue, Red Jewell, and Finish Line are multiple award winners and tasting room favorites. "When people think of wine, they think of Napa Valley and vinifera grapes, but those are not native grapes, they are an Old World European variety," says Perry. "Muscadine grapes are native plants and they produce great Georgia wines."

2873 Georgia Highway 76, Nashville (Berrien County), 229-686-9463, www.horsecreekwinery.com

## Meinhardt Vineyards and Winery

Although wines produced at Meinhardt Vineyards are available at more than 350 restaurants and retailers, the patio at the winery is the best place to sip the muscadine varietals. "People come to the winery to do the same thing they do on their front porch—relax," says winemaker Ken Meinhardt.

In what Ken calls "a hobby that got out of hand," production increased from 1,000 gallons when the winery opened in 2004 to 30,000 gallons. The winery produces white, red, and fruit wines ranging from very dry to very sweet. With names like Southern Eagle and Eagle Run, both a nod to the Georgia Southern University mascot, the wines are meant to pay homage to the region where the grapes are grown. "When the sun sets over the hayfield, there is nothing more beautiful," he says. "The wine and the view make this a popular spot, especially on weekends."

305 Kennedy Pond Road, Statesboro (Bulloch County), 912-839-2458, www.meinhardtvineyards.com

## Butterducks Winery

It all started with a duck. Sort of. Bill and Barbara Utter noticed a mallard in their pond. They named him Lenny. Worried that he was lonely, the couple bought more ducks, letting them swim in their bathtub until they were old enough to share the pond with Lenny. Around the same time, Bill and Barbara were experimenting with fruit wines. When the time came to name their blueberry, peach, muscadine, and blackberry wines, the couple drew inspiration from the ducks, and Butterducks Winery was born.

More than a dozen wines are bottled under the Butterducks label. Fruit wines like Super Sweet Fuzzy Berry, Sweet Scuppernong, and Sweet Peach are the most popular, but the winery also makes Cabernet Sauvignon, Merlot, and Sangiovese. Samples of the wines are poured in the tasting room, tours are offered by appointment, and visiting the ducks is highly encouraged.

3332 Blue Jay Road, Guyton (Effingham County), 912-728-9463, www.butterduckswinery.com

## Watermelon Creek Vineyard

Charles and Deborah Tillman planted their first muscadine grapevines in 2007 and opened a tasting room to share their first vintages five years later. "We didn't know anything about growing grapes or making wine; we bought books to learn about winemaking," Deborah Tillman recalls. "We took it one step at a time, learned as we went along."

Transitioning from careers in real estate and pharmaceutical sales to pursue their passion for winemaking was just part of the challenge the couple faced in launching Watermelon Creek Vineyard. When the Tillmans purchased the fifteen-acre homestead, which had been in the family since the 1820, most of the buildings were covered in wisteria. "We had no idea some of the buildings were even here," Charles Tillman says.

During nearly a decade of careful restoration, the couple uncovered and preserved several original buildings, including a barn, corncrib, cane syrup mill, and turpentine well. Three acres of muscadine grapes are interspersed among the structures, creating a setting that is both picturesque and historically significant. To honor the land, all of the wines—Lower Mill White, Ohoopee River White, Mill Pond Blush, Altamaha River Red, and Lane's Bridge Red—are named after local natural areas.

2977 Mt. Zion Church Road, Glennville (Tattnall County), 912-654-0107, www.watermeloncreekvineyard.com


## FESTIVALS AND EVENTS

### North Florida and South Georgia Farm Tour

New Leaf Market, a natural food co-op in Tallahassee, Florida, hosts an annual farm tour in October to highlight local farms and introduce shoppers to the farmers who grow some of the foods stocked in the co-op. The fall tour includes upwards of thirty farms in North Florida and South Georgia ranging from cattle ranches and dairies to wineries and organic produce growers. Several of the farms on the tour are not normally open to the public and offer unprecedented access during the farm tour. The participating farms also set up mini farm stores, selling their products directly to the public.

850-942-2557, www.newleafmarket.coop/events/farm_tour/

## Georgia Blueberry Festival

Peaches may be Georgia's official state fruit, but they take a backseat to blueberries in Alma, Georgia's blueberry capital. Since the 1970s, this tiny town has produced more than its share of the berries, which now outpace their fuzzy cousin in revenue for the state. Alma celebrates the importance of this little blue fruit during its annual Georgia Blueberry Festival, started in 1975. During this three-day celebration on the first weekend in June, visitors are served up a blueberry pancake breakfast (complete with Georgia blueberries, blueberry syrup, and homegrown sausage), a blueberry gospel performance, a blueberry "jam" session, and a blueberry street dance. There are also plenty of contests, including a 5K and a 1-mile fun run, sports tournaments, a beauty contest, a sidewalk chalk contest, a Big Bass Fishing contest, a blueberry cook-off, and of course, a blueberry-pie-eating contest. Non-blueberry events include carnival rides, an art fair, a theater production, and a parade.

Goldwasser Park and other venues throughout Alma (Bacon County), 912-310-7399, www.georgiablueberryfestival.org

## Brooks County Skillet Festival

To promote tourism in rural Brooks County, the local tourism commission, Destination Brooks, launched the Brooks County Skillet Festival. The first annual event took place in 2011 when Georgia governor Nathan Deal tossed out the inaugural skillet as part of the skillet-throwing contest. Held in the courthouse square in October, the festival features culinary exhibitions, a farmers' market, and live entertainment. The highlight of the weekend is the Cast Iron Chef competition, a competition between two local cooks who battle to prepare the best dish from a secret local ingredient in a cast-iron skillet.

100 East Screven Street, Quitman (Brooks County), 229-263-9085, www.skilletfestival.com

## Chicken City USA

The chickens roaming the streets of Fitzgerald did not escape from a poultry house or backyard coop. The feathered fowl are wild. While no one knows how many wild chickens call Fitzgerald home, downtown development director Alesia Davis says it's not uncommon to see up to twenty chickens scratching up median strips, parks, and, to the dismay of some local residents, gardens in search of bugs and worms to eat.

The U.S. Department of Natural Resources released flocks along the banks of the Ocmulgee River in the 1960s in the hopes that the Burmese chickens would become the next big game birds. "The alligators ate the chickens and the snakes ate their eggs, so the project didn't take off," says Davis. "We like to say that the chickens didn't like it down [at the river], so they walked back to town."

Instead of banishing the chickens, the town turned them into a tourist attraction. At the annual Wild Chicken Festival in March, tourists and residents alike compete in crowing contests and do the chicken dance in the streets while vendors sell chicken-themed arts and crafts. "The chickens are so quirky that people are willing to drive from out of town to see them," Davis says. "When you live here, they become part of the landscape."

## Turpentine Festival

In the 1930s, turpentine was a staple in most households, used for everything from cough syrup and disinfectant to paint thinner and moth repellant. Turpentine has been replaced with modern products, and turpentine distilling has gone from a popular process to a lost art.

The E. C. Carter Turpentine Still in Portal is one of the last remaining operational turpentine stills in the South. In October, the Portal Heritage Society hosts the Catface Turpentine Festival, which got its name from the slash marks distillers cut into pine trees to start the flow of the pine gum that was distilled into turpentine. The festival celebrates the history of turpentine production and the lost art of distilling the historic liquid.

The historic still operated from the 1930s to the 1960s and still sits in its original location. The Heritage Society restored the still and turned it into the centerpiece of the annual festival. A parade, vendors, and concessions are all part of the fun, but it's the still that draws crowds. There are demonstrations to showcase how the still operates, along with an overview of the important role turpentine played in rural life at the turn of the century, followed by samples of the best rosin-baked potatoes around (rosin is made from the same pine gum used to make turpentine).

217 Turpentine Drive, Portal (Bulloch County), 912-865-2566, www.portalheritagesociety.org

## 700 Kitchen Cooking School

Chef Darin Sehnert doesn't have a set menu for his Fresh from the Market class. Instead, he lets produce from a trip to the Forsyth Farmers Market dictate the dishes students prepare. Sehnert talks about what's in season and makes suggestions for dishes, like pork tenderloin with muscadine grape sauce; shrimp succotash with okra, tomatoes, and corn; or peach tarts. "I started the class with a selfish motivation," he explains. "I wanted to have a chance to have off-the-cuff inspiration and experiment with creative dishes based on what we could find at the market."

With a tentative list of recipes and ingredients in hand, the class follows Sehnert across the street to the farmers' market, where he offers tips on choosing produce—green tomatoes should be green and blemish-free or it's okay for peaches to be soft if they are being used immediately—and introduces students to vendors. With ingredients secured, it's back to the kitchen at the Mansion at Forsyth Park, where several dishes are prepared and, finally, devoured.

700 Drayton Street, Savannah (Chatham County), 912-721-5006, www.mansiononforsythpark.com/cooking_school

## Collard Greens Festival

For lovers of collard greens, the historically African American community of Port Wentworth, just northwest of Savannah, may well be the promised land. It was here in March 1997, on Promised Land Farm, that owners (and brothers) Willie and Robert Johnson found themselves with a bumper crop of this leafy southern staple. Instead of plowing the plants under, the brothers decided to give them away to senior citizens. The free event turned into an annual festival, held the first Saturday in March, complete with a parade, gospel music, a Collards 'n' Cornbread Cook-off, and barbecue dinners. The festival also features food and craft vendors and seasonal fruits and vegetables plucked from the Johnsons' thirty-acre farm. The collards are still free for seniors, veterans, and disabled persons and cost others just $5 for all you can stuff into two grocery bags.

7532 Highway 21, Port Wentworth (Chatham County), 912-965-1999

## Sunbelt Agricultural Exposition

More than 1,200 vendors set up booths at the Sunbelt Agricultural Expo, enticing farmers to check out the newest tractors, agricultural implements, fertilizers, feeds, and seeds. While the expo targets production farmers, there is no shortage of exhibits that appeal to the agri-curious. Perhaps the most interesting component of the expo is the 600-acre research farm where fields of cotton, peanuts, corn, and other row crops are used to demonstrate tillage, irrigation systems, and harvesting techniques. The expo also features livestock events, an antique tractor display, and hunting and fishing demonstrations.

290-G Harper Boulevard, Moultrie (Colquitt County), 229-985-1968, www.sunbeltexpo.com

## Shrimp and Grits: The Wild Georgia Shrimp Festival

All the wild Georgia shrimp you can eat in a minute. Home-cooked shrimp and grits smothered in gravy. Celebrity chef cooking demos and book signings. Professional chef cook-offs: During its annual Shrimp and Grits Festival, Georgia's Jekyll Island resembles an episode of the reality TV show *Top Chef*. Set during National Wild Shrimp Month in September, the popular three-day festival celebrates shrimp from the island's thriving wild shrimp harvesting business, which it pairs with another southern favorite: grits. Visitors can taste shrimp and grits samples, purchase shrimp and grits dinners, or participate in the shrimp "peel and eat" contest. Thirty lucky tasters also get to judge the winners of the chefs' cooking competitions. Shrimp boat tours, live music, an arts and crafts fair, "brew cruise," and a slew of kids activities round out the celebration, which was named Best Festival in 2011 by the Southeast Festivals and Events Association.

Glynn County, 877-4-JEKYLL, www.shrimpandgritsfestival.com

## Sweet Onion Festival

Tattnall County grows more Vidalia onions than any of the other sweet-onion-growing counties in the state, and the annual Sweet Onion Festival, held the second Saturday each May, kicks off the harvest. The Vidalia onion is the star of the festival. It's incorporated into parade floats and amusement games, vendors sell onion-inspired preserves and crafts, and, of course, sweeties are on the menu. Blooming onions and sweet onion rings are crowd favorites. Instead of having a mascot, the festival crowns a Miss Georgia Sweet Onion during the festivities.

Tattnall County, www.glennvillesweetonion.com

## Vidalia Onion Festival

When Vidalia farmer Moses Coleman first picked onions from his fields in the 1930s, he was surprised by their sweet, apple-like flavor. Other farmers were impressed by the high prices Coleman fetched for these odd onions during the Great Depression. Soon the Vidalia sweet onion became the state's official vegetable, celebrated each April with a four-day festival in the town that bears its name. The festivities, which draw 75,000 annual visitors, include a children's parade, street dance, rodeo, car show, arts and crafts fair, and carnival, as well as live music and fireworks. There's also plenty of oniony fun, with onion-eating contests, onion-cooking demonstrations, and a Vidalia onion cook-off. Visitors can also tour onion fields and check out the Vidalia Onion Museum. The festival, which started in 1978, has been featured on the Food Network and hailed by MSNBC as one of the five "don't-miss festivals across the U.S."

100 Vidalia Sweet Onion Drive, Suite A, Vidalia (Toombs County), 912-538-8687, www.vidaliaonionfestival.com

## National Grits Festival

In 2002, Georgia passed a law making grits the state's "official prepared food." The following year, it christened Warwick, Georgia, as the "official Grits Capital of the World" for its role in hosting the National Grits Festival. Every April since 1997, this tiny town of 500 swells to thousands for the festivities, which kick off with an official grits breakfast, followed by a grits cook-off, grits-eating contest, corn-shelling contest, beauty pageant, and parade of "Grits Queens." The festival also features live entertainment—including the Marine Corps Marching Band—food and craft vendors, pony rides, and an antique car and tractor show. But for many, the festival's highlight is the Quaker Grits Pit, the world's largest bowl of cooked grits. Visitors weigh in before and after jumping in this giant pool of porridge, and those with the biggest weight gain claim a cash prize.

Emerson Park, 109 Schoolhouse Street SW, Warwick (Worth County), 229-869-5550, www.gritsfest.com

## SPECIALTY SHOPS

### Freeman's Mill

The product line at Freeman's Mill reads like the shopping list for a southern restaurant: grits, cornmeal, whole wheat flour, wheat bran. . . . All of the products sold at the mill are ground in a granite mill that dates back to the early 1900s. Harry Freeman started grinding grits and meal for his family, but repeated requests for traditionally milled whole grains led him into retail markets. The products are sold in several farmers' markets, including the Main Street Farmers Market in Statesboro and the Richmond Hill Farmers Market. But, since it's the only operating grits mill in southeast Georgia, the Freeman family wanted to open the mill to the public (call ahead) to share the agricultural tradition of milling corn and wheat.

Third-generation miller Stacy Freeman operates the mill, continuing his family's legacy. He has also preserved old milling equipment, turning the mill into a de facto museum.

518 Country Club Road, Statesboro (Bulloch County), 912-852-9381, www.freemansmill.com

### Brighter Day Natural Food Market

Janie and Peter Brodhead opened a natural foods market on the southern tip of Forsyth Park in 1978. Three decades later, Brighter Day remains the best local market in the historic district. The small store is stocked with hard-to-find items, including gluten-free and vegan groceries along with a selection of local produce, fresh herbs, bulk goods, and prepared foods. A smoothie bar in the back of the store turns fruits and vegetables into delicious beverages. A certified nutritionist is on staff to answer health questions and ensure that Janie and Peter are choosing top-quality products for the store.

1102 Bull Street, Savannah (Chatham County), 912-236-4703, www.brighterdayfoods.com

### Savannah Bee Company

Ted Dennard has created quite a buzz for his artisanal honey. O, the Oprah magazine, named honey from the Savannah Bee Company as one of her Favorite Things in 2005. After a stint in the Peace Corps, where he taught beekeeping, the hobbyist-turned-entrepreneur decided to sell his honey to the masses. The Broughton Street store opened its doors ten years ago and has grown to include several varieties of award-winning honey, including sourwood, black sage, and winter white. Not sure what to choose? Step up to the tasting bar for what general manager Kellen Gray calls "a baptism into honey culture." It's part product sampling, part beekeeping education and one of the tastiest experiences in Savannah.

Almost all of the honey sold in the store, including the famous tupelo honey, which comes from a small area of South Georgia and North Florida, is produced within a three-state radius. The store also stocks an amazing selection of body care products from lotions to lip balms because, as Gray explains, "everything a bee makes is good for the human body."

104 West Broughton Street, Savannah (Chatham County), 912-233-7873, www.savannahbee.com

## Lauri Jo's Southern Style Canning

Every Christmas, Lauri Jo Bennett made jars of green tomato pickles and red pepper jelly for her husband to give to the clients he served along his long-haul trucking route. When he started getting requests for her preserves, Bennett decided to turn her once-a-year gifts into a year-round business, and Lauri Jo's Southern Style Canning was born.

Bennett started making jams, jellies, and preserves in a single pot in the kitchen of her Norman Park home in 2009. She worked as a teacher during the day and spent nights—often working until 4 A.M.—in the kitchen making preserves. Business exploded in the first year, and Bennett traded her classroom for a commercial kitchen. Her motto, "Preserving the South one jar at a time," reflects her commitment to using Georgia-grown produce to create her signature product line.

Bennett has a farm in nearby Worth County where she grows most of the ingredients she uses in preserves like candied jalapeños, peach jam, muscadine jelly, mayhaw pepper jelly, dilly beans, and green tomato pickles.

The retail store in Norman Park stocks all of her products, and a viewing room into the commercial kitchen where local ingredients are minced, measured, and mixed offers a glimpse of the action. Bennett also offers classes on canning.

4428 Highway 319 North, Norman Park (Colquitt County), 229-769-3391, www.laurijossouthernstylecanning.com

## Abraham Baldwin Agricultural College Country Store

A haven of locally produced products, the store sells everything from produce, preserves, and peanuts to cornmeal and cane syrup. Most of the items sold in the store are grown or produced by the college's Museum of Agriculture; the rest are sourced from local farms. One of the students from the college gins cotton that is grown on-site and turns it into T-shirts that are sold in the store. On Saturday mornings, a small, producers-only farmers' market operates in a pole barn adjacent to the store. The store also houses the National Peanut Museum, a small display of equipment used for planting and harvesting peanuts, along with a range of peanut products. A small crop of peanuts grows outside the back door.

1392 Whiddon Mill Road, Tifton (Tift County), 229-391-5205, www.abac.edu/museum/attractions/store.html

## Vidalia Valley

It's almost impossible not to cry during a tour of Vidalia Valley. The pungent aroma of the Vidalia onions used in dressings, sauces, salsas, and relishes permeates the plant, making tissues an essential part of the tour.

The Stanley family started Vidalia Valley in 1983. As the growers behind Stanley Farms, a farm in Toombs County where 4,000 acres of the patented onions are grown each season, the family wanted to create gourmet foods made from the Vidalia onions grown on the farm. Their line includes more than fifty custom products, all with Vidalia onions as the key ingredient. Opening the factory for tours allowed the family to share the process of transforming fresh Vidalia onions into prepared foods (and perhaps to watch visitors tear up after learning how much work it takes to create a line of signature products). For a less aromatic but equally interesting onion experience, tours of Stanley Farms are also offered by appointment.

4320 Georgia Highway 178, Lyons (Toombs County), 800-673-6338, www.stanleyonions.com

# FARM-TO-TABLE RESTAURANTS

### Sugar Magnolia Bakery & Café

"The traditional crops around here were cotton, peanuts, and soybeans, which made it difficult to source produce locally, but the diversity of stuff being grown in this region [has] really opened up," says chef Steve Jones. The abundance of fresh organic produce provided an opportunity for Jones to create a menu based on the availability of seasonal fruits and vegetables when the café opened in 2004. In addition to sourcing local ingredients for soups, salads, sandwiches, and pizzas, Jones bakes breads, pastries, and pizza crusts every morning.

The café is so committed to supporting area farmers, it serves as a pick up location for a Heritage Farms CSA and sells locally produced gourmet products. All of the tableware, including the cups and straws, are biodegradable. "No one has the determination to do seasonal and local that we do," says café owner Barry Turner.

106 Savannah Avenue, Statesboro (Bulloch County), 912-764-2090, www.sugarmagnoliabakery.com. $

### Alligator Soul

The menu at Alligator Soul reads like a who's who of Georgia farmers. Meat, produce, and cheese come from local providers like Flat Creek Lodge, Georgia Buffalo, Savannah River Farms, and Sweet Grass Dairy; even the grits are ground at a regional mill. Executive chef Christopher DiNello has relationships with dozens of Georgia farmers and uses their bounty to shape the menu. Even the cocktails, blended with organic liquor and hand-squeezed juices, have local flair.

114 Barnard Street, Savannah (Chatham County), 912-232-7899, www.alligatorsoul.com. $$$

## Café Florie

Laytoya Rivers and Theo Smith wanted to make southern soul food like their grandmothers. Sort of. The cousins envisioned staples like collard greens, sweet potato pie, and biscuits with an uber-local twist. Instead of using canned green beans and pounds of imported sugar, the pair shops for produce at the farmers' market and substitutes local ingredients like honey to sweeten sweet tea. To take advantage of local bounty, Rivers and Smith offer several vegan and vegetarian versions of traditional southern dishes.

Unlike other farm-to-table restaurants in chic Savannah, Café Florie takes an understated approach to local food. The colorful awning and bamboo exterior make the restaurant stand out, but the description of it in the *New York Times*—"a soul food shack . . . on the edge of the historic district"—is perhaps most apt. The restaurant is open for breakfast and lunch. Reservations are not accepted, but it's worth the wait to snag a table and tuck into the farm-fresh fare.

1715 Barnard Street, Savannah (Chatham County), 912-236-3354. $

## Cha Bella

Every visit to Cha Bella feels like the first time because executive chef Amie Linton is constantly changing the menu to reflect the availability of local meat and produce. Flagship dishes like risotto and ravioli get seasonal makeovers, featuring fresh ingredients sourced from local farms. Since the restaurant opened in the historic district in 2007, the goal has been to source as many ingredients locally as possible. At one point, Cha Bella sourced the bulk of the vegetables served in the restaurant from its own three-acre farm, where staff put in time weeding, watering, and harvesting. Now Linton works with local (and mostly organic) producers who supply everything from cheese and chicken to strawberries and salad greens.

102 East Broad Street, Savannah (Chatham County), 912-790-7888, www.cha-bella.com. $$

## Green Truck Pub

At Green Truck Pub, legions of hungry followers wait patiently for a table, listening to Johnny Cash on the jukebox or sipping Terrapin at the bar until their names are called. Josh Yates never planned for the pub, named after the mint-green truck parked out front, to be an instant hit. As soon as the restaurant opened in 2010, word spread and the kitchen was overwhelmed with orders for burgers with names like El Jefe and The Whole Farm. One of the burgers, The Relinda, was named for Relinda Walker of Walker Farms who supplies organic carrots and radishes to the pub.

All of the burgers are made with grass-fed beef from Hunter Cattle, the produce comes from local growers (Josh and his wife, Whitney, often shop for vegetables at the Forsyth Farmers Market), and most of the toppings, including pimento cheese, ketchup, and pickles, are made in-house. The efforts have paid off, helping Green Truck Pub earn accolades for the best gourmet burger, best veggie burger, and best locavore dining in Savannah.

2430 Habersham Street, Savannah (Chatham County), 912-234-5885, www.greentruckpub.com. $

## Local 11ten

When executive chef Brandy Williamson joined the Local 11ten team in 2010, she had never worked in a farm-to-table restaurant. "I love being able to talk to farmers and change the menu seasonally," she says. "It's also unbelievably difficult sometimes."

Williamson rises to the challenges, sourcing ingredients from dozens of local farmers, ranches, and fisherman, including Georgia Buffalo, Vince Baker Farm, Southern Swiss Dairy, and Adam Metzer Farm, to create dishes like braised bison short ribs, sautéed wild Atlantic shrimp, and grilled Berkshire pork chops. The farm-to-table fare is served up in a renovated bank building on the edge of Forsyth Park in the historic district. An evening of appetizers, entrees, and dessert will make it clear why Savannah is called The Hostess City.

1110 Bull Street, Savannah (Chatham County), 912-790-9000, www.local11ten.com. $$

## Thrive Carry Out Café

The first certified organic restaurant in Savannah is the place to go for fast food with a conscience. Chef Wendy Armstrong works with dozens of local and organic farmers to source ingredients for tomato, spinach, and Parmesan frittatas; organic Asian slaw; and curried red lentils with mixed vegetables, to name just a few of the cafe's signature dishes. The restaurant even has its own vegetable garden at Oatland Island Wildlife Center to supply additional produce for homemade dishes. The commitment to farming extends beyond the menu: The takeout containers are made from corn, and utensils are made from potato starch. Although it's called a carry-out café, seating is available in the restaurant.

Thrive also operates as a gourmet market with an impressive selection of fresh produce, grass-fed beef, pastured pork, and free-range chicken and artisanal cheese, all from local producers. Organic and biodynamic wines are also available.

4700 Highway 80 East, Savannah (Chatham County), 912-898-2131, www.thriveacarryoutcafe.com. $

## Crossroads Café

Crossroads Café's tagline, "where main streets meet and locals eat," fails to mention the best thing about the restaurant: Most of the ingredients used in the soups, salads, and sandwiches are sourced from local farmers and producers, including Southern Swiss Dairy, Flat Creek Lodge, and East Georgia Produce. A small on-site herb garden provides truly local flavor. Not only does the café support vendors at the fledgling farmers' market across the street; it's one of few places in town to get a farm-to-table meal.

113 South Main Street, Swainsboro (Emanuel County), 478-237-8008. $

## Halyards Restaurant

It's not uncommon for diners to walk through the doors of Halyards with a cooler of fresh catch. Executive chef Dave Snyder, who opened the restaurant in 2000, encourages diners to bring their own food. "I loved the concept of letting the guests participate in the meal," he says. "They love it when they can bring in their own catch that is less than six hours old."

Reeling in your supper isn't a prerequisite, though. There are plenty of local seafood options on the menu: triggerfish, flounder, and grouper are brought in by local fishermen like Larry Kennedy, captain of *Braves Bream*, and turned into dishes like triggerfish with boiled peanut succotash, flounder with smoked arugula pesto, and grouper with toasted almond quinoa. "I have a passion for fishing and want to serve local seafood on the menu," Snyder says. "It helps that on the island there is a huge demand for fresh catch." Snyder also partners with Baker Farms, Sapelo Farms, and McIntosh Seed to source local produce.

55 Cinema Lane, Street Simons (Glynn County), 912-638-9100, www.halyardsrestaurant.com. $$

## Georgian Room

At Sea Island Resort, Georgia ingredients have attracted national attention thanks to chef de cuisine Daniel Zeal. Using products sourced from local farms, Zeal helped the Georgian Room earn a coveted Forbes Five-Star award. It's the only restaurant in the state to achieve the honor. Dishes like squab with grilled peaches, polenta, collard greens, and red peas; red snapper with white beans, fennel sausage, and carrot and celery chowchow; and other southern-inspired dishes are served on hand-painted china with silver flatware at the upscale restaurant. Zeal also offers a five-course tasting menu to truly showcase the diversity of Georgia-grown products.

100 Cloister Drive, Sea Island (Glynn County), 912-638-3611, www.seaisland.com/dining/five-star-dining. $$$

## LODGING

### Greyfield Inn

Most of Cumberland Island, the southernmost barrier island in Georgia, is undeveloped. The National Park Service manages the beaches, maritime forests, salt marshes, and dunes, but a private swath of land still belongs to the Carnegie family, who built a colonial home on the island in 1901. The Greyfield Inn, accessible by ferry from Fernandina Beach in Florida, retains much of its historic charm. In addition to the sixteen rooms filled with period furnishings and family heirlooms, innkeepers still maintain a kitchen garden just like the original owners. Most of the produce served in the dining room at the all-inclusive hotel comes from the two-acre garden where all of the vegetables, fruit, and herbs are grown organically. "We've always pulled [produce] from the garden for the dining room, but we became much more focused on serving guests food from the garden around 2005," explains Mary Ferguson, general manager. "We definitely highlight the foods on the menu that come out of the garden to let guests know that we are committed to serving local foods."

Inn guests often explore the garden during their stay, chatting with gardeners about what is growing and sampling vine-ripe vegetables. "There is a resurgence of people wanting a connection to the land," Ferguson says. "They are so appreciative of such a beautiful place and the chance to explore the gardens and all of the untouched natural areas on the island."

Cumberland Island (Camden County), 904-261-6408,
www.greyfieldinn.com. $$$$

## Azalea Inn and Gardens

Teresa Jacobson started planting roses, dracaena, pomegranates, magnolias, and, of course, azaleas, at Azalea Inn after she purchased the historic bed and breakfast in 2005 in the hopes of re-creating the gardens that the original owners might have tended when the house was built in 1885. "I looked at historical archives to find out what was growing in the gardens in Savannah at that time," she explains.

Located in the historic district, the gardens have attracted a lot of attention: Azalea Inn has been featured on the Savannah Tour of Homes and Gardens multiple times. The latest addition to the eight-room inn is a vegetable garden. Growing fruit, vegetables, and herbs is an example of historic preservation—the original owners likely had their own kitchen gardens—as well as an effort to embrace the farm-to-table craze. When Jacobson serves eggs pomodoro with oven-roasted tomatoes or basil pesto, there are always requests for seconds. "I could put anything out on the buffet and say it was from the garden and guests would eat it up," she says.

217 East Huntingdon Street, Savannah (Chatham County), 912-236-6080,
www.azaleainn.com. $$$$

## Green Palm Inn

When Diane McCray moved from Michigan to Savannah to open a bed and breakfast, she embraced all that the southern city had to offer, from its historic charm to its food. She wanted to infuse the same local flavor into her inn, a Victorian cottage with four guestrooms that was built in 1847. The Green Palm Inn sits just a few steps from Greene Square. As the innkeeper of the Green Palm Inn, McCray prepares gourmet breakfasts, afternoons desserts, and hors d'oeuvres, all made with local ingredients. "There are a lot of local farms, so much fresh food, and I wanted to take advantage of it and incorporate it into all of the foods we serve to guests," she says.

548 East President Street, Savannah (Chatham County), 912-447-8901, www.greenpalminn.com. $$$

## Gin Creek

As a kid, Richie Demott rode into town with his father to pick up farmhands for help in the fields. When he learned the rustic cottages where the laborers once lived were slated for demolition, he stepped in and purchased six of them for $1 each. "All of the neighbors thought I was crazy," he says. But Demott had a plan: He relocated the cabins to his forty-two-acre farm and restored each one, adding them to a trio of log cabins from the 1800s, turning them into farm accommodations. Demott, a third-generation farmer, grows cotton, peanuts, tobacco, and corn but transitioned a portion of the farm to a relaxing retreat in 2003 to share the spirit of the farm with guests.

251 Demott Road, Hartsfield (Colquitt County), 229-941-2989, www.gincreek.com. $$

## Flat Creek Lodge

It's hard to categorize Flat Creek Lodge. The 1,860-acre property is home to a hunting and fishing reserve; a oyster-mushroom-growing operation; acres of blueberries, raspberries, and blackberries; a dairy that produces artisan cheeses; a farm-to-table restaurant; and a twelve-room lodge. The diverse functions all have one thing in common: a commitment to preserving the land. "We have a love for this land and this place," says general manager Cathy McDaniel. "This is more than just a place to get away and relax; it's also a real education about agriculture and the environment."

At the dairy, a herd of fifty jersey cows produces milk for thirty-five varieties of cheese, from cheddar and Havarti to Gouda and Parmesan. Guests who stay at the lodge often visit the dairy to see the cows being milked and learn more about the process of making the artisan cheeses, which are featured on the menu in the lodge restaurant, along with oyster mushrooms, vegetables, fruits, and herbs that are also grown on-site. Guests often bring in quail, rabbits, and fish that are hunted or caught on the property to create one-of-a-kind dishes. "It's a dream for a chef to be here, using ingredients that are grown right outside the back door," says executive chef Joey Williams.

367 Bishop Chapel Church Road, Swainsboro (Emanuel County), 478-237-3474, www.flatcreeklodge.com. $$

## Little St. Simons Island

At Little St. Simons Island, creating the menu for the sixteen-room inn is a team effort. Executive chef Matthew Raiford and sous-chef Paula Garrett coordinate with local boat captains and garden manager Amy Hagan to incorporate as much local catch and fruits, vegetables, and herbs grown on the island as possible. "We try to stay as true to our location as possible," says Raiford.

Guests at the all-inclusive resort indulge in family-style meals made from locally grown foods. Raiford has a personal interest in farm-to-table fare. He also farms on land his family has owned since the 1800s. Some of the eggs and fruits he grows are used in the kitchen at Little St. Simons Island; he also sources ingredients from local growers to supplement the produce Hagan grows in the USDA-certified organic garden on the island.

Raiford and Hagan host "garden walks" to showcase the raised beds and composting program, educating guests about the challenges of growing food on a island surrounded by swampland and salt marshes. "Along with growing food to use in the restaurant, we want to be a good model and show guests how to replicate what we're doing in their gardens at home," Hagan says.

1000 Hampton Point Drive, St. Simons (Glynn County), 912-638-7472, www.littlestsimonsisland.com. $$$$

On Little St. Simons Island, executive chef Matthew Raiford and sous-chef Paula Garrett prepare meals using ingredients harvested from the island garden.

## Dunham Farms

The minute Laura Devendorf said, "I have an idea," her daughter, Meredith, knew she was in for a wild ride. The pair decided to turn a horse barn on the family plantation into a bed and breakfast, transforming their timber farm into a haven for visitors.

Palmyra Plantation is still a working timber farm—Laura oversees the timber operation, and Meredith runs the sawmill and the inn—but the 10,000-acre site is so vast that guests never see heavy machinery. Instead, the sound of Clementine the mule braying in the pasture, porpoises swimming in the salt marsh, or Meredith whipping up a soufflé in the kitchen are the sounds of Dunham Farms. The farm spans two plantations, Palmyra Plantation and Springfield Plantation, the oldest intact plantation in Georgia still in the hands of the original owners; it's been in the Devendorf family since the original land grant in 1755. "People are becoming more and more disconnected from the land, and we knew the only way we could reconnect them was to bring them out here," says Meredith.

5836 Islands Highway, Sunbury (Liberty County), 912-880-4500, www.dunhamfarms.com. $$

# RECIPES

## Wild Georgia Shrimp and Grits with Grilled Corn Salsa

*Teresa Jacobson, innkeeper at the Azalea Inn and Gardens in Savannah, takes advantage of her coastal location and proximity to the Forsyth Park Farmers Market to source ingredients for one of her favorite southern dishes. Adding grilled corn salsa gives the meal a seasonal twist.*

SERVES 4

### FOR THE SALSA:

1    pound garden-fresh corn (2 ears corn)

2    cups diced garden tomatoes (4 tomatoes)

1    medium red onion, diced

2    tablespoons red wine vinegar

2    tablespoons chopped fresh cilantro

    Salt and freshly ground black pepper to taste

### FOR THE GRITS:

4    cups water

1    tablespoon chicken stock

1    cup Georgia grits

½    teaspoon salt

½    cup chopped green onion (2–3 green onions)

2    ounces cream cheese

    Salt and freshly ground black pepper to taste

### FOR THE SHRIMP:

1    pound wild Georgia shrimp, peeled and deveined

1    tablespoon Cajun seasoning

3    tablespoons salted butter

½    cup fresh lime juice (2–3 limes)

### TO PREPARE THE SALSA:

Grill the corn. Scrape the corn into bowl and combine it with the tomatoes, onions, vinegar, and cilantro. Season with salt and pepper and set aside.

### TO PREPARE THE GRITS:

Bring the water and chicken stock to a boil. Stir in the grits and salt and cook on medium-high heat for 1 minute. Reduce the heat; cover and simmer, stirring occasionally, until creamy. Stir in the green onions and cream cheese. Season with salt and pepper. Turn off the heat.

### TO PREPARE THE SHRIMP:

In a small bowl, toss the shrimp with the Cajun seasoning. Melt the butter in a large heavy skillet over medium-high heat and add the shrimp; sauté just until shrimp are cooked through, about 3 minutes. Remove the skillet from the heat and stir in the lime juice.

### TO SERVE:

Put a scoop of grits onto the center of a plate. Place a heaping spoonful of corn salsa onto the grits and arrange the shrimp on the salsa. Drizzle with the lime and butter mixture from the skillet, if you like.

**Vidalia Onion and Summer Squash Sauté**

*The Vidalia Onion Committee knows a thing or two about cooking with Vidalia onions. While it's possible to eat the sweet onions raw, Wendy Brannen, executive director of the committee, suggests cooking them with summer squash, which is harvested at the same time as the trademarked onions, and creating a light summer dish.*

SERVES 4

| | |
|---|---|
| 2 | tablespoons olive oil or butter |
| 1 | medium Vidalia onion, thinly sliced |
| ¼ | teaspoon salt |
| ¼ | teaspoon freshly ground black pepper |
| 2 | medium yellow squash or zucchini, or a mix, cut into ¼- inch-thick coins |
| ¼ | cup chopped fresh dill |
| ¼ | cup toasted almond slivers |

In a large cast-iron skillet heat the oil or butter over medium-high heat. Add the onions, salt, and pepper and cook until the onions begin to soften and take on a bit of color, about 3–4 minutes. Add the squash and cook for about 8–10 minutes, stirring occasionally until the squash is browned. Remove from the heat and stir in the dill and almonds. Add more salt and pepper, if desired.

## Pear Relish

*Preserving the fall harvest inspired Caroline Ables of Red Brick Farm to create a recipe for pear relish. It's a sweet accompaniment best paired with pork chops or served over chicken (and good enough to eat by the spoonful)!*

MAKES 10 TO 12 PINTS

| | |
|---|---|
| 14 | pears, cored and coarsely chopped |
| 8 | medium sweet onions, coarsely chopped |
| 2 | green bell peppers, seeded and coarsely chopped |
| 2 | red bell peppers, seeded and coarsely chopped |
| 1 | quart apple cider vinegar |
| 1½ | cups sugar |
| 1 | tablespoon turmeric |
| 2 | tablespoons freshly ground black pepper |
| 2 | tablespoons salt |
| | Pickling spice to taste |
| 10–12 | pint-size jars, ready to use |

In a food processor, working in batches, grind the pears, onions, and bell peppers, 6–8 pulses. In a large pot, combine this mixture with the vinegar, sugar, turmeric, pepper, salt, and pickling spice. Bring to a boil over medium-high heat. Cook for 30 minutes, stirring occasionally.

Fill the prepared jars with relish and seal with lids.

# *Piedmont*

Tucked between the Blue Ridge Mountains and the Upper Coastal Plain—almost smack in the center of the state—the Piedmont stretches from South Carolina to Alabama. It was once home to acres of cotton crops, but urbanization forced the transition from cotton fields to skyscrapers, and the agricultural landscape changed from acres of production farming to small-scale sustainable farms and urban farms. Outside of Metro Atlanta, which is part of the Piedmont, the farms, dairies, and historic homesteads are as diverse as the geography of the region.

## FARMS

### Lazy B Farm

Keeping bees, growing vegetables, and raising chickens, sheep, and goats required a huge learning curve for Cyndi Ball. She was determined to be as self-sufficient as possible on her seven-acre homestead. In the process of harvesting honey, shearing sheep and spinning wool, splitting wood, processing chickens, and canning vegetables, Ball realized that others shared her interest in homesteading. Instead of just farming for her family, she became a teacher, too, leading workshops on skills ranging from beekeeping and raising chickens to making herbal tinctures. "I never intended for this to be a public farm," she says. "I was surprised that people were willing to pay me to come and learn about these things; being able to teach my passion has been incredible."

In addition to homesteading classes, Ball started the Ladies' Homestead Gathering to help cultivate a local homesteading community; she also opens the farm for special events and tours. "There is a trend of going back to the land and being more independent from the grocery store, and that's what we're promoting here," she says. "I want to bring people together for the common purpose of learning how to homestead."

1938 Parker Drive, Statham (Barrow County), 770-289-2301, www.thelazybfarm.com

## Heritage Farm

It's not just children eager to pet goats and chase chickens who love spending time at Heritage Farm. The fertile fields and productive pastures attract locavores in search of a connection to their foods, foodies who want to pick fresh berries for homemade jams and jellies, and beginning farmers looking for advice on organic growing methods. And farmers Greg and Lainya Hutchins welcome them all. "Growing up, it was a big treat to spend a weekend on my grandparents' farm with the chickens and cows; that was the seed for giving tours here," says Greg. "The next thing we knew, it was Old McDonald's Farm personified."

Heritage Farm is a sustainable farm that produces pastured meats and fresh produce. Many of the Certified Naturally Grown fruits and vegetables on the farm, including beets, green beans, kale, peppers, okra, strawberries, tomatoes, and watermelons, are heirloom varieties. The fields are available for U-pick, and produce is also sold alongside heritage pork, pastured chickens, and grass-fed beef and lamb in the farm store. The star of the tours is Buddy, a 750-pound Berkshire boar who roots for acorns in the woods. "There are always animals to feed, pet, and cuddle on the farm," Greg says. "The hands-on interactions with the animals are definitely one of the most popular parts of the tours."

205 Day Road, Bowdon (Carroll County), 770-854-6174, www.heritage-farm.net

## Ole McDermitt's Farm

As soon as the temperatures dropped and the leaves started changing color, Kenny and Kayla McDermitt would travel to North Georgia to take their seven children to a pumpkin patch and corn maze. "There was no place in West Georgia that had those kinds of activities," Kenny recalls. Recognizing an opportunity to launch an agritourism enterprise in Carrollton, Kenny transformed a portion of his land into a festive fall destination. In an effort to keep the farm authentic as possible, the McDermitt's decided not to add jumping pillows or playground equipment. Instead, all of the activities are centered around agriculture, which Kenny calls "my first love."

A pumpkin patch, corn maze, and petting zoo are the big draws, but there is another reason families line up to get into Ole McDermitt's Farm: The collection of cornstalks, pumpkins, and fall foliage adorning the barn are worthy of a spread in *Southern Living*, making it one of the most picturesque places in the region. "We have a lot of people who want to come out to the farm to take pictures because it's so pretty," Kenny says. "They are making memories here."

102 Baxter Road, Carrollton (Carroll County), 678-850-8948, www.olemcdermittsfarm.com

## Athens Corn Maze

For row crop farmers Rodney and Kendra Miller, growing a corn maze was a fun experiment. The Millers partnered with Jerome and Tina Beggs to start the Buford Corn Maze in Buford, Georgia, in 2009. The maze was so successful that the couple replicated the maze on their farm. Since their inaugural season in 2011, the agritourism activities have expanded to include hayrides and displays of antique tractors and farm equipment. In the petting zoo, calves, horses, goats, and rabbits are ready to be nuzzled. Unlike other farms where the corn boxes are filled to the brim, Miller Family Farms has attached traditional corn-shellers to the box and encourages guests to turn the hand crank and add more shelled corn to the box before diving in.

1035 Cleveland Road, Athens (Clark County), 404-308-4028, www.athenscornmaze.com

## Will Farm for Food

Across the nation, informal groups called Crop Mobs bring together wannabe agrarians and farmers to exchange labor for knowledge. Once a month, groups of farmers-in-the-making descend on farms to pull weeds, stake tomatoes, build chicken coops, repair fences, and harvest squash. In exchange for their hard work, the mobs get firsthand knowledge of what it takes to manage a farm, as well as a meal provided by the farmer.

The first Crop Mob took place in Raleigh, North Carolina, in 2008. Since then, Crop Mobs have popped up all around the United States, embracing the idea that farming requires the collective efforts of entire communities to be successful. In Georgia, Crop Mobs have been held on farms in Atlanta, Savannah, and Athens. The Crop Mob Georgia website (www.cropmobgeorgia.com) posts notices about upcoming events.

## Roots Farm

Thanks to a lot of passion and hard work, Chris Lutz manages to turn a few acres of land into upwards of thirty varieties of vegetables and cultivate a living from the land. Lutz believes in sustaining the community as well as the land, inviting working members to trade farm labor for fresh foods. All of the fruits, vegetables, and herbs grown on the farm are sold at local farmers' markets and on-farm sales. One evening a month, the farm hosts a Beaverdam SlowDown Dinner, a five-course meal prepared by a rotating cast of local chefs using ingredients from the farm. Following the meal, Lutz offers tours of the farm.

46 Beaver Trail, Winterville (Clarke County), 706-742-0010, www.rootsfarm.org

## University of Georgia Horticulture Trial Garden

UGA horticulture professor Allan Armitage receives shipments of seeds from companies all over the country. As founder of the Horticulture Trial Garden, it's his job to propagate the seeds and assess their performance. Armitage started the garden in 1982 and turned it into one of the premier trial gardens in the nation. And it's open to the public.

The garden is a little hard to find, hidden between the garbage bins outside the dining hall and a loading dock, making it feel even more like a secret hideaway. It's a place to see a collection of the most unusual and colorful plants found anywhere. Both annuals and perennials are included in the trial garden.

New trials are planted in April and May, but the temperate climate in Athens means the garden is almost always in bloom. One of the best times to visit is March, when the annual Plant-a-Palooza event transforms the trial garden into a retail nursery, where native plants are sold to the public and top-notch horticulturalists and master gardeners are available to answer questions and help with plant selections.

1111 Plant Sciences Building, Athens (Clarke County), 706-542-2471, www.ugatrial.hort.uga.edu

## Twisted Fence Ranch

Judy Maxwell thought opening a fiber shop in downtown Harlem would be the perfect way to showcase the roving and yarns made from the alpacas she raises on her farm. The shop did not do as well as she hoped, but instead of giving up on the concept, she closed the downtown store and set up shop on her farm. And it became more popular than ever.

The store stocks fiber, yarn, and knitting and spinning supplies. In addition to sheering the alpacas and washing and spinning yarns, Maxwell also dyes and custom blends fibers. But it's not the availability of locally raised fiber that is a boon for business: at the farm, the alpacas are the real draw. Customers often spend time on the ranch, knitting and spinning, slipping treats to a small herd of alpacas grazing in the pastures, in between knitting and purling.

Maxwell also offers tours of the farm by appointment, introducing visitors to the herd and teaching them about their fiber.

134 Misty Woods Drive, Grovetown (Columbia County), 706-863-2120, www.twistedfence.com

## 180 Degree Farm

Not long after their son, Mason, was diagnosed with cancer, Scott and Nicole Tyson began researching its causes and discovered that pesticides and GMO foods might have contributed to his illness. The couple planted a garden to grow organic produce and from then on purchased grass-fed, organic meat and raw milk. In conjunction with surgery to remove a tumor, the family changed their eating habits and minimized their exposure to pesticides and other chemicals. To their delight, Mason was declared cancer-free one year later. With the trauma of his illness behind them, the couple turned their attention to sharing their newfound knowledge with others. Their belief that food played a crucial role in healing their son inspired them to start a farm. Unlike other small-scale farms that hope to turn a profit from selling produce, 180 Degree Farm is a nonprofit organization. Scott and Nicole set it up as a charity and embrace the motto, "Grow, Give, Teach," which means holding workshops, nutrition classes, and tours, along with running a CSA and on-farm sales.

The farm produces fruits and vegetables, chickens, and lamb as well as duck eggs, which contain high alkaline proteins that are said to be good for cancer patients. The farm grows crops and raises livestock organically with no added hormones or antibiotics. As part of their mission, the couple donates produce grown on the farm to those who are struggling with illness and unable to afford organic foods and to ministries in the Coweta and Fayette areas. In the first half of 2012, 180 Degree Farm donated 6,000 pounds of produce.

237 Emory Phillips Road, Sharpsburg (Coweta County), 678-481-3367, www.180degreefarm.org

## Dickey Farms

Between May and August, all of the rocking chairs on the wide wooden porch that overlooks the packing shed at Dickey Farms are taken. With the hum of the packing equipment in the background, visitors indulge in homemade peach ice cream and cobbler while they watch peaches roll through the assembly line.

Started in 1898, the fifth-generation family farm is the oldest continually operating packinghouse in Georgia. Although the process of growing and harvesting peaches has remained almost the same over the last century, the interest in observing the process has changed. "More and more people kept asking about the packing shed, [so] we built the porch so they could see how it runs," says Cynde Dickey. "It's a commercial operation, but it doesn't have a commercial feel. We wanted to keep the old-timey feel of how things were when the farm first started."

Most of the peaches harvested on the 1,000-acre farm are shipped to retailers like Winn Dixie, Publix, and Walmart, but the just-picked fruit is also sold on the porch alongside peach bread, pies, fritters, and other goodies that are made on-site daily. A conveyor belt behind the packing shed removes overripe peaches from the packing line, offering customers who want to bake with the fruit or put it up for the winter a great deal on fresh fruit. "We grow thirty different varieties of peaches, so every week there is a new variety to try," Dickey says. "They all taste great in ice cream."

3440 Old Highway 341 North, Musella (Crawford County), 478-836-4362,
www.dickeyfarms.com

## Greenway Farms of Georgia

Greenway Farms embraces a greener way of farming. On the sustainable farm, owned by Kerry and Robin Dunaway, all garden waste is turned into vermicompost, sawdust from the on-site mill is used as bedding in the chicken coops, animals are raised without hormones, and crops are grown without chemicals. It's all part of the couple's goal to safeguard the environment, ensuring their farm is fertile for the next generation and their foods are safe for their customers.

What started out as a hobby farm in 2008 turned into a diverse operation with produce, goats, pigs, broilers, laying hens, bees, and several vegetable crops. The couple also runs a cannery to produce value-added goods. "We like to do things the way our grandparents did," says Robin. "When our grandparents farmed, they had some of everything so that they could sustain themselves."

The growing popularity of sustainable farming inspired Kerry and Robin to open the farm to visitors. Tours educate visitors about all aspects of farming, from growing tomatoes without chemicals and raising hens to processing chickens; stories and crafts help pint-sized guests learn about life on the farm. "We want to be good stewards of what God has given us, and we want to share those things with visitors, explaining how all of the different [elements] on the farm work together and support each other," Robin explains.

1100 Beasley Road, Roberta (Crawford County), 478-836-3774,
www.greenwayfarmsofga.com

## Fancy Feather Farms

The ostriches, emus, and rheas are the most unusual and captivating animals on the farm. Their plump, feathered bodies, long necks, and beady eyes attract curious stares and inspire kids to giggle and ask, "What is *that?*" Jim and Kelly Scott have been raising the odd-looking birds since 1991 and decided to open the farm to visitors to share their love of the exotic creatures. The birds share the farm with other feathered companions, including chickens and ducks. All of the feathered farm animals are eager to accept food pellets and pose for pictures.

3571 Bowman Highway, Royston (Franklin County), 706-246-0214, www.fancyfeatherfarms.us

## Indian Creek Angus

When Carol Corbin met Dennis Burton, he was raising cattle to sell at auction, knowing the cows would end up on feedlots, pressed together on concrete pads and fed a diet of low-grade grain before being sent to the slaughterhouse. Corbin, a college professor who taught environmental communications, had ethical issues with the operation. After the couple got married, Corbin convinced Burton to take a different approach to cattle farming. As of 2009, all of the cattle raised on the farm are grass-fed, Certified Naturally Grown, and sold directly to the consumer. "We were able to merge our expertise, to put the health of the animals and the planet first, to provide healthy food for our community," says Corbin. "We made our first sale in March 2010, and the interest has rapidly increased."

The couple also raise registered Angus, Hereford, and Charolais cattle on their ranch alongside the more unusual Murray Grey, an Australian breed with a silver coat. All of their grass-fed beef is sold on the farm, where Corbin and Burton regularly offer tours. "We think that everything needs to be transparent, which is the opposite of what happens on a feedlot—no one wants you to see what goes on there. We want people to come to the farm, to see where their food comes from and ask questions," Corbin says. "We're taking a different approach, and our customers appreciate it."

1515 Georgia Highway 198, Carnesville (Franklin County), 706-384-2648, www.grassfedbeefgeorgia.com

## Walnut Knoll Farm

Fairbanks, Legato, Treasure, and All That Jazz-Bo love to meet new people. In fact, all of the alpacas at Walnut Knoll Farm are eager to check out the visitors who come to the pasture gates. While most of their guests are there to meet ranchers George and Judy Dick to learn more about alpaca ownership, the farm also welcomes curious visitors who want to get a closer look at the animals. In addition to special events like National Alpaca Farm Days and an annual holiday open house, farm tours and alpaca meet-and-greets are available by appointment.

466 Stone Lane, Canon (Franklin County), 706-245-0821,
www.walnutknollfarm.com

## Callaway Gardens

Callaway Gardens isn't a traditional agritourism destination. The 13,000-acre property started out with a golf course and a stocked lake for fishing and has grown to include zip lines, a beach, a tennis center, and guest accommodations. Look beyond the resort atmosphere and there are elements of agriculture to explore. Mr. Cason's Vegetable Garden was planted in 1962 and is filled with corn, beans, tomatoes, squash, zucchini, and other vegetables. The seven-acre garden was used as the set for a public broadcasting station in Boston that wanted to film its TV program *The Victory Garden* in the South. It also serves as a teaching garden, showcasing growing techniques and hosting annual plant trials as part of the American Garden Award competition. "We wanted people from the North to see how to grow vegetables and collard greens and people from the South to see kohlrabi and kale," says garden director Patricia Collins.

In the summer, the garden hosts scavenger hunts, giving visitors clues that lead them through various plots in search of information about the crops. Although there is a strict "no sampling" rule, there is a farmers' market on Friday evenings from May to October to sell produce from the garden along with products from producers within 150 miles of Callaway Gardens. The produce is also used in The Gardens Restaurant on-site.

5887 Georgia Highway 354, Pine Mountain (Harris County), 800-225-5292,
www.callawaygardens.com

Georgia farmers grow a huge variety of vegetables.

## Jenny Jack Sun Farm

Jenny Jackson's interest in growing food was piqued when she was studying horticulture at the University of Georgia. After graduation, she worked in the vegetable garden at Callaway Gardens and volunteered on an organic farm in Hawaii. When she returned to Georgia in 2007, her parents encouraged her to start an organic garden on their land. She started with a 5,000-square-foot plot and sold the produce at local farmers' markets. "We were surprised at how receptive people in this area were to organic produce," she recalls. "I didn't realize that there was an awareness of organic produce and people looking for it in smaller towns."

Thanks to skyrocketing demand, Jenny and her husband, Chris, expanded the plots every season. The couple currently grows 150 varieties of fruits, vegetables, and herbs as well as eggs and honey, which are sold at farmers' markets and an on-farm market and distributed to a 130-member CSA. "We try to keep it as diverse as possible," says Jenny. "It's fun to introduce people to new things like purple peppers and kohlrabi."

During annual farm dinners in the spring and fall, the couple partners with local chefs to showcase their produce. Since starting the dinners in 2008, the events have grown to feed up to 200 diners. "It's something fun to do and a way to serve produce right on the farm," Jenny says.

707 White Cemetery Road, Pine Mountain (Harris County), 706-333-4479, www.jennyjackfarm.com

## Frolona Farm

Even though the Davis family has been farming in Heard County since the 1870s, Josh Davis never planned to continue the tradition. He finished graduate school and, unsure what to do next, signed up for a guitar-building workshop in the Northeast. Davis returned to Franklin and set up a workshop in the old barn with plans to start a custom guitar shop. "I always loved being on the farm, loved the work," he recalls. "When I started working in the barn, it seemed like all of my interests dovetailed."

In 2008, Davis committed to farming. He raises grass-fed beef, pastured pork, and heritage breed turkeys and chickens and grows several varieties of vegetables—all Certified Naturally Grown. He sells produce at the farmers' market but encourages customers to come to the farm to purchase fruits, vegetables, meat, and eggs. "For folks interested in naturally grown and raised foods, coming to the farm is the next step in understanding where their food comes from," he says. "My job is as much about connecting with consumers and educating them as it is about growing and selling produce, and that means inviting people to the farm."

3232 Frolona Road, Franklin (Heard County), 706-506-1878, www.frolonafarm.com

## Shields Ethridge Heritage Farm

Actively farmed since 1789, the Shields Ethridge Heritage Farm is also an outdoor farm museum showcasing Georgia's agricultural and natural history. Listed on the National Register of Historic Places, the 152-acre farm boasts over twenty intact historic buildings—including a wheat house, milking barn, blacksmith, and carpenter's shop—along with original farm equipment. Visitors can take virtual tours on the farm's comprehensive website or use signage, brochures, and an iPhone app to navigate the farm's self-guided walking tour, during which they can peek inside the general store and other buildings. Once a year, at the farm's annual Black Pot Cookin' event, some of the buildings open their doors, including the working gristmill, cotton gin, and restored schoolhouse. The event also features food cooked the old-fashioned way—over an open fire—as well as bluegrass and gospel music. Visitors can also purchase grits, cornmeal, and honey produced on the farm.

2355 Ethridge Road, Jefferson (Jackson County), 706-367-2949, www.shieldsethridgefarminc.com

### Greenleaf Farms

For most of the year, Greenleaf Farms isn't open to visitors. Instead, Greg Brown sells his vegetables through farmers' markets like the Emory Green Market, Peachtree Road Farmers Market, and Decatur Farmers Market. But during Till and Fill in the spring and Weed and Feed in the fall, Brown invites the agri-curious to put in a day of work on the farm in exchange for a meal prepared from the season's harvest. During breaks from hoeing, weeding, and sowing, Brown discusses the processes of growing produce like asparagus, blueberries, figs, peaches, and pecans using Certified Naturally Grown methods and what it takes to operate a successful farm.

201 Highway 36 Bypass, Barnesville (Lamar County), 678-596-6803

### Carroll Farms

Carroll Farms grows twenty-five varieties of peaches on 250 acres. Between May and August, the offerings range from Flame Prince and Red Prince to Gala and Dixie Red, all sold from the packing shed. In the 1950s, the orchards were among the largest in Georgia. Though operations have scaled back since T. H. Carroll started the farm, his daughter, Kay Carroll Barnes, preserves the tradition of growing Georgia peaches. Most of the peaches that go through the packing shed are shipped to supermarkets, but it's possible to purchase peaches from the shed, too. A small retail shop also sells peach butter, peach preserves, peach salsa, and other specialty products.

4040 Carroll Chunn Road, Woodbury (Meriwether County), 706-553-2795, www.carrollfarms.com

### Greendale Farm

All of the grass-fed beef and lamb, pastured pork and chicken, free-range eggs, and artisanal cheese produced on Greendale Farm are available at the Athens Farmers Market, Peachtree Road Farmers Market, and restaurants like Bacchanalia and Restaurant Eugene, but farmers Russ and Christel Green encourage their customers to make a trip to the farm to get a closer look at the source of their food. The couple, both from South Africa, moved from Atlanta to Madison in 2007 and started farming. Although the learning curve was steep, it didn't take long for the farm to gain a loyal following and for their products, which are all Certified Naturally Grown, to become sought after by chefs and foodies alike.

4410 Lower Apalachee Road, Madison (Morgan County), 706-752-1482, www.greendalefarm.com

## Verner Farms

"We didn't decide to sell meat because we had a small farm and a few cows," says Adam Verner. "We run 200 head of cattle on a 1,500-acre farm; this is not a small operation." Verner Farms is a Georgia Centennial Farm that has been in the family for more than 130 years. It's always operated as a cattle ranch, but the approach has changed from one generation to the next, shifting from 500 head of beef cattle and dairy heifers, to a commercial cattle operation, to a small herd of breeding cattle. According to Verner, a fifth-generation rancher who oversees a herd of registered Angus and Simmental cattle, the cattle are raised on pastures with no added hormones or antibiotics. "We like to say that we raise cows the right way," he says.

The family has always processed steers for their tables. After friends started placing orders for grass-fed beef, which led to friends of friends calling the farm to request cuts of meat, Verner Farms ran with the demand. "The demand snowballed and more people started saying, 'Dang, you should sell this,'" Verner recalls. "In 2010, we got our own meat label and started selling meat from the farm. It's not something we set out to do, but it's been a good experience."

4990 Davis Academy Road, Rutledge (Morgan County), 706-474-0091, www.vernerfarms.com

## Burge Organic Farm

Burge Organic Farm grows all of the usual suspects—okra, asparagus, tomatoes—for its CSA members, but it also offers rare varieties of fruits and vegetables, including wild plums, heirloom garlic that grows wild on the farm, and specialty Asian vegetables like komatsuna. Most of the produce, honey, and eggs produced on the organic farm are distributed through a CSA and local farmers' markets, but farm manager Cory Mosser offers on-farm pickups and tours by appointment.

The farm is part of Burge Plantation, a 930-acre plantation that has been in the same family for seven generations. Most of the amenities on the 1,000-acre historic plantation are available only to members of Burge Club; but picking up produce directly from the farm also offers a chance for a rare glimpse of the private club and its beautiful grounds.

44 Jeff Cook Road, Mansfield (Newton County), 912-257-9865, www.burgeclub.com

## Mitcham Farm

When Henry and Molly Boggus operated the farm in 1884, they raised just enough chickens, hogs, and cattle to sustain themselves. Tommy Mitcham wanted to continue the tradition of farming on the Centennial Family Farm but decided to share his bounty with the community. Mitcham, a fifth-generation farmer, and his wife, Emy, sell strawberries, tomatoes, onions, and other fresh vegetables from their farm stand in the spring; the farm also opens its strawberry patch for U-pick. Corn is still a staple crop on the farm, just like it was when Tommy's great-grandfather worked the land. While some of the sweet corn is grown for the table, a field is reserved for the Colonel Cob's Corn Maze. The seven-acre corn maze is one of a number of fall activities on the farm, including a petting zoo, a corn silo, a cow train, hayrides, and a pumpkin patch.

797 Macedonia Church Road, Oxford (Newton County), 770-855-1530, www.mitchamfarm.com

## Hidden Springs Farm

"Most people have no idea that there are different varieties of honey," says Donna Lopes. "They think that all honey is the same." On Hidden Springs Farm, Lopes introduces visitors to dozens of varieties of honey, including wildflower, tupelo, orange blossom, kudzu, blackberry, strawberry, and blueberry honey. She harvests the honey from 200 hives—40 on the farm and 160 more located on farms across the Southeast.

Sampling different varieties of honey is one of the highlights of a farm tour. "As soon as they taste it, they ask if I've added flavor," Lopes says. "They can't believe how different each different kind of honey tastes." But Lopes, who has been raising bees, cattle, and chickens and growing pecans on the farm since 1995, also takes visitors to the honey room to see an observation hive and to watch the process of extracting honey. At the end of the tour (held regularly and by appointment), Lopes sells fresh honey from her hives.

974 Bethany Road, Williamson (Pike County), 770-412-1703, www.hsffarm.com

## The Rock Ranch

The Rock Ranch might belong to S. Truitt Cathy, founder of Chick-fil-A, but there isn't a chicken in sight. Instead, the 1,250-acre ranch is home to a herd of cattle that seem oblivious to the squeals of delight as guests race through the corn maze or ride the zip line over the pasture. "Growing healthy families and being good stewards of this property is what we're all about," says Adam Pugh, director of events and marketing.

During annual events like Fun in the Summertime and Fall Family Fun Days, families explore the petting zoo, ride the farm train, try cane-pole fishing, shoot the pumpkin cannon, or bounce on the jumping pillow. For a true Wild West experience, overnight guests can camp in Conestoga wagons.

It's not just an agritourism destination; the Rock Ranch is a working ranch where U-pick patches are bursting with strawberries, blueberries, and sweet corn and a produce stand is stocked with fresh fruits and vegetables as well as beef and honey raised on the farm.

5020 Barnesville Highway, The Rock (Upson County), 706-647-6374, www.therockranch.com

## Back River Farm

Richard Brown sells produce at both the Snellville and East Lake farmers' markets, but shoppers love making the trek out to the farm to purchase fresh fruits and vegetables. "I like planting a seed and seeing things grow and I think other people like that, too," Brown says. "A lot of families who come out to the farm live in subdivisions and want to show their kids that their food comes out of the ground." As a child, Brown knew exactly where his food came from: He helped with corn and soybean production on a 500-acre family farm. It was the memories of those experiences that led Brown to trade a career in engineering and construction for farming in 2010.

All of the squash, zucchini, turnips, okra, tomatoes, bell peppers, sweet corn, and other produce he grows on the eighteen-acre farm is Certified Naturally Grown. He sells produce on the farm and encourages customers to ask about how it was grown. The process is much different than that on the conventional farm he worked on as a teen. His commitment to the environment, much like the fruits and vegetables on the farm, has grown significantly since he started farming. "I believe in protecting the land for the next generations," he says. "Being all natural helps with that."

4121 Bullock Bridge Road, Loganville (Walton County), 770-842-5642, www.backriverfarmga.net

## William Harris Homestead

Melissa Basta calls William Harris Homestead "one of Georgia's hidden treasures." The 50-acre historic homestead was part of a 500-acre land lottery granted to William Carr in the 1800s. Once planted in cotton, it's now a designated historic site where several original buildings, including the farmhouse, barn, corncrib, and salt house, serve as classrooms for visitors. "It's one of very few preserved farms with original outbuildings that depict how rural Georgia farm families would have lived," says Basta, the facilities coordinator for the site. To protect the homestead from development, it was placed on the National Register of Historic Places in 1980. After being abandoned for almost seventy years at the turn of the century, the once-dilapidated farmhouse and outbuildings underwent extensive restoration between 1986 and 1990.

On the first and third Saturdays of the month, docents dressed in period costumes demonstrate food preservation and open-hearth cooking using foods from the on-site vegetable garden; cotton picking from the cotton patch for carding, spinning, and dyeing; sheep herding; and blacksmithing on a period forge.

3636 Georgia Highway 11, Monroe (Walton County), 770-267-5844,
www.harrishomestead.com

## Ogeechee River Mill

Running a gristmill is the hardest thing Missy Garner has ever done. A cattle farmer from Florida, she had no experience milling corn, but the 1847 mill came with the farm she bought in 2000 and it seemed wasteful to let it sit idle. "I decided to turn it into a living classroom," she says. Garner restored the mill and got the original stones and belts working again. A turbine is powered by water from the Ogeechee River. Garner grinds corn into cornmeal and hush puppy mix that are sold through local retailers and at the mill. The process, she believes, honors the heritage of the area. "I want to continue to preserve what we have," she says. The mill also offers tours by appointment.

262 Reynolds Road, Warrenton (Warren County), 706-465-2195

## Moore Acres

Moore Acres bills itself as a "real farm experience." The 275-acre cattle ranch is home to a herd of Angus cows as well as chickens, rabbits, and goats, and the fields are planted with crops like hay, corn, and timber. In October, the farm transitions into an amusement park for agriculture lovers, complete with a zip line, climbing fort, bucking bull barrel rides, and pedal carts. As a working farm, Moore Acres also offers activities with an agricultural focus, including a corn maze, a pumpkin patch, a livestock barn, and mock steer roping.

1277 Tignall Road, Washington (Wilkes County), 706-678-5705, www.mooreacresfarm.com

## FARMERS' MARKETS

### Cotton Mill Farmers Market

When the Cotton Mill Farmers Market started in 2002, there were not many places to shop for local foods in Carroll County. "We felt like there was a need," says Melanie Drew, a board member and vendor. Between April and September, up to twenty local vendors selling produce, meat, bread, eggs, and value-added products like jellies, granola, and pasta set up tents in the parking lot of a strip mall on the edge of downtown. Along with the vendors, there are often demonstrations: Chefs create recipes using seasonal ingredients, or artists share their creative processes. "It's more than just a place to shop," Drew says. "It's where our community comes together."

401 Rome Street, Carrollton (Carroll County), www.cottonmillfarmersmarket.org

## An Online Alternative to Farmers' Markets

In 2002, software developer and sustainable farmer Eric Wagoner developed a website to help farmers in his hometown of Athens connect with consumers. The premise: Setting up a booth at the farmers' market required farmers to anticipate sales and guess how much produce to harvest. Often, leftover produce was sold at a fraction of the market price at the end of the market or thrown away. Setting up a system where shoppers placed their orders *before* the produce was harvested eliminated speculation. To address the issues, Wagoner created locallygrown.net

Through the website, farmers can upload basic details about their offerings, which range from fresh produce and meat to honey and grains, set a price for their products, and wait for customers to place their orders. Once orders are received, farmers harvest only what has sold and drop it off at a central location at a predetermined date and time.

Unlike CSAs, where consumers partner with one farm and might end up with too much of one item and not enough of another, placing an order through locallygrown.net allows shoppers the flexibility to order anything they want from any farmer who has it available. Once their orders are placed, shoppers pick up their purchases from the same location where farmers drop them off.

The concept has been incredibly popular. Since Wagoner introduced locallygrown.net, it has expanded from Athens into more than 300 other markets across the United States and Canada.

## Athens Farmers Market

Athens is known for its thriving music scene, so it should come as no surprise that the farmers' market operates to a backdrop of local musicians. On Saturday mornings, shoppers weaving between the booths at Bishop Park may be buying blueberries to the sound of bluegrass or stocking up on rhubarb during a rock-and-roll riff. All of the vendors, whose products must be Certified Naturally Grown, often sing along to the tunes while counting change.

The Wednesday evening market at City Hall (301 College Avenue, Athens) is slightly more subdued, but the produce sells out just as quickly. At both locations, it's a good idea to arrive early for the best selection; to chat up any of the twenty vendors, showing up just before the market closes is a better bet.

705 Sunset Drive, Athens (Clarke County), 706-613-3592, www.athensfarmersmarket.net

## Downtown Commerce Farmers Market

When the Downtown Commerce Farmers Market debuted in 2008, only about five vendors showed up. By 2012, the market boasted almost three times that number—and it keeps growing. Arts and crafts were recently added to the list of products, all of which are grown or made in Georgia. There's also a plethora of produce—from zucchini squash to peppers to melons—and baked goods ranging from cookies, cakes, and pies to dog biscuits. Vendors, who sometimes sell products right out of their pickup trucks, are friendly and available to discuss recipes or growing methods, which are often organic. Some popular items include the fresh-cut flowers and herbs, which tastefully accentuate meals prepared with the market's other items. Other products include baked bread, honey, nuts, free-range chicken or duck eggs, jams, and jellies.

1573 South Elm Street, Commerce (Jackson County), 706-335-2954, www.commercega.org

## FARM STANDS AND U-PICKS

### Farmers Fresh CSA

Patricia Gladney knew it was hard for farmers to commit to setting up a booth at the farmers' market every Saturday morning and hoping sales would cover their operating costs. To help expand their reach, she helped start a CSA program in Carroll County. In 2009, demand peaked and she transitioned the CSA into a storefront market.

Farmers Fresh CSA still serves as a CSA pickup location but also sells produce, meat, cheese, milk, eggs, and grains from its storefront. "The storefront allows people to keep local on their minds," says Gladney. "They don't have to wait until the farmers' market on Saturday mornings to buy fruits, vegetables, herbs, and meat."

At least 90 percent of the products sold in the market come from producers within a fifty-mile radius of Carrollton. Both farmers and backyard gardeners sell their products in the market. A deli serves ready-made foods made from local, organic, and fair trade ingredients. To encourage the community to support local farms, Gladney offers a work/trade program: workers who help stock shelves or fill CSA boxes earn store credit to stock their cupboards. "It's important to encourage the community to support our farms," she says.

207-B Adamson Square, Carrollton (Carroll County), 770-633-6261, www.farmersfreshcsa.com

### Country Gardens Farm

Most of the grass-fed beef, pastured pork and chicken, raw milk, free-range eggs, wildflower honey, shitake mushrooms, and vegetables that Country Gardens Farm produces are sold through CSA subscriptions. Often, farmers Mike and Judy Cunningham have excess meat, dairy, and produce, which they make available at their farm stand. The self-service stand operates on the honor system; customers choose their items from the cooler, tally up their purchases, and leave their payment in a box. Judy admits that while the process is impersonal, there is an added benefit to an on-farm stand. "People like to come out to the farm and see where their food is grown," she explains. "It helps them feel connected to the farm."

## The ABCs of CSAs

CSA is the acronym for Community Supported Agriculture. As part of a CSA, consumers buy shares (also known as memberships or subscriptions) in a farm and farmers supply a box of seasonal produce each week during the farming season.

The size of a CSA varies from farm to farm; smaller farms may operate CSAs with as few as ten members while others might grow produce for hundreds of subscriptions. Some CSAs pack boxes with produce while others provide meat and eggs. By accepting payment for shares up front, farmers have access to funds to purchase seeds and livestock.

CSA members agree to pick up their produce at a predetermined location and time. The inclusions change from week to week; the produce included in the box reflects the harvest, which means there is often more variety at peak growing season. Farmers often include recipes, especially for fruits and vegetables their members might not be familiar with. Members benefit from weekly boxes of farm-fresh goodies as well as the knowledge that purchasing a share in a CSA helps support a local farm.

In 2011, the couple closed their landscaping business and turned their attention to farming full time. Their passion for growing things led Mike to launch a workshop series that includes classes on organic gardening, seed starting, raising chickens, and pruning fruit trees. "We wanted to teach people about all of the different things they could do to be more sustainable," Judy says. "The classes have been really popular."

2050 McCollum Sharpsburg Road, Newnan (Coweta County), 770-251-2673, www.countrygardensfarm.com

## The Veggie Patch at Bouchard Farm

The white clapboard house at the end of a gravel road used to be home to a farming family. When James Bouchard decided to start growing tomatoes, corn, cucumbers, peppers, chard, collards, and other vegetables on the farm in 2009, he turned the house into a rural produce stand. "Folks want to come and shop at the farm," says sales manager Tony Young. "We have great farm stand sales and we're growing all the time." All of the produce grown in the fields and in the greenhouses is certified organic. According to Young, the market has created opportunities for other local farmers. "We help support other farmers in the area by offering their produce to a wider audience and create a really strong community for locally grown produce," Young says.

594 Nunn Road, Commerce (Jackson County), 706-616-7869, www.simplyfreshveggies.com

## Native Sun Farm

On the Appalachian Trail, somewhere between Georgia and Maine, Brent and Amy Lopp decided to start a farm. The revelation came when the couple, who met while studying agriculture and ecology in Costa Rica, through-hiked the trail in 2008. "We believe in the importance of local communities and local foods," says Brent. "We wanted to be a family that served the community by providing fresh, flavorful food."

Brent and Amy grow thirty varieties of Certified Naturally Grown vegetables and raise chickens on their Oconee County farm. Their farming practices mimic those that were used 100 years ago; they use crop rotation, cover crops, and rotational grazing while eschewing pesticides. Brent relishes the interaction with his customers that he has during tours and through sales at the farmers' markets. "Everything we sell is grown right here, and buying it on the farm is a special interaction because I'm the only vendor," he says. "There is much more of a feeling of supporting the community than you find anywhere else, even at a farmers' market."

1560 Jimmy Daniel Road, Bogart (Oconee County), 706-254-4231, nativesunfarm.com

## Washington Farms

From the road, the sheer size of the strawberry, blueberry, and blackberry fields makes Washington Farms looks like a commercial grower, not a U-pick farm. Between April and June, though, fourteen acres of strawberries are ripe for the picking and empty buckets are snapped up as fast as the staff can sell them. As soon as strawberry season is over, the blueberry and blackberry patches are bursting with berries and the race to fill containers with sweet summer fruit begins again.

5671 Hog Mountain Road, Watkinsville (Oconee County), 706-769-0627, www.washingtonfarms.net

## Whippoorwill Hollow Organic Farm

Whippoorwill Hollow Farm might be a working farm, but Andy Byrd will happily stop what he is doing to welcome visitors. During informal tours of the farm, Andy explains the organic growing techniques used to produce fruits, vegetables, herbs, and flowers. Depending on the season, it's possible to step into the fields and pick produce, and the harvest is always available for sale from the on-farm stand.

Andy and his late wife, Hilda, bought the farm in 1997 with plans to build a house and enjoy a simpler life. "We were clearing the land and underneath all of the briars and brush, we saw pretty pink and white flowers and found about half an acre of blueberries," Andy recalls. "Hilda looked at me and said, 'What are we going to do with all of these blueberries?'" Andy put a "U-Pick Blueberries" sign at the roadside, and cars started stopping. After picking blueberries, customers noticed the small garden where Andy and Hilda were growing vegetables for their table and asked whether the produce was available for sale. "And that's how we got into farming," Andy says.

Whippoorwill Hollow Farm operates a CSA, sells produce on the farm, and provides produce to local chefs. To encourage other growers to adopt organic principles, the couple sells organic animal feed like cracked corn, field peas, and oats and organic fertilizers, insecticides, and soil amendments like bone meal, hot pepper wax, and compost; they will happily make recommendations to help both backyard gardeners and small-scale farmers achieve organic growing success.

3905 Georgia Highway 138, Covington (Walton County), 770-601-0110, www.whippoorwillhollowfarm.com

Jeff and Karen Green use milk from cattle raised at Berry College to make cheddar, Jack, Gouda, and alpine cheeses.

## DAIRIES

### Udderly Cool Dairy

"Neither of us knew we'd end up making cheese," says Karen Green. Although it was never part of the plan, Karen, a former teacher, and her husband, Jeff, an entrepreneur who installed milking parlors on farms across the Southeast, left their jobs to pursue their passion for making artisanal cheeses. It took months of experimentation to come up with the perfect cheese. Once the Gouda, Jack, and cheddar hit store shelves, Karen and Jeff quickly became award-winning cheesemakers: Their cheeses won multiple medals at the North American Jersey Cheese Awards in 2011, helping the couple gain national attention for their work.

Eventually, Jeff and Karen plan to raise cattle on the farm and add a milking parlor and viewing room; for now, the all-natural milk comes from a herd of Jersey cows at Berry College near Rome, Georgia. All of the pasteurization, milling, pressing, and aging are done at the creamery in Roopville. Their cheeses are available at farmers' markets and restaurants across Georgia as well as in the farm store in Roopville, where the couple offers tours. "The feeling we get when our cheeses are ready is such a joy," Karen says. "Being able to sell everything we make right from the creamery is icing on the cake."

300 West Drive, Roopville (Carroll County), 770-854-6300, www.udderlycoolcheese.com

## Capra Gia Cheese Company

A herd of 300 Alpine, Nubian, LaMancha, and Saanen goats graze the pastures in Carrollton, producing milk that is made into award-winning artisanal goat cheeses, including feta, roasted garlic and red pepper chèvre, onion and chive chèvre, peach chèvre, and honey lavender chèvre. "We truly have the freshest cheese in Georgia because our milk never sets," explains cheesemaker Mark Stevens. "We milk our goats every twelve hours and turn the milk into cheese immediately using the same processes that were used 500 years ago."

Stevens, an experienced and award-winning cheesemaker, teamed up with Matthew David Williamson, Jenny Livingston O'Connor, Jeremy Bethel, Brian Hager, and Heidi Lewis to start Capra Gia in 2011. All of the cheeses are made in-house, by hand. Stevens admits that their process is labor intensive but says, "It makes for a much better product."

During open houses and scheduled tours, visitors can meet the goats and tour the cheesemaking facilities to watch and learn about the process. Spring is one of the best times to visit because upwards of 200 newborn kids are in the barn waiting to be nuzzled. There are also opportunities to purchase cheese. Outside of the open houses, Capra Gia cheeses are also sold at farmers' markets in Atlanta, Alpharetta, and Marietta. Classes in cheesemaking and goat husbandry are also offered on the farm.

3325 Shady Grove Road, Carrollton (Carroll County), 770-712-8465, www.capragia.com

## Decimal Place Farm

Although she was an experienced cheesemaker, Mary Rigdon had always purchased milk from farmers. When she decided to start her own herd, she started attending goat keepers meetings in Atlanta. "Everyone laughed at me because I was Mary-No-Goats," she recalls. "I wanted to learn everything I could before I started." Rigdon also spent weekends farm-sitting on goat farms, getting comfortable with the animals and learning the ins and outs of maintaining a herd. In 1995, she purchased her first goats, two

Saanen females. Since then, her herd has grown to twenty-five milking goats, whose milk Rigdon turns into cheese. "I chose [Saanen goats] for their gentleness," she says. "We do everything we can to keep the goats happy because the less stressed they are, the better their milk is, and that comes through in the cheese."

Decimal Place Farm cheeses, including chèvre, feta, cheddar, and tuma, an Italian basket cheese similar to mozzarella, are sold through the East Atlanta Village Farmers Market, Peachtree Road Farmers Market, and Grant Park Farmers Market. It's also a staple on the menus of farm-to-table restaurants all over town.

The farm, eighteen acres just outside of Atlanta, in the flight path of Hartsfield-Jackson International Airport, is open for tours by appointment. "I love seeing the farm through the eyes of the people who visit," she says.

4314 Almach Avenue, Conley (Clayton County), 404-363-0356, www.decimalplacefarm.blogspot.com

## Steed's Dairy

Jim Steed recalls telling his late father, who started Steed's Dairy in 1946, of his plans to add agritourism activities to the farm. "He said, 'No one is going to pay you to walk through our corn field,'" Steed recalls. "I wish he could see it now." When Steed turned ten acres of the family dairy into an agritourism destination in 2010, 20,000 visitors traveled to Grovetown to pick pumpkins, navigate the corn maze, and meet the cows, rabbits, goats, and pigs in the petting zoo during the first season, proving that times have changed on family farms!

Steed visited other agritourism operators across Georgia to learn about the most popular activities. He installed a jumping pillow and a corn kernel pit while putting his own spin on things. "I didn't want this to be a cookie-cutter operation," he explains. To personalize the experience, Steed designed one-of-a-kind playground equipment, including a climbing apparatus that looks like a tractor and a mini zip line. Standing at the top of a climbing tower overlooking the corn maze, Steed muses, "If my dad could see this now, he wouldn't believe it."

4634 Wrightsboro Road, Grovetown (Columbia County), 706-855-2948, www.steedsdairy.com

## Johnston Family Farm

The dairy has grown significantly since J. H. Johnston milked seventeen cows in 1956. Today, second-generation dairyman Russell Johnston milks up to 100 cows, producing up to 800 gallons of milk per day. "Believe it or not, most of the people who come to the farm expect me to walk out of the dairy wearing overalls and a straw hat and sit down on a three-legged stool to milk the cows by hand," he says. "It's unreal how little people know about what we do here."

To educate the public about dairy farming, Johnston started offering farm tours. During springtime tours of the pasture and milking parlor, guests have the chance to explore the barn, pet the calves, feed pregnant heifers, watch the cows being milked, travel around the farm on a hayride, and make (and eat) ice cream. In 2012, the dairy stopped bottling milk and started making cheese. Johnston installed viewing windows into the processing plant to showcase mozzarella-making in progress. The farm store sells fresh mozzarella along with raw milk. "People leave the farm with a totally new outlook on dairy farming," he says.

2471 Broughton Road, Newborn (Newton County), 706-247-5023, www.johnstonfamilyfarm.com

## Mayfield Dairy Farm

Mayfield Dairy is best known for the yellow milk jugs that are ubiquitous in southern supermarkets. "Most [of our] fans believe the Mayfield yellow milk jug simply reinforces the brand image, but in fact, the opaque plastic helps protect the flavor and nutrients of the milk," explains Jamaison Schuler, senior manager of corporate communications.

Despite the name Mayfield Dairy Farm, there are no Holsteins grazing in the pastures on the tour. In fact, there are no pastures. The "farm" is a milk-processing facility where visitors can learn how milk goes from a dairy farm to the dairy case. The dairy processes approximately 154,000 gallons of milk per day. "The [dairy] represents the history, agriculture, nutrition, technology, research and development, entertainment, and art [of operating a dairy]," says Schuler. The tour includes a short video, views of tanker trucks unloading milk, and a glimpse of the homogenizers, pasteurizers, and packaging lines. All tours end in the ice cream parlor, where huge scoops of Mayfield Dairy ice cream are dished out as tasty souvenirs.

1160 Broadway Avenue, Braselton (Jackson County), 706-654-9180, www.mayfielddairy.com

# CHOOSE-AND-CUT CHRISTMAS TREES

## Spring Brook Farm

David and Beth Taylor purchased farmland in Carrollton with plans for a quiet retirement, but the idea to grow a handful of Christmas trees for their grandchildren led them out of retirement and into business. The couple planted trees in a field once filled with kudzu and cut their first trees in 2004. Beth died the following year, but David continued with their plans, opening the farm every weekend between Thanksgiving and Christmas. The farm is more than just a place to grab a Christmas tree, though. Families have built traditions around visits to the farm, sipping hot chocolate while wandering through the rows of cypress and Fraser firs in search of the perfect tree, climbing aboard a wagon for a hayride, or shopping for wreaths in the big red barn.

1520 Mandeville Road, Carrollton (Carroll County), 770-861-5333, www.springbrooktrees.com

## 7 G's Farm

When Greg Smith's uncle passed away in 1999, the farm that had been in the family since 1943 was given to Greg and his six siblings, whose names also begin with "G." Together, the "7 Gs" started a Christmas tree farm, believing it would require less labor than a "real" farm. The family soon realized their mistake but embraced the endeavor anyway. The "Gs" now work around the clock to maintain twenty-five acres of Leyland cyprus trees as well as a newly planted crop of blackberries and raspberries. Visitors can choose among fresh-cut trees, which are all pre-measured and priced, or cut their own with assistance from the 7 G's staff. The staff will also shake, load, and tie your tree—and even custom drill the bottom to fit a tree stand. Stands, as well as ornaments, wreaths, jams, and jellies are all available for sale at the on-site gift store.

2331 Old Kings Bridge Road, Nicholson (Jackson County), 706-757-2526, www.7gsfarm.com

### Bring One for the Chipper

To encourage Georgia residents to recycle their Christmas trees, the Keep Georgia Beautiful campaign launched "Bring One for the Chipper." Through the program, communities host pick-up programs or establish drop-off sites to turn Christmas trees into mulch used on playgrounds and beautification projects across the state. Since its inception in 1990, the program has recycled four million trees.

### Jack's Creek Christmas Tree Farm

As a high school junior, Mark Batchelor had no idea that his after school job would turn into a lifelong career. While he was learning to tend to trees and interact with the public, Batchelor found a mentor in an old-school tree farmer, and in 2000, he bought the farm.

Along with his brother-in-law and business partner Damon Malcom, Batchelor grows fifty acres of choose-and-cut Christmas trees, including Leyland cypress, Virginia pines, red cedars, and Green Giants. The pair also brings in precut Fraser firs and white pine trees from North Carolina and Virginia. "Instead of having three or four varieties, we want to make sure our customers have a lot of selection to choose from," Batchelor says. The most popular tree, according to Batchelor, is the Murray cypress.

The farm opens the weekend before Thanksgiving, and families drive for miles to pick out Christmas trees. Although the opportunity to trek out onto the tree farm to pick the perfect tree is the main draw, the farm also offers hayrides that wind through a festive "Tunnel of Lights" filled with twinkling, colorful Christmas lights, as well as a shop stocked with ornaments, garland, and boiled peanuts. There is even a small petting zoo on the farm, and Santa stops in on weekends to pose for pictures. "This is a place where families come to spend time together picking out trees and making memories," Batchelor says. "They can get away from the rush of the city, get out onto the farm, and have fun."

2291 Price Mill Road, Bostwick (Morgan County), 706-343-1855, www.jackscreekfarm.com

### Berry's Tree Farm

Preservation is a passion for the Berrys, who have owned and operated the same farm in Covington since the 1890s. In the 1970s, the family began planting Christmas trees on the land as a way to prevent soil erosion, provide shelter for wildlife, and reintroduce oxygen into the air. They also hoped to create Christmas memories for families by offering them the opportunity to choose and cut their own trees. There are acres of trees to chose from, as well as assistance cutting, shaking, and tying the trees. They'll even "snow-flock" the trees, if Mother Nature doesn't cooperate. The farm also features fresh-cut Fraser firs and container landscape trees and shrubs, ripe for replanting. Visitors can pick up decorations and tree stands at the Berry store, as well as snacks and hot beverages. Berry's also offers train rides for little passengers and hayrides for the whole family.

70 Mt. Tabor Road, Covington (Newton County), 770-786-5833,
www.berrystreefarm.com

### Crooked Pines Farm

When Duncan and Angela Criscoe opened their farm to the public in 2010, their goal was to provide agritourism experiences to families who wanted rural adventures. In the fall, the Pumpkin Festival offers all of the traditional harvest activities: a pumpkin patch, petting farm, and hayrides. Vendors set up booths on the eighty-two-acre farm to sell Georgia-made, Georgia-grown products during the festival. In December, the annual holiday celebration includes live music, hot apple cider, crafts for kids, vendors, a petting farm, and a Christmas tree lot with precut trees from regional farms. Santa also makes a guest appearance during the festival.

355 Harmony Road, Eatonton (Putnam County), 706-347-0274,
www.crookedpinesfarm.com

# VINEYARDS AND WINERIES

## Boutier Winery and Vineyard

Victor Boutier preferred beer to wine. A home brewer from Holland, he was familiar with hops and yeast but had no experience with making wine. On a whim, his wife, Mary Jakupi-Boutier, bought him a winemaking kit and encouraged him to experiment with something new. "We weren't wine drinkers, so we had no idea if the wine was good," says Victor. But friends raved about the wines he was making, and Victor decided to see if they were right: He entered the wines in several competitions and won. Success in international competitions led Victor and Mary to pursue careers as winemakers. In 2008, they bought a vineyard and built a winery. Together they produce wines like Pinot Noir, Cabernet Sauvignon, Riesling, Chardonnay, and Merlot as well as rose petal and fruit wines. "Victor has no formal training, but that turned out to be a blessing because he's not afraid to try new things," says Mary. The creativity doesn't end with the winemaking. Their wines have names like The Cranky Bastard, Kick Ass, and Sun of a Berry.

4506 Hudson Rivers Church Road, Danielsville (Madison County), 706-789-0059, www.boutierwinery.com

## Warm Springs Winery

Ed Rocereta wanted to honor the region with his wines. He chose names like River Walk Red for the Columbus RiverWalk, White House White for the Little White House in Warm Springs, and Kudzu Rose for the ubiquitous southern vine to ensure his muscadine wines had a strong sense of place. Rocereta, a pharmacist-turned-winemaker, makes all of his wines from estate fruit. He even picks the blueberries for seasonal fruit wine from a nearby farm. While sampling wines in the tasting room, it's possible to watch the fermenting and bottling operation. The winery also hosts special events like Cork and Pork, a seasonal supper served in the vineyard.

7227 Roosevelt Highway, Warm Springs (Meriwether County), 706-655-2233

## FESTIVALS AND EVENTS

### Ag Heritage Days
Every October, the University of Georgia Cooperative Extension in Carroll County and the Carroll County Farm Bureau sponsor annual Ag Heritage Days to teach visitors about the history of agriculture in the county. Ag Heritage Days is the longest-running event in Carroll County focused on the agricultural history of the community. On weekdays, it's open for field trips and homeschooled groups; the public is welcome to attend the free event on Saturday.

A replica gristmill on the banks of Buffalo Creek showcases the process of grinding corn into grits and meal, while a historic homestead, complete with vegetable gardens, fruit trees, and antique farming equipment, illustrates how settlers lived off of the land. There are demonstrations of churning butter, making soap, preserving food, and blacksmithing. Egg hatching incubators and beehives are also on-site, and hands-on activities like milking goats round out the event.

900 Newnan Road, Carrollton (Carroll County), 770-836-8546, www.caes.uga.edu/extension/carroll

### Bicycle Farm Tour
Forget overalls and rubber boots, on the Bicycle Farm Tour hosted by the Athens Food Tour Company, the preferred attire is bicycle helmets and spandex. The tours, hosted in the spring, summer, and fall, lead groups of cyclists to local farms, where farmers explain their farming operations, answer questions about producing local foods, and share their bounty. "There are so many farms within biking distance of Athens that it just made sense [to start a bicycle farm tour]," says Mary Charles Howard, the landscape-architect-turned-entrepreneur who founded the Athens Food Tour Company in 2010.

Howard plans routes between twenty and forty miles in length to some of the top organic farms, dairies, and apiaries in the region. Howard grew up on a farm and relocated from Chapel Hill, North Carolina, to Athens to lead foodie tours like the Farmers Market Tour and Bicycle Farm Tour that connect people to local food through visits to farm-to-table restaurants and farms. "Buying organic food from local farms and biking are both [trendy] right now," she says. "With these tours, connecting people to farmers, we hope that it becomes more than a trend, that it inspires people to make it part of their lifestyle."

No bike? No problem. Bicycles are available for rent, or the tour routes can be followed by car.

Clarke County, 706-338-8054, www.athensfoodtours.com

## Digging Roots Educational Farm

Naomi Davis was the first organic farmer in Crawford County. In 2005, she offered a canning workshop to teach members of her CSA how to preserve seasonal vegetables. The workshop was so popular that Davis, who grows certified organic vegetables and strawberries on a twenty-five-acre farm that has been in her family since the 1800s, had an idea: Start a nonprofit organization to grow sustainable food. Digging Roots Educational Farm was incorporated in 2009 and offers popular workshops on topics ranging from growing strawberries and making cheese to baking bread. The canning workshop that kick- started the organization remains one of her most popular classes.

701 Hortman Mill Road, Roberta (Crawford County), 478-836-4564

## Cotton Pickin' Fair

Cotton used to be king in Meriwether County. After the last batch of cotton was ginned and bailed in 1971, the cotton mill operated by the Gay family was shut down. Instead of tearing the building down, the family turned the mill—and their farm—into the centerpiece of the Cotton Pickin' Fair. Over time, the festival morphed from a celebration of agriculture into an arts festival. Beyond booths filled with pottery and paintings, the farm still retains its farming roots. Tour the 1891 farmhouse, cotton gin, cotton warehouse, seed houses that stored cottonseed, and the scale that weighed cotton, all original to the farm.

The pastoral setting and historical significance of the farm have attracted the attention of Hollywood. Several movies have been filmed on the site, including *The War*, starring Kevin Costner and Elijah Wood, and *Lawless*, with Jessica Chastain and Shia LaBeouf.

The 1911 Society, a nonprofit that supports farm preservation and sustainable rural development, and Ellen Gay McEwen, whose family has owned the land since the 1830s, host the festival every May and October.

18830 Georgia Highway 85, Gay (Meriwether County), 706-538-6814, www.cpfair.org

## Bostwick Cotton Gin Festival

At first glance, it looks like the millers left the cotton gin at the end of their shift in the 1960s and never returned. But the Bostwick Cotton Gin still operates, ginning 3,000 bales of cotton between September and November. All of the cotton baled in the gin is grown in Morgan, Walton, and Oconee Counties and shipped through a co-op in Mississippi before hitting the open market, where it's used to make products like textiles, cotton swabs, and flour. The husks are used for cattle feed, and cottonseed oil is used in food products like Crisco. "Almost all parts of the plant are used," says John Ruark, a fourth-generation cotton farmer and gin operator. "A lot of people are surprised by all of the things cotton is turned into."

The gin, operational since the 1940s, is one of just two operational gins north of Interstate 20. It's also the centerpiece of the Bostwick Cotton Gin Festival, which takes place on the first Saturday of November. The annual event started in 1988 and attracts up to 7,000 visitors who are curious about the process of ginning cotton. During the festival, the gin is operational and tours highlight how cotton goes from the field to bales and into production. "People are fascinated by the gin and the fact that we come together to celebrate our agricultural heritage," says festival chairperson Angie Howard.

5951 Bostwick Road, Bostwick (Morgan County), 706-342-0182, www.bostwickga.com

## The Sunflower Farm Festival

In 2002, after catching several photographers sneaking onto his farm to snap pictures of blossoming sunflowers and asking permission to cut the fresh flowers, Wes Holt decided to change his business plan. "My grandfather was a cotton farmer, and he started growing sunflowers in the 1980s because Pennington [Seed Company] needed someone to grow them for their wild bird mix," Holt recalls. "It's not a great crop to grow in South Georgia because it's too humid, so it didn't last long."

The fields of colorful flowers attracted so much attention that Holt opened the farm as a sunflower farm: During June and July, when the sunflowers are in full bloom, Holt welcomes photographers to the farm to shoot pictures and charges visitors to cut sunflowers.

The Sunflower Farm Festival, which started in 2002, has grown to be one of the most popular festivals in middle Georgia. The fifteen acres of sunflowers are the centerpiece of the annual festival, which also features live music, heritage crafts, wagon rides through the sunflower fields, a

Acres of sunflowers are in full bloom during the annual Sunflower Farm Festival.

petting zoo, and milking demonstrations, as well as a tractor parade that winds through the rural streets. Tours of the 1811 McCowan-McRee House, an 1891 sharecropper's cabin on the farm, and the Holts' heritage gardens honor the history of the farm, which has been in the family for almost a century. "It's more than just a field of sunflowers; we also have art, music, and a lot of activities," Holt says.

1430 Durden Road, Rutledge (Morgan County), 706-557-2870, www.sunflowerfarmfestival.com

## Field of Greens

Field of Greens should be called "The Festival Sure to Get You Lost" for its lack of signage and an address that challenges even the most up-to-date GPS. Keep asking for directions, though, because the hunt for Whippoor-will Hollow Farm, the certified organic farm where the festival is held in October, is worth it.

The festival features a small farmers' market, where vendors sell items ranging from garden supplies and mushroom-growing kits to soap and cupcakes, and educational exhibits with information about raising hens and goats, all while live music plays in the background. The heart of the festival is the tasting tent. At least thirty of the best farm-to-table chefs create bite-sized portions of delectable fresh, local foods. In the past, chefs from Bantam + Biddy, Farm Burger, Ecco, Cakes & Ale, and Woodfire Grill have participated. My advice: Go early, go hungry.

3905 Highway 138, Covington (Newton County), www.fieldofgreensfestival.com

### Strawberry Festival

It's hard not to feel inspired to pick a pint of strawberries and start experimenting in the kitchen after checking out the creative entries in the strawberry cook-off. The competition for Best in Show is a new addition to the annual event, held in April at Washington Farms. Ogling the tarts, pies, and shortcake works up a craving for something sweet, but it's nothing a double scoop of homemade strawberry ice cream can't satisfy. While the festival was inspired by the strawberry season, there is a lot more to do than pick and eat the plump red berries. Take a hayride through the fields, ride the cow train, race around the tricycle track, zip down the tunnel slide, bounce on the jumping pillow, and feed the animals in the petting farm. And then order another scoop of strawberry ice cream.

5691 Hog Mountain Road, Bogart (Oconee County), 706-769-0627, www.washingtonfarms.net

### Southern Heritage Festival

Locals call the Southern Heritage Festival "Mule Days" because the beasts of burden are the highlight of the event, which takes place the second Saturday of October at Callaway Plantation. Mules are used to demonstrate traditional plowing techniques and to grind cane into syrup just as it would have been done when the Callaway family ran the farm in the 1800s. The mules might be the biggest draw at the annual event, but the Southern Heritage Festival is about more than mules. There are also spinning, weaving, and blacksmithing demonstrations; tours of the historic homes, which date back to 1790 and 1869; and visits to the gardens, overflowing with apples, muscadine grapes, black walnuts, and figs; and corn and cotton patches.

The city acquired fifty-six acres of the former cotton farm in the 1960s and turned it into a living history museum that is open to the public year-round. Mule Days is the flagship event at the plantation, attracting upwards of 4,000 visitors.

2160 Lexington Rd, Washington (Wilkes County), 706-678-7060, washingtongeorgia.net/callaway

# SPECIALTY SHOPS

## Daily Groceries Co-op

When Angie Grass learned that her employer, Daily Groceries, planned to close its doors, she came up with a plan to save the small supermarket—and her job. Without enough cash to purchase the store on her own, she decided to see if the co-op model would work. Her plan: If people agreed to buy a share of the market for $60, she could buy the store. The plan worked, and the Daily Groceries Co-op opened in 1992. After twenty years in business, it's still the only co-op in Athens. The shelves are stocked with locally grown and produced goods, including lots of vegan fare.

523 Prince Avenue, Athens (Clarke County), 706-548-1732, www.dailygroceries.org

## Lucky Lady Pecans

Georgia is the top pecan-producing state in the nation with 144,000 acres of orchards that produce up to eighty-eight million pounds of pecans annually. In Columbia County, Lucky Lady Pecans sells the popular nuts in a variety of forms, including shelled, roasted, candied, and mesquite-barbecue-flavored, and, of course, in pecan pies.

The idea for a store came about after the staff at Tracy Luckey, a plant that has shelled and processed pecans for retailers, wholesalers, and confectioners since the late 1800s, started receiving an increasing number of emails and phone calls from consumers who wanted to purchase pecans. The shop in downtown Harlem features products once available only through mail order, including the sweet and salty pecans that were chosen as finalists in the Flavor of Georgia competition hosted by the University of Georgia.

220 North Louisville Street, Harlem (Columbia County), 706-556-6216, www.luckyladypecans.com

## Nearly Native Nursery

In the 1990s, Gwinnett County was one of the fastest-growing counties in the nation. Jim and Debi Rodgers noticed fields and forests filled with native plants being ripped up to make room for subdivisions and office buildings. Their frustration with urban sprawl led them to seek refuge in rural Georgia and, inspired by the loss of habitat in the cities, prompted Jim to leave a career in the printing business to go back to school to study botany. With a newfound passion for preserving the environment, the couple opened

Nearly Native Nursery in 1996. Their focus on native plants, including edibles, has made them a favored destination for eco-conscious gardeners.

"There has been a lot more interest in attracting [wildlife] to the garden," Debi says. "A lot of our customers want plants that will draw butterflies and bees or produce berries for the birds. And, a lot of native plants are edible and growing edibles is really popular." According to Jim, American persimmon, American hazelnut, and pawpaw trees, serviceberries, and black cap raspberries are among the most popular native edibles sold at the nursery. In addition to a robust selection of plants, the nursery also showcases native plants in several demonstration gardens. "The gardens are a place for customers to see what different native plant species will do once they are established in their gardens," Debi says. "We want to show our customers that it is possible to have a diverse landscape that is beautiful and low maintenance."

776 McBride Road, Fayetteville (Fayette County), 770-460-6284, www.nearlynativenursery.com

### The Madison Produce Company

*Budget Travel* magazine voted Madison one of the most picturesque villages in the world, and its historic square is part of the charm. The commitment to preserving and supporting the local community led Andy and Gary Oller to open a produce market on the square with displays of fresh fruits and vegetables that are as pretty as the town itself. "Around here, people like shopping at a market that is locally owned," says Gary. "They tell us that the local grocers don't do it like we do it, and that's because we have a lot of products from around here, not stuff that is shipped 1,000 miles."

Their motto, "A little store, a lot of fresh," describes their mission of providing a boutique produce-shopping experience similar to what you'd expect at European markets. Most of the produce stocked at the Madison Produce Company, which opened in 2010, comes from local producers like Hillside Orchard Farm, Nora Mill Granary, Stone Mountain Pecan Company, Southern Swiss Dairy, and Fickle Pickles, but there is a lot of imported produce, too. "We get local stuff when it's available, but sometimes we have to bring [produce] in from other places to keep it on the shelves," Gary explains. "Mostly, we focus on quality rather than quantity even if it means smaller amounts of local products."

132 East Washington Street, Madison (Morgan County), 706-342-1908

## Waste Not, Want Not

The farmers' market is filled with temptations: the sweet aroma of fresh peaches, carrots just pulled from the soil, cartons of eggs in gorgeous shades of blue and brown. But think twice before filling a canvas bag with farm-fresh foods: In the United States, 160 billion pounds of food are tossed into the landfill every year, according to the U.S. Department of Agriculture. Of course, choosing frozen fruits and vegetables or processed foods with an endless shelf life is not the answer. But making a list—even for shopping at the farmers' market—planning meals, and purchasing only as much produce as you can eat can all help cut down on food waste, according to Jonathan Bloom, author of *American Wasteland: How America Throws Away Nearly Half of Its Food*.

Bloom notes that the average American family spends upwards of $2,200 annually on food that ends up being tossed in the trash. It's more than just an expensive problem: Food waste also wreaks havoc on the environment. Up to 97 percent of the food wasted every year, approximately thirty-four million tons, ends up in landfills or incinerators, where it generates methane gas and contributes to climate change.

Reducing food waste is as simple as shopping for smaller amounts more frequently—a good excuse to stop by the farmers' markets on Saturday morning and one evening during the week—and using about-to-spoil food in baked goods or preserving the harvest in jams, jellies, and spreads.

## Noring Farms on Floyd

Christina and Andrew Norman started out growing vegetables in their Atlanta backyard and selling them at local farmers' markets. As the popularity of local produce grew, so did their garden plot. The couple expanded their garden several times before purchasing ten acres of farmland in Covington. Sixty-five different varieties of heirloom tomatoes grow on the farm alongside vegetables like purple asparagus, okra, greens, peppers, and corn.

Christina, a former mortgage broker, and Andrew, a wine rep, started selling their heirloom produce to restaurants in Atlanta and looked for opportunities to sell to their community, too. "You had to go to farmers' markets in Atlanta to get the heirloom varieties we're growing," Christina says. "There was no place in Newton County to buy all of the great produce that is grown here." Instead of joining the local farmers who schlepped boxes of produce to farmers' markets in Atlanta on Saturday mornings, Christina and Andrew decided to retrofit a former Thrift Oil station, transforming it into a produce market. "I call it a mini Whole Foods," says Christina. The market also serves as a co-op for other local producers. Products from Johnston Family Farm, Burge Organic Farm, Verner Farms, Snapola Farms, and Tewksbury Farms are sold alongside the produce and free-range eggs that Christina and Andrew raise on Noring Farms.

5177 Floyd Street, Covington (Newton County), 678-712-6577


## Piccadilly Farm

Sam Jones, a retired botany professor at the University of Georgia, and his late wife, Carleen, started Piccadilly Farm in 1982. The nursery is known for its impressive selection of native plants, perennials, and rare shrubs and trees, earning accolades as one of the Best of Atlanta by *Atlanta Magazine*. An expansive display garden shows customers how plants will perform and serves as an inspiration for home gardens.

A passion for plants runs in the family. Valerie Hinesley, a registered landscape architect, joined the business her parents founded three decades ago to provide design services to customers.

1971 Whippoorwill Road, Bishop (Oconee County), 706-769-6516

## FARM-TO-TABLE RESTAURANTS

### Five & Ten

When executive chef Dean Neff determines the daily menu, he looks first to local farmers. While the menu changes with the seasons, the Frogmore stew with Gulf shrimp, fingerling potatoes, andouille, corn, and tomato and leek broth is a staple. To truly appreciate the seasonal fare, make a reservation for the prix fixe menu. The three-course meal changes every night to reflect the availability of the freshest local meat and produce from farms like Grass Roots Farm and Sweet Grass Dairy.

Neff uses seasonal ingredients not only to support local farmers but also because they result in more flavorful dishes. "The products are so amazing when sourced locally and seasonally, it makes our job easy," says Neff. He cites tomatoes from Woodland Gardens Farm, their most consistent vendor, as an example. "They're so perfect, we just have to slice and season them" to receive raves. And the restaurant, started in 2000 by James Beard Award–winning chef Hugh Acheson as a fresh take on southern cooking, is no stranger to raves, having snagged dozens, including Restaurant of the Year by the *Atlanta Journal Constitution*.

1073 South Milledge Avenue, Athens (Clarke County), 706-546-7300, www.fiveandten.com. $$$

### Heirloom Cafe and Fresh Market

Growing up, Jessica Rothacker helped her mom pick vegetables from their backyard garden to serve for dinner. Memories of those seasonal meals served up the inspiration for Heirloom Cafe. Heirloom serves breakfast, lunch, and dinner in a small café that once operated as a gas station. The gas pumps have been replaced with colorful umbrellas and overflowing flowerpots; inside, wooden tables topped with floral tablecloths and light fixtures made from mason jars fill the former service bays. Packets of heirloom seeds act as table markers to help servers deliver meals to the correct tables. To emphasize the breadth of locally sourced ingredients, a chalkboard highlights the growers whose produce is featured on the menu. Greendale Farm, Dragonfly Farm, AtlantaFresh Creamery, Three Pigs Farm, and Sundance Farm are just a few of the producers Rothacker works with.

815 North Chase Street, Athens (Clarke County), 706-354-7901, www.heirloomathens.com. $$

## Product of the Peach State

Agriculture commissioner Gary W. Black wants to tell the world that Georgia produces some of the best agricultural products in the nation. Instead of shouting from the rooftops, he spearheaded the Georgia Grown program. The marketing and economic development program is operated by the Georgia Department of Agriculture and promotes locally grown and raised products. Since its launch in 2012, the program has attracted 300 members from across the state who use the "Georgia Grown" label on products ranging from jams and grits to alpaca fiber and watermelons. The strict standards restrict who can use the label, providing consumers assurance that they are getting true local products

## Shotgun Dinners

Shotgun Dinners started out when a group of friends—Damien Schaefer, Randolph Dudley, Patrick Stubbers, Eddie Russell, Matt Palmerlee, and Nancy Lind—started getting together for Saturday suppers. Several members have culinary backgrounds: Patrick is the sous-chef at The National restaurant; Eddie is a butcher at Earth Fare; and Matt is the head chef at Farm 255. Over seasonal dishes made with ingredients from local farms, the group swapped stories and drank wine for hours. During one of their Saturday suppers, they made the decision to grow the gatherings outside of their Athens kitchens.

In 2008, they launched a supper series called the Four Coursemen, inviting friends (and friends of friends) who shared their passion for sustainable agriculture and local foods to join them for dinner at a shotgun house in Athens. The suppers were an instant hit. The five-course dinners are held twice a month. A week before an event, an email goes out to the mailing list with instructions about how to RSVP. There are just twenty-eight seats at the table, and the spots fill fast. The menu is kept a secret until diners sit down to supper, in part because the dishes aren't decided on until the morning of the event, when the organizers go to the farmers' market to shop for ingredients.

Clarke County, www.shotgundinners.com. $$$

## The National

Athens is a college town with more than its fair share of casual eateries. The National is different. Modeled after the sidewalk cafés in Europe, the restaurant serves up Mediterranean-inspired meals like stuffed Medjool dates with Manchego cheese and smoked paprika; beet salad with chickpeas, escarole, and goat cheese dressing; and chicken roulade with roasted red potatoes and green bean salad. An ethnic menu prepared using straight-from-the-farm ingredients helped chef Peter Dale earn accolades, like the People's Choice award for best new chef in the Southeast from *Food + Wine* magazine. The prices are lower than other farm-to-table restaurants in town, helping The National draw an eclectic crowd. During special events like the Autumn Harvest Dinner, Dale partners with local chefs to make a prix fixe, family-style meal using ingredients from the Athens Farmers Market.

232 West Hancock Avenue, Athens (Clarke County), 706-549-3450, www.thenationalrestaurant.com. $$

## The Caboose

In 1995, Ed Hogan bought a boxcar with plans to turn it into an ice cream shop. The boxcar, built in 1910 and used to transport munitions during World War II, became a popular spot in historic Rutledge, and it didn't take long for Hogan and his wife, Molly Lesnikowski, to expand the menu at The Caboose to include casual fare like burgers, sandwiches, and milkshakes.

Operating a restaurant out of an upcycled boxcar was just the start of their sustainable efforts. The couple sought out local farms to supply ingredients for their menu, using grass-fed beef from Verner Farms for burgers, chili, and meatloaf subs; fruits and vegetables from producers like Crystal Organic Farm; and milk for their milkshakes from Johnston Dairy. Lesnikowski even uses local produce to make her popular fried pies. "We have always bought fruits and vegetables from local producers," she says. "Anytime I can choose a local product, I will. It's a philosophy that works for us."

102 West Main Street, Rutledge (Morgan County), 706-557-9021. $

## Blue Willow Inn

Judging by the lineup of guests who are dressed in their Sunday best and waiting for a table at the Blue Willow Inn, it seems fitting that the historic-home-turned-restaurant sits in the heart of Social Circle. It helps that Billie Van Dyke, who opened the Blue Willow Inn with her late husband, Louis, in 1991, makes the rounds in the dining rooms to ensure her guests are enjoying their meals. Van Dyke stops to talk to regulars and accepts compliments on her southern cooking from diners, many of whom made the trek to Social Circle after reading rave reviews of the restaurant in the likes of *Southern Living*, *Gourmet*, and *USA Today*.

The accolades are due to a buffet overflowing with traditional southern foods like chicken livers, fried chicken, collard greens, green beans, mac and cheese, cheese grits, and the fried green tomatoes that guests beg for. It's food that inspired Van Dyke to pen several cookbooks, including *The Blue Willow Inn Bible of Southern Cooking*. In the summers, the Blue Willow Inn goes through upwards of fifty pounds of green tomatoes per day, all purchased from local farmers. "We're cooking southern food, so we use southern ingredients whenever we can get 'em," says Van Dyke. "It takes a lot of farmers to keep up with the volume we do here, especially the fried green tomatoes."

294 North Cherokee Road, Social Circle (Walton County), 770-464-2131, www.bluewillowinn.com. $$

## LODGING

### The Farmhouse Inn at 100 Acre Farm

Crystal Johnson traded the concrete jungle of Hong Kong for the pastoral landscapes of Madison, leaving her job as a retail buyer to act as the innkeeper for The Farmhouse at 100 Acre Farm. Her husband, Ellis, bought the farm two decades ago as a nod to his childhood. "His grandfather had a 100-acre farm and [Ellis] always dreamed of having his own 100 acres," she explains. Instead of rushing between buying appointments, Johnson has adopted a slower pace, gathering eggs while Sugar, the resident turkey, follows her into the historic barn and working in the garden, a gorgeous space

At the Farmhouse Inn at 100 Acre Farm, innkeeper Crystal Johnson collects fresh eggs for gourmet breakfasts for guests.

filled with grapes, tomatoes, eggplants, cucumbers, squash, and herbs. Johnson had no gardening experience when she moved to the farm ten years ago, but she has developed a green thumb and a love of growing her own food. In the mornings, Johnson fixes a gourmet breakfast using fresh produce and eggs she collected just hours before. All of the excess produce that isn't used in the inn's kitchen is donated to the local food bank.

Each of the ten rooms has its own theme—the River Cottage is a favorite. Guests are welcome to lounge in front of the fireplace in the common room, fish in the pond, nuzzle the goats, get acquainted with the chickens and Sugar, who Johnson calls "a very friendly turkey," or walk the trails. "It's such a peaceful place," she says.

1051 Meadow Lane, Madison (Morgan County), 706-342-7933, www.thefarmhouseinn.com. $$

## RECIPES

### Macaroni and Three Cheeses

*Mac and cheese is the ultimate southern comfort food, and cheesemakers Karen and Jeff Green have perfected the recipe using cheeses they produce at Udderly Cool Dairy.*

SERVES 6

| | |
|---|---|
| 1 | pound macaroni |
| 5 | tablespoons unsalted butter |
| ¼ | cup all-purpose flour |
| 2 | cups milk |
| 1½ | cups Udderly Cool Creamery grated Gouda |
| 1 | cup grated Udderly Cool Creamery Jack-style cheese or Monterey Jack cheese |
| 1 | teaspoon sea salt |
| ½ | teaspoon freshly ground black pepper |
| 3 | medium farm-fresh tomatoes or 4 Roma tomatoes |
| ¼ | cup dry breadcrumbs |
| 2 | tablespoons grated Udderly Cool Creamery Southern Alpine–style cheese or Parmesan cheese |

Preheat the oven to 375 degrees. Bring a large pot of salted water to a boil. Add the macaroni and cook according to package instructions. Drain well.

In a large saucepan, melt 4 tablespoons of the butter over medium-high heat. Add the flour and cook for about 2 minutes, stirring with a whisk. While whisking, add the milk and cook until thickened. Remove from the heat and stir in the Gouda and Jack cheeses, salt, and pepper. Stir in the pasta.

Pour the macaroni into a 3-quart baking dish. Arrange the sliced tomatoes on top of the macaroni.

In a medium saucepan (or bowl using the microwave), melt the remaining butter and add the breadcrumbs and Southern Alpine or Parmesan cheese. Sprinkle the breadcrumb mixture over the tomatoes. Bake for 30 minutes or until bubbling and golden brown. Serve immediately.

## One Cup Peach Cobbler

*Peach cobbler is the quintessential dessert during peach season in Georgia. At Dickey Farms, thirty varieties of peaches pass through the historic packing shed every season, and Cynde Dickey always sets aside a few bushels to make peach cobbler. Her recipe is a simple twist on an iconic dessert.*

SERVES 8 TO 10

| | |
|---|---|
| 3 | cups peeled and sliced Dickey peaches (3–4 medium peaches) |
| 1 ½ | cups sugar |
| 1 | stick unsalted butter |
| 1 | cup self-rising flour |
| ¼ | teaspoon salt |
| 1 | cup milk |
| 1 | teaspoon vanilla or almond flavoring |

Sprinkle the peaches with ½ cup of the sugar. Toss and set aside.

Melt the butter in a 9×13-inch casserole dish in the oven while it is heating to 350 degrees.

In a medium bowl, combine the remaining sugar, the flour, and the salt. Add the milk and flavoring and stir to combine. Pour the mixture evenly over the melted butter. Spread the peaches evenly over top of the batter.

Bake for 45 minutes or until the batter rises through the fruit and the top is golden brown.

Serve the cobbler warm, topped with vanilla ice cream.

Dade

Catoosa

Whitfield

• Ringgold

Murray

Walker

Chattooga

Gordon

Floyd

Rome•

Bartow

Cartersville
•

Polk

Paulding

Haralson

# Appalachian Region

The Appalachian Region, a small section of the northwest corner of the state, gets its name from the mountain range that runs through it. The high altitude and rugged terrain of the mountainous region provide more than great views: The Appalachian Region has some wonderful agricultural assets from family farms and dairies to U-picks and alpaca ranches, proving that when it comes to agritourism, the smallest region in the state has a lot to offer.

## FARMS

### Pettit Creek Farms

Twenty years ago, Scott Allen volunteered his farm when his son's teacher needed a place to take a kindergarten class on a field trip. During the visit, one of the boys in the class expressed disgust when Allen explained that eggs came from chickens. "We are so far removed from the source of our food," he says. "We realized that we had an opportunity to educate kids on the farm."

Fall is the busiest time on the farm, thanks to a corn maze and pumpkin patch. The farm is home to all of the traditional petting zoo animals, including goats, sheep, chickens, and donkeys, but Allen and his wife, June, also raise exotic breeds like camels, zebras, and wallabies. The rare animals grazing in the pasture fascinate visitors, but the real draw, according to June, is the atmosphere. "People love the fact that this is a working family farm," she says. "They think it's a fantasy life."

341 Cassville Road, Cartersville (Bartow County), 770-386-8688, www.pettitcreekfarms.com

Peanut pumpkins (pumpkins with peanuts attached to their skins) attract a lot of attention.

### Pumpkin Patch Farm

The collection of pumpkins, Indian corn, gourds, and cornstalks surrounding the red barn at Pumpkin Patch Farm looks like a scene from a Hallmark Channel movie. Add families wearing Fair Isle sweaters and rosy-cheeked children in rubber boots, and all that's missing is a director calling, "Quiet on the set!" But there is nothing quiet about fall weekends at the farm. Larry and Elaine Erwin want to hear squeals of delight as children rush to pick out pumpkins, get up close with the animals in the barnyard, gallop on stick horses in the corral, navigate the hay maze, and ride pedal tractors pretending to be farmers.

It wouldn't be a pumpkin patch without the pumpkins. The Erwins grow most of the pumpkins, which range from minis to some that weigh as much as the kids who try to carry them.

230 Old Dixie Highway NW, Adairsville (Bartow County), 770-773-2617, www.pumpkinpatchfarm.net

## B&B Family Farm

When Russ Bates transitioned from a career in computer engineering to life on a sustainable farm, deciding which breeds of cattle, pigs, and chickens to raise was simple: he consulted with the American Livestock Breeds Conservancy to see which breeds were endangered or threatened. As a result, the farm he operates with his wife, Elizabeth, a former union rep for the United Auto Workers, and his brother, Scott, has Pineywoods cattle, Dominique chickens, and large black pigs grazing in the pastures. "I wanted to focus on cattle, hogs, and chickens because, in my opinion, those are the animals that are most abused in conventional farming," Bates says.

Bates became passionate about sustainable agriculture after reading Michael Pollan's *The Omnivore's Dilemma*. He took classes, read dozens of books about raising livestock, and relocated from Michigan to Georgia to work the land. Instead of sitting at a desk reviewing computer code, he rides a four-wheeler through the pastures to check fences and feed acorns to the hogs and sweet corn to the cows; he provides meat to restaurants in Cave Spring and Atlanta and to consumers through on-farm sales. The farm also offers tours by appointment. "We love sharing our farm with people who are passionate about sustainable agriculture and want to know more about the source of their food," he says. "If you really want to understand what you are eating, you have to see where it comes from."

650 Padlock Mountain Road SW, Cave Spring (Floyd County), 248-841-7224, bandbfamilyfarm.com

## Lowrey Farms

"Ten years ago we started growing some sweet corn to sell from a wagon on the side of the road, and things evolved from there," explains Ivy Lowrey. It wasn't long before a wagonload of corn wasn't enough to meet the demands of customers who were eager to buy produce from the farm. Instead of just raising cattle and grain, third-generation farmer John Lowrey added a fifteen-acre plot to produce okra, tomatoes, squash, zucchini, peppers, and other vegetables to sell at a roadside stand that his wife, Ivy, manages. "We take a lot of pride in what we do and work really hard to provide a quality crop to the community," she says. "Everything we sell is picked fresh every day." Lowrey Farms also sells all natural Angus beef and whole hog sausage, bratwurst, and bacon as well as jams and preserves. It's open from May to December.

2416 Turkey Mountain Road, Rome (Floyd County), 706-295-1157, www.lowreyfarms.com

## The Fight for Fair Food

Fair trade certification ensures that the farmers in other countries receive a fair price for their products and guarantees workers a living wage and safe working conditions. But what about the farmers in Georgia who are growing lettuce, harvesting peaches, or producing corn? Currently, there are no domestic programs offering the same protections to U.S. farmers.

Food Justice Certification is working to change that. Introduced by the Agricultural Justice Project, a coalition of four nongovernmental organizations, the new certification is part of the domestic fair trade movement to guarantee that domestic farmers and food processors meet a rigorous set of standards for best practices. "We wanted to find a way to put fairness back into organic and sustainable practices," explains Elizabeth Henderson of the Agricultural Justice Project. "In twenty years, we hope Food Justice Certification will be as prevalent as organic [certification] is now."

To date, seventy farms in Canada and eight in the United States have earned the certification. While Henderson expects it'll be 2014 before Food Justice Certification labels will start showing up on food packaging, consumers can get involved now. Here's how:

*Learn about the label*: Achieving Food Justice Certification requires adherence to a rigorous set of standards, including fair wages and benefits for workers, fair pricing for farmers, and the elimination of toxic chemicals. Understanding what the label stands for—and spreading the word about its importance—will help the certification gain traction.

*Encourage producers to get involved*: Asking "Have you heard about Food Justice Certification? Do you plan to apply?" lets farmers and ranchers know that consumers value the label and want to support certified producers.

## Wright Family Farms

Todd and Carolyn Wright believe in raising cattle and sheep in open pastures where the herds have room to roam and lots of fresh grass for grazing. In addition to benefiting the environment and the animals, practicing sustainable agriculture helps the couple produce a superior product. Cuts of "Rome Grown" grass-fed beef and lamb are sold at the farm.

420 Scoggins Road, Rome (Floyd County), 706-766-1445, www.southerncomforteventing.com/wrightfamilyfarms.html

## Little River Farms

Marisa Poarch spent three decades cutting and coloring hair in Gordon County. While Poarch loved her career, she dreamed of living on a farm. Her dream came true in 2004 when she retired from hairdressing and started raising goats, llamas, horses, pheasants, turkeys, peacocks, and a passel of other animals. "I love sitting on the front porch, I can see the whole farm and hear all of the animals," she says.

Poarch wanted to share her love of agriculture and decided to turn the farm into an agritourism destination. The farm is open to visitors in the spring and fall. During visits, guests spend hours getting lost in the corn maze, bumping across the pastures on a hayride, riding horses on the nature trails, and feeding and nuzzling the animals.

669 Nickelsville Road, Resaca (Gordon County), 706-280-7393, www.littleriverfarms.com

## Steadman Farms

Farming has changed a lot since Charles Williams started his dairy farm in the 1960s. To teach a new generation that farming wasn't always about high-tech milking equipment and tractors with GPS systems, he started hosting an annual fall festival on the farm in 2010. During weekends in October, visitors explore a gristmill and blacksmith shop and check out antique harrows, plows, cultivators, and tractors. "People love to make pictures of their kids on the antique tractors," he says. On a hayride, Williams stops the wagon in the pasture and lets visitors feed mules from buckets of corn. The experience, he says, is one of the most popular on the farm.

The fall festival features modern agritourism activities, too, including a corn maze, pumpkin patch, hayrides, and a petting farm. On chilly evenings, Williams lights a bonfire for an old-fashioned marshmallow roast.

### Help Wanted

During harvest season, ripe cucumbers are dying on the vine and unpicked peaches are dropping from the branches and rotting on the ground. A study by the Georgia Department of Agriculture estimated that Georgia farmers had suffered upwards of $10 million in crop losses in 2011. The problem: A controversial new immigration law, House Bill 87, which passed in the Georgia legislature in 2011, cracking down on undocumented immigrants. The Georgia Agribusiness Council opposed to the bill, arguing that it could reduce the labor force up to 30 percent and cost state farmers between $300 million and $1 billion.

Farmers often find guest worker programs, which allow them to hire seasonal workers to harvest crops, ineffective because of the extensive paperwork involved. Moreover, critics of guest worker programs argue that it's harder to fill positions through such formal channels, especially among Latino workers who tend to rely on word of mouth to find work in the fields.

To address labor shortages, Republican governor Nathan Deal introduced a state-run program to replace migrant workers with probationers in search of work. The program took effect in late 2011 with mixed results.

After a long break from farming (he closed the dairy in 2005) he looks forward to seeing the farm come alive in the fall.

3283 Steadman Road, Tallapoosa (Haralson County), 770-574-2611, www.steadmanfarms.com

### Wake Robin Alpacas

Turk likes to give kisses. The frisky alpaca saunters right up to Karen Cross and plants one on her cheek. "We wanted [our alpacas] to be well-socialized, and I think we've succeeded," jokes Bruce Cross. Bruce and Karen spend a lot of time in the pasture, stroking and nuzzling the alpacas, help-

The alpacas at Wake Robin Alpacas are eager to pose for photos and give visitors kisses.

ing their prized herd win the hearts of visitors. Owning alpacas has been a dream for the couple, both pharmacists, ever since Karen saw a late-night infomercial about the animals in the 1990s. "She woke me up and said, 'Can we get alpacas?'" Bruce recalls. "I reminded her that we lived on a quarter-acre lot in a subdivision, so it was not a good idea."

A decade later, the couple moved to rural Georgia and purchased enough land for four alpacas. Since then, their herd has grown to fifteen alpacas, whose fiber is shorn and turned into roving and wool sold in the farm store. As a nod to their careers in medicine, all of the alpacas born on the farm are named after medicinal herbs and flowers such as Trillium, Solomon's Seal, Evening Primrose, and Star Anise, and all of the animals are as sweet as their names. To honor their herd, Karen fills the garden with the flowers for which the alpacas are named.

During farm tours, the couple introduces visitors to alpacas in three pastures, offering plenty of opportunities to interact with the animals and learn about the farm. "This is our passion, and we love sharing it with others," says Karen.

1968 Old Bush Mill Road, Bremen (Haralson County), 770-537-4210, www.wakerobinalpacas.com

## Carlton Farms

Although the Carlton family has operated a dairy farm in Polk County since 1946, making a living from milk grew increasingly difficult. A decade ago, Bobby Carlton and his sons, Chad and Brad, halted commercial milk production and focused on diversifying the farm. To a small herd of Jersey cows, the family added pigs and chickens and constructed a farm store to sell raw milk, eggs, pork, and grass-fed beef; they also partnered with local vegetable growers to start a CSA. "We try to help out other local farmers by carrying their produce in the store, too," Brad says.

All sales in the farm store are on the honor system: Customers pick up what they need, add up their purchases, and slide cash or a check into a box on the counter. It's the old-fashioned way of doing business that Brad believes still makes sense in Polk County.

A desire to educate the community about the importance of family farms inspired the addition of agritourism activities in 2001. "We did it to save the farm, and it's become a tradition for a lot of families," says Brad. In October, the farm operates a corn maze, a pumpkin patch, and an animal barn where visitors can bottle-feed calves and pet goats, sheep, donkeys, ponies, pigs, and chickens. During the hayrides, the tractor stops in the middle of the pasture so riders can feed hay to the cattle.

1276 Rockmart Highway, Rockmart (Polk County), 770-684-3789, www.carltonfarm.com

## Paradise Arabians

Paradise Arabians is one of the largest breeders of Egyptian Arabian horses in the world. Nestled in the mountains of North Georgia, the pastures are home to upwards of 150 champion horses, including adorable, silken foals that are eager to munch on apples while their ears are scratched.

Owners Gary and Wanda Kenworthy love showing off their horses. In addition to welcoming visitors who want to spend an hour nuzzling the mares, the couple turned their home into a bed and breakfast; three guestrooms are available to overnight guests who want to spend more time helping with feeding and grooming the horses or just watching them grazing in the pastures.

721 Gowin Road, LaFayette (Walker County), 706-397-9950, www.paradisearabians.com

### Freeman Springs Farm

Freeman Springs Farm dates back to 1836, when Benjamin Freeman left North Carolina to take advantage of available land in Georgia. Although fourth-generation farmer William Freeman Collins uses tractors instead of mules to plow the fields, the tradition of the farm remains the same: The land is dedicated to agriculture, ranging from cotton crops and horse breeding to chicken houses and beef cattle.

In the fall, Black Angus and Simmental cattle share the farm with visitors who come to experience the corn maze, pumpkin patch, hayrides, and petting zoo. The farm also hosts an Antique Tractor Show and Miss Fall Harvest pageant. A country store in the old dairy barn is stocked with jams, jellies, and handmade soaps.

3895 Freeman Springs Road, Rocky Face (Whitfield County), 706-270-2402, www.freemanspringsfarm.com

## FARMERS' MARKETS

### Bartow County Farmers Market

On Wednesday and Saturday mornings, under the shade of a towering oak tree, farmers and backyard gardeners flip down their tailgates and sell excess produce from the back of their trucks. With a mission to "help Bartow County grow," the market started in the 1980s and draws up to thirty vendors. Most of the produce is grown in Bartow County, but some of the vendors come from elsewhere in the region, including Tennessee.

10 North Public Square, Cartersville (Bartow County), 770-607-3480

## Access for All

For some shoppers, the organic tomatoes, just-picked peppers, and ripe melons at the farmers' market are too expensive to add to the weekly grocery list. Wholesome Wave Georgia (wholesomewavegeorgia.org) wants to change that. The nonprofit organization works tirelessly to make it easier for Georgia residents to access fresh, local foods.

Wholesome Wave Georgia doubles each dollar spent at farmers' markets for those who receive federal or state nutrition benefits through programs like the Supplemental Nutrition Assistance Program (SNAP) or Women, Infants and Children (WIC). In short, $1 in nutrition benefits equals $2 for shoppers, allowing them to stock up on fresh, local produce at producer-only markets that would otherwise be unaffordable.

When the program launched in 2009, three Georgia farmers' markets participated. In 2011, Wholesome Wave Georgia partnered with fifteen markets across the state, doubling the purchasing power of 3,500 individual card swipes, increasing sales from $61,500 to $123,000. The organization operates through grants, private donations, and the support of local partners.

## Berry College Farmers Market

Twice a year, a farmers' market on the campus of Berry College features agricultural products created by students. Students set up tents at the spring and fall markets to sell beef, cheese, fruits, vegetables, and herbs grown and raised on the 26,000-acre campus. "It started out as a showcase for some of the Student Enterprise projects and grew from there," says Mary Chambers, a junior who majors in marketing at Berry College and directs the Student Enterprise programs. In addition to Berry College students, the farmers' market is open to farmers from throughout Floyd County, drawing upwards of sixty vendors to the biannual event, turning the campus into a cornucopia of seasonal delights.

2277 Martha Berry Highway NW, Mount Berry (Floyd County), 706-232-5374, www.berry.edu

# FARM STANDS AND U-PICKS

## Browns Produce

David Brown grew tired of loading his truck with produce and hauling it 100 miles to set up a stall at the Atlanta Farmers Market. "We had people stopping by all the time wanting to buy stuff," he recalls. The long commute combined with the increased demand for locally grown produce led Brown to build a produce market, allowing people to shop on the farm for the first time since his family started working the land in the 1970s.

The farm stand is open from April to November. There is some imported produce at the roadside stand—bananas from Guatemala and onions from Peru—but most of the fruits and vegetables displayed on folding plastic tables are grown on the seventy-nine-acre farm behind the shop.

158 Georgia Highway 41, Ringgold (Catoosa County), 423-364-8719

## Payne Farm

Operating a roadside produce stand was never part of the plan for third-generation farmer Sam Payne. But Highway 41 bisected his farmland, making it difficult to operate the equipment he needed to grow row crops and raise beef cattle. At the same time, the garden he grew with his wife, Ann, started producing more vegetables than the couple could eat. Payne set up a booth at the Calhoun Farmers Market to sell excess produce. "We got tired of hauling everything to the market and started selling produce from the farm," he says. He built a farm stand in 2006 and developed it into a popular local stop, helping Payne Farm transition thirty acres of pastures and row crops into a veggie patch.

In addition to the produce stand, the farm is open for U-pick strawberries from April to June. At the end of strawberry season, Payne Farm hosts a Strawberry Festival. In the fall, fifty varieties of pumpkins are sold on the farm. But the veggies—tomatoes, squash, beans, cucumbers, eggplant, peas, and corn—are a staple of the farm.

Payne strikes a balance between full service and U-pick, keeping the farm stand stocked and letting customers who want a true farm experience pick their own vegetables.

336 Salem Road, Calhoun (Gordon County), 770-480-7004,
www.paynefarm.net

## Willoughby Farms

In the summer, for several mornings a week, Allen and Donna Willoughby invite the public to try their hand at harvesting. The crops: blueberries and blackberries. Several varieties of the Certified Naturally Grown berries are grown on the farm, and pickers aren't shy about testing the berries before filling their buckets.

2342 Corinth Poseyville Road, Bremen (Haralson County), 770-646-9080,
www.willoughbysberries.com

## The Blueberry Farm

The instructions for picking blueberries, blackberries, and muscadines are posted on a whiteboard in a small gazebo on the side of the road: look at the map for directions to the fields that are ripe for picking, grab a one-gallon bucket, fill the bucket with fresh berries or grapes, refer to the pricing guide on the whiteboard, and put the money into a wooden box attached to a fencepost to pay for the fruit. There are just two rules: do not take the buckets or steal from the cash box.

The farm operates seasonally, offering blackberries in June and July, blueberries in July and August, and muscadines in September and October. Although it's a self-serve farm, hours are limited to from dawn to dusk. It's a simple setup with a delicious payoff.

1363 Highway 151, LaFayette (Walker County), 706-638-0908,
www.theblueberryfarm.com

## An Alternative to Organic

A growing number of Georgia farmers are promoting their products as Certified Naturally Grown. The program, started in 2002, was designed to complement the organic certification offered by the U.S. Department of Agriculture. "There were a lot of farms that wanted a way to convey their values to their customers but felt that the scale of the National Organic Program, because of the cost and the amount of paperwork, didn't fit with their farm," explains Alice Varon, executive director of the Certified Naturally Grown program.

The main difference between the Certified Naturally Grown and USDA National Organic programs is the certification model: Unlike organic certifications, which require an inspection and approval by a government official, the Certified Naturally Grown program relies on a peer review inspection process, which "is recognized internationally as a way to support small-scale sustainable agriculture," according to Varon.

Since its inception, more than 740 farmers and beekeepers across the nation have been Certified Naturally Grown. Most are small-scale farmers who sell directly to the public through farmers' markets, CSAs, and on-farm sales. Approximately 5 percent of farms that are Certified Naturally Grown are also certified organic.

While farmers who are Certified Naturally Grown are proud of the program, it doesn't have the same name recognition with consumers as organic certification, in part because most of the farms that obtain the certification are not selling their products to the mass market. The organization is working to boost its public profile, launching awareness campaigns through social media and grassroots marketing efforts. Eventually, Varon hopes the Certified Naturally Grown label will be as recognizable as the green-and-white USDA Organic seal. "We have big plans," she says. *For more information about Certified Naturally Grown, visit www.naturally grown.org.*

## DAIRIES

### Berry College

All-nighters are common at Berry College. At 3:30 A.M., animal science majors are coaxing twenty-nine Jersey cows into the milking parlor for their morning milking. "It's a completely student run dairy, so it's different," says sophomore Taylor Sautter. The dairy is part of the Student Enterprise program, an on-campus student work experience program, and is just one of several agricultural operations on campus. Through the program, students also run Season's Harvest, Martha's Herbs, and Angus beef operations, selling vegetables, herbs, meat, and cheese through the local farmers' market and on-site sales. "All of the enterprises incorporate education for the students," explains Mark Detwiler, director of agricultural operations for the campus.

The newest student enterprise, AgriEducation, coordinates tours and field trips for the public. Students in the program lead educational tours of the barns to talk about the sheep, goats, and cattle raised on campus as well as the gardens and greenhouses where vegetables and herbs are grown.

2277 Martha Berry Highway NW, Mount Berry (Floyd County), 706-232-5374, www.berry.edu


## WINERIES

### The Georgia Winery

Georgia's first farm winery started by accident. Dr. Maurice Rawlings, a cardiologist in Chattanooga, bought fifty acres of land as an investment in 1982. He asked the Tennessee Department of Agriculture what to do with the land, and an extension agent suggested planting vines. He took the advice to heart. Now a third-generation family farm, The Georgia Winery makes thirty varieties of wines and offers tastings and tours from its tasting room in Catoosa County.

All of the muscadine wines, including Rawlings Ruby Red, Dixie Divine, and Tara Bella, are made from estate fruit. Wines like Tail Gate Red, Napoleon, and Southern Blush are made from grapes like Concord, Niagara, and Cayuga that are imported from other U.S. vineyards. Tastings are offered daily, and tours of the winery are conducted on Saturdays. Although the winery isn't located on the vineyard, there are some sample vines outside the tasting rooms (and muscadine grapes can be plucked from the vine and bought by the bunch). The biggest event, the Grape Stomp, is held annually in October.

6469 Battlefield Parkway, Ringgold (Catoosa County), 706-937-9463, www.georgiawines.com

## FESTIVALS AND EVENTS

### National Alpaca Farm Days

In an effort to educate the public about alpacas, cloven-hoofed camelids from South America, the Alpaca Owners and Breeders Association, Inc., launched National Alpaca Farm Days. The event features alpaca encounters and fiber demonstrations with ranchers who are eager to answer questions and share their fascination with the breed. In Adairsville, two alpaca ranches participate in the event, which is held annually in September. Southern Estate Alpacas and Deer Hollow Alpaca Farm show off their herds, talk about the breed and its prized fibers, and sell products made from alpaca, including hats, scarves, and socks. It's one of few opportunities in Bartow County to learn about the workings of an alpaca ranch and interact with the animals.

Southern Estate Alpacas, 85 Bailey Road NW, Adairsville (Bartow County), 678-618-2880, www.southernestatealpacas.com

Deer Hollow Alpaca Farm, 15 Hunt Club Lane, Cartersville (Bartow County), 770-862-7102, www.deerhollowfarm.com

### The Great Valley Exposition

Sam Lowery collects antique tractors, farm implements, and tools. Instead of leaving them in the barn collecting dust, he decided to host an expo to show them off. In 2005, he threw open the barn doors, polished up the tractors, and launched the Great Valley Exposition. It's grown to include exhibitors from across the state. "We want to educate people about the agricultural history and culture of our state," says Ivy Lowrey, Sam's daughter-in-law. "The event showcases the evolution of farming from mules pulling plows to tractors with GPS that drive themselves."

It's possible to spend hours wandering in the barn, which is stocked to the rafters with oil cans, rusted tractor seats, and old advertising signs, all set up to resemble a farming museum. The annual event, which takes place in July, also features live entertainment, wagon rides, and mule plowing demonstrations.

2416 Turkey Mountain Road, Rome (Floyd County), 706-295-1157, www.lowreyfarms.com

## Prater's Mill Country Fair

In 1855, after Benjamin Franklin Prater built his water-powered gristmill, farmers lined up outside the mill in the predawn hours, waiting for millers to grind their corn and wheat using the most modern cleaning, grading, and shifting machines in the region. The mill operated until the 1960s but then fell into disrepair until the Prater's Mill Foundation, a nonprofit group dedicated to preserving the mill as part of the cultural history of Southern Appalachia, stepped in to restore it. "We thought it was a magnificent piece of history," says Judy Alderman, president of the board of directors for the Prater's Mill Foundation. "It's a nineteenth-century building that made food for our daily bread; you can't get much more important than that."

With restoration efforts under way, the foundation set about creating an event to honor its cultural importance. The annual Prater's Mill Country Fair includes tours of the gristmill, cotton gin, and barn as well as exhibits and demonstrations featuring period handicrafts such as spinning, quilting, and woodcarving.

Volunteer millers run the mill, grinding corn and wheat into cornmeal, grits, and whole wheat flour that are sold at the foundation offices. The mill also operates during the festival, and several vendors use cornmeal in foods like hoecakes, a coarse cake that used to be baked on the blade of a garden hoe. Alderman calls them "the best southern food this side of heaven." The mill is listed on the National Register of Historic Places and is represented in the Local Legacies Project headed by the Library of Congress.

5566 Georgia Highway 2, Dalton (Whitfield County), 706-694-6455, www.pratersmill.org

## SPECIALTY SHOPS

### Last Stop Gift Shop

The Rome Convention and Visitors Bureau knew that the tourists who stopped in for maps and brochures were also interested in souvenirs to commemorate their visit to the North Georgia mountains. Instead of filling the visitors center with mass-produced products, staff connected with local farmers and artisans to stock shelves with Georgia-grown, Georgia-made products. "People want to take home something that was made in the city, county, or region that they are visiting," says Luke Chaffin, special projects coordinator for the Rome Convention and Visitors Bureau. "We wanted to promote and support local authors and craftspeople, not just to visitors but to locals who might not know about the diverse talents of the people who live here."

Along with directions to the Martha Berry Museum or recommendations for restaurants, visitors can find a selection of jams, jellies, barbecue sauces, salsa, honey, and other value-added products made from local ingredients.

402 Civic Center Drive, Rome (Floyd County), 706-295-5576, www.laststopgiftshop.com

# FARM-TO-TABLE RESTAURANTS

### Swheat Market

Kari Hodge got tired of driving 100 miles to buy organic groceries in Athens. In an effort to bring organic foods closer to home, she opened an organic market in Cartersville in 2005. Despite the location in the historic downtown district, business was slow. Shoppers that did come into the market were more interested in homemade muffins, soups, and salads than organic produce. "It's a small town and there is a lack of education about what organic means and why it matters," she says. With produce sales flagging, Hodge needed to make a change. She transitioned the organic market into a restaurant focusing on farm-fresh fare. Hodge sources most of the ingredients for the soups, salads, and sandwiches on the lunch menu from regional farms, choosing organic products whenever possible. The restaurant is popular, though Hodge still finds herself educating diners about the importance of local, sustainable foods. "A lot of people still don't understand what I do here, but they love the food and keep coming back," she says.

5 East Main Street, Cartersville (Bartow County), 770-607-0067, www.swheatmarket.com. $

### Farm to Fork

In a town with an abundance of fast-food joints and few locally owned restaurants, Farm to Fork is a welcome addition. In fact, since it opened in spring 2012, the most common phrases overheard in the restaurant are "Wow, this is *good*" and "We've been waiting for a place like this." Mike Manis and chef Joseph Black partnered to open the restaurant to serve southern favorites like fried green tomatoes, country fried chicken, and squash casserole, which are made with ingredients from local farms.

While the farm-to-table concept has been slow to catch on in Ringgold, the quality of the food has locals hooked. "We make everything by hand, fresh from the farm to the table," says Black. "You can tell the difference between a canned turnip green and a fresh turnip green."

118 Remco Shops Lane, Ringgold (Catoosa County), 706-937-3675. $

## Harvest Moon Café

A cardboard box filled with hot peppers sits on a table outside Harvest Moon Café in downtown Rome with a sign that reads, "Please, pick me!" "We grew a lot more peppers than we could use," explains Ginny Kibler.

Kibler grew the peppers on Big Cedar Creek Farm, the farm she operates with her husband, Doc. Most of the produce grown on the farm is served in the restaurant, adding local flair to dishes like tomato pie and sweet potato soufflé. "I don't think people realize how much of the produce served in most restaurants comes from places like Florida and Mexico and China," notes kitchen manager Jeff Beard. "We started using fresh produce straight from the farm, and everything tasted better, people noticed."

Not all of the meats and vegetables on the menu are from Big Cedar Creek Farm, but the restaurant has relationships with several regional farms and fisherman and strives to use ingredients from local sources whenever possible.

234 Broad Street, Rome (Floyd County), 706-292-0099, www.myharvestmooncafe.com. $

## Water Club

Jeff and K. C. Myers operate two successful restaurants in Atlanta, but their hearts are in the small community of Cave Spring. In 2012, the couple opened Water Club and designed the menu to take advantage of the abundance of produce available from local farms. Through relationships with B&B Family Farm and Berry College, the restaurant serves seasonal dishes with southern flair. Even the water has a local connection: K. C. hauls buckets to a natural spring across the street each morning and serves the award-winning water at the restaurant.

18 Broad Street, Cave Spring (Floyd County), 706-777-8811. $$

## RECIPES

### Jaemor's Peach Pudding

*When Mrs. Jimmy Echols, whose husband runs Jaemor Farms in Hall County, calls her children and grandchildren to the supper table, few things get them more excited than the news that she made peach pudding for dessert.*

SERVES 8

| | |
|---|---|
| 6–8 | medium ripe peaches, cored and thinly sliced |
| 1 | (5.1-ounce) box vanilla instant pudding mix |
| 3 | cups milk |
| 1 | box Nilla Wafers |
| 1 | (12-ounce) container Cool Whip |

Place a layer of Nilla Wafers in the bottom of a 9×13-inch baking dish. Arrange half of the sliced peaches on top, and then another layer of wafers. Arrange the remaining peaches on top of the wafers. In a blender, mix the pudding and milk. Pour over the peach-wafer layers. Top with Cool Whip. Chill for at least 4 hours, up to overnight and serve. Refrigerate leftovers.

## Fresh Strawberry Rhubarb Sauce

*You could eat a plain scoop of vanilla ice cream, but Joni Kennedy of Melon Head Farm thinks it tastes better when it's topped with strawberry rhubarb sauce made with produce that comes straight from the farm. Not in the mood for ice cream? The sauce is delicious over biscuits or drizzled on pancakes.*

MAKES 4 CUPS

| | |
|---|---|
| 2 | tablespoons unsalted butter |
| 4 | cups thinly sliced fresh rhubarb (about 1 pound) |
| 4 | cups sliced fresh strawberries (about 1 pound) |
| 1 | cup sugar |
| | Pinch of salt |
| 1 | teaspoon vanilla |
| 1 | teaspoon fresh lemon juice |

In a medium skillet, melt the butter over medium heat. Add the rhubarb, strawberries, sugar, and salt, stirring constantly, until the rhubarb and strawberries begin to soften, about 8 minutes. Add the vanilla and lemon juice and serve warm.

# Blue Ridge & Valley Region

The Blue Ridge and Valley Region is hailed as the premier region in the state for growing grapes, apples, and Christmas trees. It's home to Apple Alley, the Georgia Wine Trail, and the highest concentration of Christmas tree farms in Georgia. The region extends across the top of the state, connecting Georgia with Tennessee, Alabama, and North Carolina. Thanks to sharp changes in elevation across the region, the Blue Ridge and Valley Region has both the highest point in the region—and the state—in the Blue Ridge Mountains and the lowest in the Chickamauga and Great Valleys. The changes in elevation result in a huge variety of vegetation. In addition to apples, grapes, and cypress trees, there are also pumpkin patches, cattle ranches, and organic produce growers.

## FARMS

### Bradley's Pumpkin Patch

Bradley Weaver has been in business since he was five years old. He planted pumpkin seeds and set up a roadside stand in 1995 after his parents, Tony and Karen Weaver, told him he had to save money for college. "He gave most of the pumpkins away for the first few years, but he kept at it," says Karen.

Passersby loved the idea of purchasing pumpkins from a kid, and the business took off. Bradley specializes in selling heirloom pumpkins grown from seeds dating back to the early 1900s. The pumpkins are so popular that customers from as far away as Atlanta drive up to the farm in September to stock up. As the demand for heirloom pumpkins grew, the family converted a barn into a gift shop to expand the business, turning the middle school student into a successful entrepreneur. Bradley was only nine years old when he decided to start a second business. "His customers started telling him that if he sold Christmas trees, they would come back and buy one from him," Karen says. "He listened to what his customers wanted and started another business selling Christmas trees."

Since then, Weaver has expanded the business several more times, moving to a historic home in downtown Dawsonville and adding new products, including heirloom daylilies, boiled peanuts, honey, and U-pick blueberries—all of which he grows on his family's land. Tony and Karen, both retired teachers, joined the business, leading school tours and managing retail operations while Bradley oversees production. For the college junior who is pursuing a business degree from North Georgia College, juggling school, farming, and operating a business are all part of a day's work. "Being outdoors and working with kids in an agritourism business is his passion," Karen says.

25 Lawrence Drive, Dawsonville (Dawson County), 770-380-3636, www.bradleyspumpkinpatch.com

## Burt's Farm

Talking pumpkins Autumn and Gordie are the stars of the two-mile hayride through the woods—and it's not just the kids laughing at the songs and jokes. In fact, it was introducing a hayride in 1989 that turned Burt's from a hobby farm into an agritourism destination. "My parents [Johnny and Kathy Burt] started the farm for fun," says Casey Sanders. "Farming is something my dad has always loved, and he wanted to share it with others. He just kept adding new things and people kept coming to the farm."

Ever since the Burts purchased the farm in 1972, fall has been the busiest time at the family farm. It takes months of hard work to prepare for fall weekends, when hundreds of cars fill the parking lot, mostly because all of the pumpkins, from the minis to the 300-pound Big Macs, are grown onsite. "We give people wheelbarrows to use as shopping carts!" says Sanders.

The family also grows white and blue pumpkins and makes homemade, pumpkin-inspired treats like pumpkin pie, pumpkin bread, and pumpkin butter. The family even launched a line of body care products, Early Harvest, all made with pumpkin.

5 Burts Pumpkin Farm Road, Dawsonville (Dawson County), 706-265-3701, www.burtsfarm.com

## Cane Creek Farm

Lynn Pugh is an educator at heart. After teaching high school science for most of her career, she wanted to trade her small garden plot for acreage with enough space to grow all of the fruits and vegetables she wanted. And then she started teaching others to do the same. With the help of Georgia Organics, Pugh developed a curriculum for the first organic gardening and farming course in the state. She launched the program in 2007, inviting students to gain hands-on experience on her eighteen-acre farm.

Pugh has extended her farm beyond organic produce production, adding herds of Dexter cattle and Katahdin sheep. She runs a CSA and operates an on-farm market on Wednesdays, selling produce, herbs, mushrooms, flowers, and meat from Cane Creek Farm alongside produce, eggs, soaps, and fair trade chocolate and coffee from other sustainable farms.

During educational tours (offered by appointment), Pugh lets visitors explore the pastures, greenhouses, gardens, and chicken coops while she explains what it means to run a sustainable farm.

5110 Jekyll Road, Cumming (Forsyth County), www.candcreekfarm.net

## Cedar Hill Enrichment Center

Cedar Hill Enrichment Center started out as a goat farm and became a spiritual retreat center for women. Since it was founded in 1995, its mission has changed, and the center transitioned into a center for sustainable living. The grounds include native plants and meditation gardens that have helped the seventeen-acre rural retreat earn certification as a Wildlife Habitat through the National Wildlife Federation. The center also participates in the Adopt-a-Stream program. Executive director Kat Stratton is a certified habitat steward, master gardener, and permaculture design consultant who is committed to teaching visitors how to be good stewards of the land. The center leads workshops on permaculture, vermiculture, beekeeping, preparing for garden planting, seed saving, and food preservation.

5735 Dawsonville Highway, Gainesville (Forsyth County), 770-887-0051, www.discovercedarhill.org

## Preserving the Harvest

Sometimes there are just too many pecks of peaches, bushels of okra, and pounds of pears to eat in a single season.
A growing number of locavores are canning and preserving fruits and vegetables to increase their access to locally grown foods all year along. But "putting up" the harvest comes with risks: Research conducted by the National Center for Home Food Preservation at the University of Georgia (http://nchfp .uga.edu) found that a high percentage of home cooks use improper methods for preserving foods, putting themselves at risk for food-borne illnesses. With funding from the Co-operative State Research, Education and Extension Service and the U.S. Department of Agriculture, the National Center for Home Food Preservation created an extensive collection of resources to educate the public about safe methods of food preservation. The website features step-by-step instructions for canning, drying, freezing, pickling, and curing/smoking countless varieties of fruits, vegetables, and meats. There are also instructions and recipes for using fresh produce to make jams and jellies.

## Smokey Hollow Farm

When Frank and Pat Corker moved to the mountains, their goal was simple: buy land and raise animals. The process turned out to be a lot more entertaining. The couple transported three Oberhasli goats, two livestock guardian dogs, and two barn cats in the back of a truck while towing a trailer of hay! In a single trip, their farm dream was realized. "We were both working full-time jobs and spent a lot of time doing research and talking about [farming] and then we decided to just do it," Frank recalls. "Before you know it, we had land and goats."

The herd has grown from two goats in 2008 to seventeen. According to Frank, one of the most entertaining parts of raising goats is seeing the newborn kids in the spring "bouncing all around, cute as can be." All of the raw goat milk produced on the farm is sold on-site, by appointment. To share their knowledge and passion for living off the land, the couple turned the farm into an educational center for sustainable living, offering classes on goat husbandry, cheesemaking, processing chickens, and permaculture.

2897 Goose Island Road, Cherrylog (Gilmer County), 678-374-7473, www.smokey-hollow.com

## Melon Head Farm

"I'd be lost without Google," confesses Joni Kennedy, a sales-rep-turned-farmer who started growing blackberries, figs, persimmons, onions, cucumbers, garlic, peppers, potatoes, and several varieties of watermelon in 2011. With no farming background, Kennedy has relied on the Internet and the advice of other farmers to sprout seedlings, tackle pests, and improve soil health on her organic farm. So far, it's working. Melon Head Farm has developed a loyal following at the Clarkesville Farmers Market, and customers come to the farm to pick up the heirloom produce Kennedy has developed a reputation for growing. "I use heritage seeds to grow produce that has been around for hundreds of years but is dying off," she says.

500 Brando Trail, Clarkesville (Habersham County), 578-481-3201, www.melonheadfarm.com

## Elachee Nature Science Center

The 1,200-acre nature preserve, part of the Chicopee Woods Nature Preserve, one of the largest protected green spaces in the state, is home to an impressive collection of native plants. Hiking trails wind through four distinct habitats—woodland, wetland, stream, and lake—and the grounds feature native gardens as well as rain gardens, butterfly gardens, and a compost demonstration site. Naturalists lead special programs, including hikes, a fall festival, and master naturalist programs to introduce visitors to the extensive collection of Georgia-grown flora and fauna in the preserve.

2125 Elachee Drive, Gainesville (Hall County), 770-535-1976, www.elachee.org

## Focusing on Farmland Preservation

American Farmland Trust, a nonprofit aimed at protecting farm and ranch land, reports that Georgia loses about fifty acres of farmland to development every day. Nationwide, the statistic jumps to one acre of farmland per minute. To protect disappearing farmland, American Farmland Trust promotes environmentally sound farming practices and educates the public about the importance of supporting local farmers by purchasing food at farmers' markets or through CSA programs.

The organization also lobbies for policy changes to protect farmland, including the Federal Farmland Protection Policy Act, which was introduced as part of the Farm Bill in 1981 as the first federal law to address the loss of agricultural land to nonfarm development. The act minimizes the extent that federal programs like airports, dams, and highways contribute to the loss of farmland but doesn't address the impact of private developers.

To preserve farmland in Georgia, landowners can sell their development rights and have their land placed into a conservation easement management by the Georgia Department of Natural Resources through a program run by the Georgia Land Conservation Program. Conservation easements are made between landowner and easement holders that restrict how the land is used (there are fifty organizations in Georgia qualified to hold easements, including the Georgia Forestry Commission and the Department of Natural Resources). Most easements forbid subdivision of the land or mining but allow agriculture and recreation. To date, there are approximately 1,000 conservation easements in Georgia.

## Jaemor Farms

Thirty years ago, despite warnings from fellow farmers, Jimmy Echols bought seventy acres next to the new four-lane highway and opened a produce stand. "Everyone told my grandad he was going to lose everything he had by spending his money on land out here because the road wouldn't have any traffic," says Drew Echols.

The fears turned out to be unfounded. In fact, there are so many cars lined up to get into Jaemor Farms on fall weekends, Echols has to hire a traffic cop. More than 700,000 people pass through the farm market annually, stocking up on produce, baked goods, and preserves. Echols believes that the farm has benefited from increased interest in locally grown produce. "My granddad was doing locally grown before it was cool," he jokes.

Jaemor Farms earned its reputation for growing peaches. When Echols took the reins in 2002, he diversified the crops, growing strawberries, apples, muscadine grapes, and pumpkins. He added a corn maze and pumpkin patch in 2006, enduring some of the same comments from his family that his grandfather heard decades ago. "My granddaddy and my daddy were resistant, they thought I was crazy. Lucky for me, it's been really successful," he says. "It's much harder to get used to doing agritourism than it is to introduce a new crop. For a few months a year, the farm turns into a carnival, and I'm the ringleader!"

The farm celebrated its centennial in 2012, a milestone Echols attributes to their reputation for providing "a superior product at a reasonable price."

5340 Georgia Highway 365, Lula (Hall County), 770-869-3999, www.jaemorfarms.com

## Hillside Orchard Farm

Ask Robert Mitcham how he got into agritourism and he'll blame his wife. "Every time we went somewhere, Patsy would come up with a new idea for something we should build on the farm," he jokes. Hillside Orchard Farm started making pickles, apple butter, chowchow, and other value-added products in 1967. In addition to processing produce grown on their farm, the husband and wife team partnered with other farmers across the Southeast to create private-label products. As Robert explains, "We've grown to the point where we could never grow enough produce to suit our needs, but it's a good problem to have."

As demand grew, adding a retail store to the thriving wholesale business made sense. The store carries 600 different products and serves up homemade ice cream. And, thanks to ideas generated during countless trips to agritourism destinations, Hillside Orchard Farm also has U-pick apples and blackberries, a pumpkin patch, a corn maze, a petting zoo, and a gem mine.

In 2009, Mitcham started keeping bees. He built a honey house to process wildflower and sourwood honey that he harvests from 1,500 hives on the farm. He's perfected the process and sells jars of fresh honey in the farm store.

18 Sorghum Mill Drive, Lakemont (Rabun County), 706-782-2776, www.hillsideorchard.com

### Ladybug Farms

Ladybug Farms grows everything from arugula to zucchini. In fact, the produce raised on the fourteen-acre sustainable and biodynamic farm is as diverse as the selection of fruits and vegetables in the supermarket produce aisle—which is exactly how farmer Terri Jagger Blincoe intended it. "First and foremost, I'm a CSA farmer, and that model is all about diversity," says Jagger Blincoe. "To get all of the nutrients we need, we should have diversity in our diets. Growing diverse crops is also the best way for a farmer to manage the land."

Jagger Blincoe had no experience operating a farm when she started Ladybug Farms in 2007. Before purchasing the land on the edge of a national forest, she rented land for a small garden, volunteered at Gaia Gardens, and took an organic farming class through Georgia Organics, all with the intention of connecting to the source of her food. Most of the produce grown on the farm is sold through a CSA and at the Clayton Farmers Market; Ladybug Farms also supplies restaurants like Cakes & Ale, the Lake Rabun Hotel, and Fromage.

Thanks to a few seasons of bumper crops, Jagger Blincoe learned how to preserve much of the produce she grows on the farm. Through on-farm classes on topics like pickling okra and cooking sweet potatoes, Jagger Blincoe shares the traditional skills of food preservation. She also offers classes on seed starting, installing drip irrigation, and other essential organic growing topics. "I can touch a lot of people by teaching classes and sharing my knowledge," she says. "I feel like I have a responsibility to help other people start growing their own food. The question isn't whether small farms can feed the world—because they absolutely can—but whether there are enough people willing to do the work."

676 Coleman River Road, Clayton (Rabun County), 706-782-7244, www.ladybugfarms.net

## Cupid Falls Farm

After Steve and Patti Clark left Atlanta and purchased a farm in the mountains with plans to grow a small vegetable garden and relish the peaceful surroundings, the couple noticed something was missing. "The pasture looked so empty," says Patti. They rescued two malnourished llamas, Hope and Grace, to add life to the pasture. During the process of rehabilitating the llamas, the couple fell in love with the sound of animals on the farm and decided to add alpacas. "We went to get two [males] for fiber and came home with four; we decided to get two females and came home with five; before long, we had babies," recalls Steve. "All of a sudden we realized, We're farmers!"

After the llamas and alpacas, the farm has welcomed chickens, sheep, ducks, rabbits, bees, and dogs. To share their love of the farm and its residents, field trips are offered by appointment, and one of the alpacas, Candi, is a therapy animal that visits nursing homes to interact with residents. "We're not a petting zoo," says Patti. "When someone comes to visit the farm, we want them to leave with an appreciation for the animals."

An on-site farm store is stocked with scarves and hats made from alpaca fiber, along with soap, lip balm, and candles that are made on-site. "Our friends in Atlanta think we're crazy," says Patti.

4630 Thomas Town Road, Young Harris (Towns County), 706-379-4179, www.cupidfallsfarm.com

## Destiny Alpacas

Cathi Dietsch laughed out loud the first time she saw a picture of an alpaca. "It was so goofy looking, I thought it had to be a Dr. Seuss creature," she recalls. The photo was in a newspaper article about an agricultural fair. Intrigued with the South American animals, she dragged her husband, Larry, to the fairgrounds to check them out. She fell instantly in love, and a few months later, the couple owned four alpacas and moved from a condo in Louisville to a twelve-acre farm in Young Harris. Their herd has grown to twenty-one alpacas, all multiple award winners. "We had no livestock experience when we started the farm," says Larry. "We went to a lot of seminars and asked a lot of questions. Now, we do everything on the farm; we even do our own ultrasounds!"

In addition to breeding and showing alpacas, Cathi and Larry sell the fiber—and even began carding and spinning the fiber and knitting it into purses, hats, scarves, and socks sold in the farm store. The couple describe the fiber as high end, like cashmere, but easier to process.

The couple knows all of their alpacas by name and talk about their distinct personalities. And twelve years after seeing an alpaca for the first time, Cathi still thinks they are the oddest and most adorable animals she's ever seen.

1952 Gibson Road, Young Harris (Towns County), 706-379-2361, www.destinyalpacas.com

## Byron Herbert Reece Farm and Heritage Center

Although he was best known as a poet and author, Byron Herbert Reece was also a farmer who worked the land near the Appalachian Mountains. To preserve his legacy, the nonprofit Byron Herbert Reece Society preserved a portion of his original homestead. The Heritage Center, which opened in 2012, comprises nine acres and includes a corncrib, a smokehouse, and barn buildings filled with farming implements and antiques that highlight life in Appalachia during the 1900s. "We wanted to preserve and share not just the literary legacy of the renowned poet and novelist but also the cultural legacy and the way of life for Appalachian farmers," explains John Kay, chair of the Byron Herbert Reece Society.

The Society undertook the project in 2003 after securing a fifty-year renewable lease from Union County, the current landowner, and receiving grants for the preservation efforts. One of the most loved parts of the property is a poetry trail that winds through the grounds and is marked with stones inscribed with Reece's poems.

Reece committed suicide in 1958. During his lifetime, many of his poems reflected his agrarian roots. His poem, *I Looked Into a Dead Man's Fields*, includes the lines:

I looked into a dead man's fields
As I walked out by kettle lane;
The corn hung ripe in husky shields
Shaped to his hands that not again
Might harvest it to heaps so clean
Of waste the winter-hungry birds
Had found none in his field to glean
And mourned his thrift in mickle words

"The Reece family were subsistence farmers who had to farm out of necessity," Kay says. "It was a hardscrabble life he lived, working all day in the fields and writing late into the night; a lot of the lines of poetry he wrote were probably conceived while he was following the plow."

8552 Gainesville Highway, Blairsville (Union County), 706-745-2034, www.byronherbertreecesociety.org

## Georgia Mountains Research and Educational Center

All of the corn, tomatoes, apples, and grapes at the 400-acre farm in Union County are infected with pests and diseases like Japanese beetles, spotted wilt virus, and downy mildew. The infestations are intentional and are part of research being conducted by professors at the University of Georgia College of Agricultural and Environmental Sciences. The center, established in 1984, is the most northern research center in the state, and, at an elevation of 1,800 feet, it is also a prime site to assess cold hardiness and screen cultivars for yield—research that is essential to local farmers. "I really feel in my heart like we're enriching the community by offering these programs," says superintendent Joe Garner.

Although the UGA Research and Educational Center grows acres of edibles, Garner explains, "we want to support growers, not compete with them." Instead of selling the produce at farmers' markets or establishing a produce stand at the center, UGA works with the Department of Corrections to provide fresh fruit to the inmates. It's a program Garner calls a win-win.

The center hosts regular open houses and field trips to highlight its research and offers access to the original farmhouse and homestead, including the organic vegetable and herb gardens. During the annual Johnny Appleseed program, costumed interpreters explain how apples grow and the importance of the crop to mountain farms, and visitors can pick apples in the orchard. Private tours are scheduled by appointment.

2564 Mountain Experiment Station Road, Blairsville (Union County), 706-745-2655, www.caes.uga.edu/center/gmrec/index.html

## Lasso the Moon Alpaca Farm

Most of the visitors to Lasso the Moon are prospective alpaca owners who want to learn more about raising and caring for the exotic animals. In an effort to show those unfamiliar with the breed that alpacas are even cuter up close, Courtney and Holly Williams, who began raising alpacas in 2001, open their farm to visitors by appointment.

During tours, the husband and wife alpaca ranchers show off their herd, which includes award-winning black, white, and fawn alpacas, inviting guests to feel their fiber and expand their understanding of the Peruvian animals. The Williamses are as passionate about the animals as they are about the fiber they produce. They shear the animals on the farm and spin and dye the fiber, transforming it into scarves, hats, and fly-fishing lines that are sold in their on-site store alongside roving and yarn.

106 Agape Drive, Blairsville (Union County), 706-835-1837, www.alpacamoon.com

## Logan Turnpike Mill

George Holland doesn't mind being called old-fashioned. In fact, he's proud of the fact that he's using the same techniques to make stone-ground cornmeal, grits, and flour that millers used centuries ago. George started milling with his wife, Cecilia, in the 1980s. "In the old days, millers had to be electricians, mechanics, entomologists . . . they had to do it all," he says. "We take the same approach, getting involved in the whole process from beginning to end."

The couple built their current mill twenty-five years ago. They grind up to five tons of corn per week, selling their products through the on-site store, local farmers' markets, and festivals. To help shoppers understand what it takes to grind corn, George added a window between the retail shop and the grinders. "People love watching the process," he explains. "Part of what we offer here is tradition, a chance to get people in touch with their roots and their food."

The process is done at a lower temperature than the high-speed mills use in commercial operations, which helps preserve the nutrients and improve the taste, resulting in what George calls "tasty and convenient southern foods."

3585 Gainesville Highway, Blairsville (Union County), 1-800-84-GRITS, www.loganturnpikemill.com

Sharon Mauney prepares for GarlicFest, an annual celebration of the stinking rose, held at LoganBerry Heritage Farm.

## LoganBerry Heritage Farm

Before she sows seeds or harvests vegetables, Sharon Mauney consults the biodynamic planting calendar. Her goal is to schedule farm activities around the cycles of the moon and constellations. It's all part of restoring harmony on the farm. "It's very important to me that I get the most vitality and life force into the vegetables and grow the healthiest foods that I possibly can," she says.

Restoring the spirit of the farm has consumed Mauney since she bought the land in 2007. The sixty-two-acre former hog farm has been part of her family's homestead since 1828. Mauney "emptied [her] entire life savings to buy the farm" and has been working to protect it from development and turn it into a sustainable farm ever since. When Mauney bought the property, the land was overgrazed, the soil stripped of nutrients. Through hard work and organic growing techniques, she has made the land productive again, growing Southern Appalachian vegetables like white runner beans, field peas, okra, corn, tomatoes, sweet potatoes, and collards. "I didn't know much about organic farming when I started," she says. "This is a special place and I wanted to honor the land."

Through the farm, Mauney also wants to introduce people to healthy, organic foods. On Saturdays, she opens the farm to the public and sells produce, meat, and eggs in the market barn.

2660 Adair Mill Road, Cleveland (White County), 706-348-6068, www.loganberryheritagefarm.com

## Nacoochee Valley Farm

Nacoochee Valley Farm may feel a bit like a time warp. On this working vegetable and livestock farm, just minutes from the Chatahoochee National Forest, visitors will find not only sheep, hogs, a milk cow, and chickens but also several Percheron work horses, an Amish oak and peg barn, and a windmill. That's because former veterinarian and owner Scott Hancock and his wife, Judy, believe in farming the old-fashioned way, where crops are cultivated with draft horses and Amish-designed horse-drawn equipment rather than modern machinery. Hancock, who admits he was born 200 years too late, wants visitors to gather eggs, feed the horses, and see where milk comes from, all of which they can experience on farm tours. The fruits of the Hancocks' labor—free-range eggs, over twenty varieties of vegetables, baked goods, honey, meats, and fresh flowers—are sold at their log cabin store and directly to area restaurants.

1304 Georgia Highway 17, Sautee Nacoochee (White County), 706-878-5590

## FARMERS' MARKETS

### Clarkesville Farmers Market

The hard-to-find market, tucked behind A Garden for Wellness, features a small number of growers who come out on Saturday mornings between April and September to sell Certified Naturally Grown produce. It's the only local market where vendors like Melon Head Farm and LoganBerry Heritage Farm sell fresh produce while mind/body therapists from A Garden for Wellness offer acupuncture and massage.

140 Laprade Street, Clarkesville (Habersham County)

### Historic Downtown Gainesville Market on the Square

It might be called a farmers' market—and the fruits, vegetables, herbs, honey, flowers, and baked goods are the center of attention—but the Friday afternoon event is so much more than an outdoor produce stand. Since the first market was held on the square in 2009, market managers and vendors have worked to come up with creative events to get shoppers excited about local foods. The markets regularly offer classes and special events like a Salsa Festival and the popular Cast Iron Chef cooking competition that pits local chefs against each other to see who can prepare the best meal using a mystery box of seasonal fruits and vegetables gathered from vendors. The decision to host the market downtown was an attempt to re-create the thriving local commercial district that existed when the square was first built and, in an effort to support the "Know Your Farmer, Know Your Food" movement and support local agriculture, all of the products sold in the market were grown or made in the region and are sold by the farmers.

Main and Spring Streets (Hall County), 678-943-4442,
www.hallfarmers.org

## Dahlonega Farmers Market

The focus of this small, community-oriented farmers' market is the food—and the farmers who produce it. All of the fruits and vegetables, baked goods, jams, and jellies are grown or produced by the sellers, who hail from five nearby counties. The friendly farmers also serve as resources for recipes, offering tips on how to cook or prepare their seasonal produce. Because of its accessible location in historic downtown Dahlonega, many residents and tourists make a day of it—picking up foodstuff at the farm-ers' market before visiting the town's shops and restaurants, then stopping back to the square in the afternoon for live music.

West Main and Waters Streets, Downtown Dahlonega (Lumpkin County),
706-482-2706, www.dahlonegadda.org

## Simply Homegrown Farmers Market

This twenty-booth market, located in the new City Hall complex just west of historic downtown Clayton, features sustainable produce and products from gardeners and growers in just three northeast Georgia counties: Rabun, Macon, and Oconee. The fresh foodstuff and friendly atmosphere have attracted fervent fans, with readers of *Eating Well* magazine selecting Simply Homegrown as one of the top ten farmers' markets in America in 2007. In addition to organic vegetables, fruit, and beans, patrons can stock up on stone-ground cornmeal and grits, chutney, and fresh baked goods. This small-town market is never short on ambience, with live music, kids activities, and regular cooking and craft demos. Featured vendor and prod-uct lists are updated weekly on the market's website.

837 Highway 76 West, Clayton (Rabun County), 706-782-2420,
www.simplyhomegrown.org

## Southeastern African American Organic Farmers Network

In the 1920s, there were an estimated one million African American farmers working the land; the number has dwindled to just 29,000—and just a small percentage of those farmers are using organic farming methods, according to the Southeastern African American Organic Farmers Network (SAAOFN). The nonprofit organization wants to change that.

In 2006, fifteen African American farmers from three southern states traveled to Savannah to take part in an intensive organic certification workshop hosted by the Southern University Agricultural Center and Southern Food System Educational Consortium. It was the first workshop of its kind in the South. As word of the training spread, it was clear that there was a demand for organic certification among African American farmers, and additional workshops were planned. The desire to build a community led the farmers to create SAAOFN, a co-op of African American farmers that has grown to include 121 farms in six states and the U.S. Virgin Islands. All of the farmers in the network participate in mentoring programs to assist new African American growers interested in transitioning to organic. In addition to promoting organic growing practices, several members of the nonprofit are experimenting with ethnic crops like dasheen, callaloo, and cho-cho in the hopes of creating a niche market for SAAOFN farmers.

## Union County Farmer's Market

From its humble beginnings at the Union Country Courthouse in 2007, the Union Country Farmer's Market—which relocated to its current space in 2010—now boasts over sixty booths packed with products that are either homegrown or homemade in the Blue Ridge Mountains region. The market was started as a way to celebrate Union County's agricultural heritage, and its patron saint is Byron Herbert Reece, the late Union County farmer and Pulitzer Prize–nominated poet. Pictured on the market's promotional banner, Reece represents both the local farmers and the local artisans, whose wares range from raspberries and peaches to gourd art and belly button brushes. A community gathering place, the market regularly hosts bake-offs, cooking demonstrations, live entertainment, kids activities, and a giant Trash to Treasure yard sale. In 2012, the market also opened a cannery, allowing customers to preserve the produce they purchase.

148 Old Smokey Road, Blairsville (Union County), 706-439-6000

## Sautee Nacoochee "So Called Farmer's Market"

On Sunday mornings, a small but enthusiastic group of growers sets up tents at the Sautee Nacoochee Arts Center to spread the gospel of fresh produce. It's one of the smaller markets in the region (on some mornings there are just a handful of vendors), but market manager Ben Tanner believes that the small size is part of the appeal. "It's not as busy as other markets, so it gives people a chance to really interact with the farmers and develop relationships with the people who are growing your food," Tanner says. "At other markets, you have to show up really early to get the best selection, but with us, the selection is always good, even if you come toward the end of the market."

Thanks to its location across the street from the Nacoochee Presbyterian Church, it's not uncommon to find shoppers dressed in their Sunday best stopping in after services to pick up fixings for supper. In fact, both the location and the Sunday morning schedule were strategic, according to Tanner. "We wanted to make it as convenient as possible for people to shop for local foods," he says. Amen to that!

283 Georgia Highway 255 North, Sautee (White County)

# APPLE ORCHARDS

## Mercier Orchards

As a child, Tim Mercier filled his wagon with apples and set up a roadside stand, enticing neighbors to trade a few nickels for just-picked produce and developing a reputation for growing the best apples in the Blue Ridge Mountains. Today, thousands of visitors descend on the U-pick orchard to pluck some of the twenty varieties of apples—the farm grows favorites like Fuji and Cameo as well as rare varieties like Yates and Gold Rush—from the dwarf trees. "We were a commercial orchard with a good roadside business, but we wanted to bring people onto the farm, let them wander around the orchard, pick their own fruit, and gain a whole new appreciation for apples," explains Mercier.

A second-generation apple grower—his parents, Bill and Adele Mercier, purchased the original twenty-seven-acre orchard in 1943—Tim Mercier helped expand the orchard to 200 acres, making it the largest apple orchard in Georgia. The original apple house, built in 1925, is still in the orchard, and the views from it are some of the best in the county. Of course, the apples are pretty good, too. "One of the big advantages we have over the grocery store is that we can offer samples of lots of varieties you'll never see in the supermarket," Mercier says.

Bushels of apples are also available in the on-site Country Store along with specialty products such as apple cider and apple butter. Looking at the line in the bakery, though, it's obvious that the famous fried pies get the most attention!

8660 Blue Ridge Drive, Blue Ridge (Fannin County), 706-632-3411, www.mercier-orchards.com

## Explore Apple Alley

Ellijay is known as the Apple Capital of Georgia thanks to the orchards that grow more than 600,000 bushels of apples every fall. There are eight apple houses along a stretch of Georgia Highway 52 that runs through Gilmer County, leading locals to call the area Apple Alley. On fall weekends, just as the leaves start to change colors, most of the apple houses along the route open their doors to the public, selling more than twenty varieties of apples from Red Delicious and Jonagold to Fuji and Yates in their retail stores or loading eager apple pickers onto wagons and transporting them to the orchard to pluck pecks of apples straight from the trees. The apple houses located in Apple Alley are Oak Hill Orchards, R&A Orchards, Sellers Apple House, Hudson's Apple House, Aaron's Apple House, Mac Aaron's Apple House, BJ Reece Orchards, and Hillcrest Orchards.

## BJ Reece Orchards

The Reece family has been growing apples in Gilmer County since 1960. When Boyd Jackson Reece started selling apples, his "store" was a shed in front of his house. The apple house has grown since then, but the focus on fresh, local apples remains the same. In September, the orchard is bursting with Red Delicious, Rome Beauty, Arkansas Black, and Granny Smith apples available for U-pick. All of the apples are also sold in the apple house along with fried pies, apple Danishes, apple cider, apple butter, and other mouthwatering fall favorites that are made in-house. The overripe apples are used as ammunition in an apple cannon. Between July and September, BJ Reece also opens its peach orchards for U-pick.

9131 Georgia Highway 52 East, Ellijay (Gilmer County), 706-276-3048, www.reeceorchards.com

## R&A Orchards

Apple cider, apple butter, applesauce, and other iconic products made from the popular fruit fill the shelves in the apple house at R&A Orchards, but the offerings extend beyond the expected. Shoppers will also find apple syrup, apple salsa, and dried apples. Alongside shelves of specialty products, bushel baskets are piled high with fresh apples.

Outside the apple house, a sixty-acre orchard planted in 1947 by Roger and Ann Futch (the R and A the orchard is named for), beckons wagon-loads of eager guests to pluck fruit from the trees. The orchard is open for tours and U-pick from August to December.

5505 Georgia Highway 52 East, Ellijay (Gilmer County), 706-273-3821, www.randaorchards.com

## Hillcrest Orchards

If Costco specialized in apples, their warehouse would look like the apple house at Hillcrest Orchards. The orchard stocks its shop with bushels packed with more than a dozen varieties of apples like Red Delicious, Fuji, Campo, Gala, and Yates, all grown on the farm. The crowds surrounding the bushel baskets and stuffing apples into paper bags or clamoring for fruit hanging in the U-pick orchard are proof that fresh apples are hot commodities on fall weekends. The bakery, stocked with products made from the tree-ripened fruit, is also popular—just ask someone devouring a fried pie or sipping cider slush. "The thing we hear the most is how good it smells in the apple barn, especially when fresh doughnuts are coming out of the fryer," says second-generation farmer Janice Hale. "Everything we make definitely tastes good."

Outside of the packed apple house, a petting farm is filled with barn-yard animals, and on weekends, visitors can race pedal carts, see milking demonstrations, and cheer for their favorite swine during the pig races. A Farmhouse Museum is filled with antiques and farm implements showcasing farm life in the 1900s, and a Moonshine Museum is filled with working stills and tells the story of 'shiners making apple brandy in the mountains. "Moonshine is part of the heritage of the Appalachian Mountains," says Hale. "We thought it would be a neat thing to do, to have the stills here to show people how moonshine was made." Unlike the apple house, though, no samples are available at the Moonshine Museum!

9696 Georgia Highway 52, Ellijay (Gilmer County), 706-273-3838

## Red Apple Barn

Although the Pritchett family has been growing apples in the mountains of North Georgia since 1965, fans of the fall fruit had to purchase their apples from the barn; the orchard didn't start offering U-pick until 2010. "We were getting more and more and more requests for U-pick, so we started doing it," says third-generation farmer Barry Pritchett. "It's been a big success for us. The first day we opened for U-pick, I said, 'Daddy, we've had it wrong for years; [people] will pay us to ride out to the orchard and pick their own apples!'"

In fact, between August and October, it's hard to tell whether there are more apples or apple lovers in the orchard and apple barn. The farm grows multiple varieties, from Gala and Suncrips to Mutzu and Jonagold. Their signature apple, Pritchett Golden, was named after the patriarch of the family farm, W. T. Pritchett, who dug up a single apple tree from a ditch in the 1970s and grafted additional trees for the orchard.

During a wagon ride into the orchard, the driver shares the history of the farm and offers a brief lesson on picking apples. After that, it's all about tasting different varieties and filling bags with fresh fruit. "A lot of people who come here have never been to an orchard or tasted an apple that was just picked from a tree," Pritchett says. "We hear people say things like, 'WOW, I didn't know that's what an apple tasted like!' That is the simple, back-to-the-farm experience that we want to provide here."

3379 Tails Creek Road, Ellijay (Gilmer County), 706-635-5898, www.redapplebarn.com

# FARM STANDS AND U-PICKS

### Osage Farm

On Saturday mornings, it's almost impossible to squeeze another car in the parking lot at this roadside produce stand. Clint and Ricky James stock the stand, which operates between May and October, with tomatoes, peppers, okra, peaches, green beans, potatoes, cabbage, sweet corn, strawberries, and other produce grown on their farm. Staff wearing T-shirts with catchy slogans like "Team Cabbage" race to keep the produce bins stocked.

In addition to produce grown on their farm, the family partners with farmers around the region to offer their locally grown produce. The farm stand also stocks grits and cornmeal, honey, jams, jellies, and preserves from regional producers.

5030 Highway 44, Dillard (Rabun County), 706-746-7262

# DAIRIES

### Mountain Valley Farm

Most Saturday mornings, Susie Wright finds a line of customers waiting for her farm store to open. Located on a dead-end road in the shadow of the North Georgia mountains, Mountain Valley Farm is known for its premium cuts of grass-fed beef and free-range heritage pork. The farm, started by the Wright family in 1826, is also one of the only dairies in the region selling raw milk. Most of the milk from the 400 head of cattle on the farm is pasteurized offsite and sold in supermarkets, but Susie Wright, who operates the farm with her husband, Frank, ensures she has enough raw milk available in the store's refrigerators to meet the demand.

"In the 1950s, [brothers] Frank and Bill would carry milk around in gallon glass jugs and sell it for 50 cents," explains Susie. "We do things a little differently now!" The couple opened the farm store in 2010. Most weekends, Wright sells between 200 and 300 gallons of raw milk (labeled for pets, according to Georgia law). Customers toting coolers and ice packs come from as far away as Atlanta and Tennessee to buy raw milk from Mountain Valley Farm. "We have a lot of regulars," says Wright. "Weekends at the farm store are social events; people come to stock their freezers and catch up with each other."

2026 Homer Wright Road, Ellijay (Gilmer County), 706-889-0999,
www.grassfedgeorgia.com

## Mountain Fresh Creamery

Forget California; fourth-generation dairy farmer Scott Glover believes happy cows come from Hall County, Georgia. On Glover Farms, a herd of sixty grass-fed Holsteins graze in the pastures and, according to painted signs in the creamery, "are treated like family."

Glover opened a creamery in 2011 to make his dairy products available to the masses. The store is located a few miles from the farm and stocked with whole milk, buttermilk, chocolate milk, butter, and ice cream that are produced on-site. Mountain Fresh Creamery also carries products from other producers, like grits from Nora Mill Granary and green pepper jelly from Lauri Jo's Southern Style Canning, as well as honey, ground beef, and cheese.

In the shop, associate Donna Hayduk offers samples and explains the pasteurization process happening in the production facility, which is visible through a viewing room window in the store: Milk is bottled in the mornings and churned into ice cream in the afternoons. "A lot of old-time farmers come in and say, 'this is what the milk from my grandparents' farm tasted like,'" Hayduk says.

There is a "Moo Thru" for customers who need to pick up milk on the go.

6615 Cleveland Highway, Clermont (Hall County), 770-983-1666, www.mountainfreshcreamery.com

## CHOOSE-AND-CUT CHRISTMAS TREES

### Bottoms Christmas Tree Farm

"We have about 500 families who come back every single year to cut their own Christmas trees," says Sandra Bottoms. "They'll see us and say, 'This is our ninth year at the farm!'" Sandra and her husband, Dennis, purchased the farm in 1993. Dennis grew up on a tree farm and knew how magical it could be to be part of a treasured holiday tradition. In fact, helping their customers create lasting memories is one of the things the Bottomses like best about operating a family farm.

Between Thanksgiving weekend and Christmas Eve, thousands of people ride out to the farm in search of the perfect Christmas tree. After picking a tree from one of the seven varieties grown on the farm, including white pine, Carolina Sapphire cypress, Murray cypress (or fresh cut Fraser fir), shopping for garland and wreaths, sipping apple cider, stocking up on homemade preserves and fudge, having pictures taken with Santa, and taking a hayride through the farm, families are feeling the spirit of the season. "We want people to feel like they can come out here and get their tree in twenty minutes or spend all day," Sandra says. "When they drive off with a tree strapped to the top of their sports car or SUV, we want them to say, 'We had such a great time.'"

5880 John Burruss Road, Cumming (Forsyth County), 770-889-5235, www.bottomstreefarm.com

## Kinsey Family Farm

After their sons grew up and went off to college, Jim and Liz Kinsey decided to retire from farming. With no cattle or chickens that needed their attention, the couple started traveling. During a trip to Asheville, North Carolina, to visit their son, Geoff, Jim and Liz visited a tree farm to help choose a family Christmas tree. "We got the idea to grow Christmas trees on our farm, thinking it would be a good part-time job," Liz recalls. "When we planted our first trees in 2002, we were as naive as we could be." Most of the Carolina Sapphire, Leyland, and Blue Ice cypress trees that the couple planted didn't sell at Christmas. With the help of their sons, Kelly and Andy, they sold the excess trees to landscaping companies. It sparked an idea to start a nursery on the former cattle farm.

The Kinsey family didn't want to give up on the idea of selling Christmas trees. To attract additional customers, the family came up with new ideas: In addition to choose-and-cut trees, they brought in Fraser and Douglas firs that could be purchased from the pole barn, added a hayride and a bonfire for roasting marshmallows, served up hot cider, and invited visitors to interact with farm animals like cows and goats. The plan worked: Kinsey Family Farm has become a tradition in North Georgia. "It's not just called a family farm, it really is a family farm—and people like that," Liz says.

7170 Jot-em Down Road, Gainesville (Hall County), 770-887-6028, www.kinseyfamilyfarm.com

## Southern Tree Plantation

This sixty-acre pumpkin and Christmas tree farm, located in North Georgia's Blue Ridge Mountains, is all about fun and family. With over 30,000 Christmas trees of eight different varieties, 2,000 pumpkins, and dozens of kid-friendly activities, many families make a day of it. The farm provides saws for visitors who wish to venture out among the Colorado spruces, white pines, white spruces, and balsam firs, to cut their own tree. The plantation also offers fresh-cut Fraser firs and a variety of "balled and burlapped" spruce trees available for replanting. The craft store offers an array of decorations (wreaths, candles, tree stands), local crafts, plants, and food (cider, honey, baked goods). The activities, which include hay rides through the mountain scenery, pony rides, a wooden barnyard maze, marshmallow roasting, a twenty-two-foot inflatable slide, and a barnyard playground with rabbits, goats, and deer, are offered from October through December.

2531 Owltown Road, Blairsville (Union County), 706-745-0601, www.southerntreeplantation.com

## VINEYARDS AND WINERIES

### Crimson 'N Scarletts Vineyard

Growing up, brothers Glenn and Bob Ulmer watched their father turn rhubarb into wine, and it sparked a lifelong fascination with the process. In 2006, the pair started a family-run farm winery in North Georgia, producing southern fruit wines like Scarlett Muscadine, Perfectly Pear, and Strawberry. All fifteen of the varietals produced at the winery can be sampled in the tasting room.

36 Collins Road, Dawsonville (Dawson County), 770-480-2801, www.cnsvineyard.com

Georgia soil is perfect for growing muscadine and vinifera grapes, creating two distinct wine regions within the state.

### Cartecay Vineyards

"It took about thirty seconds for me to know this was the right piece of property," says Larry Lykins of his 2007 decision to purchase land on Highway 52. Lykins planted his first grapes in 2008 with high hopes for the resulting Merlot, Vidal Blanc, blush, and Cabernet Sauvignon. When the first Cartecay Vineyards vintages were released in 2011, Lykins was thrilled with the results. It's not just the wines that are earning accolades—the Merlot and Vidal Blanc both won awards in national wine competitions—there is also buzz about the location: Cartecay Vineyards is the first vineyard in Gilmer County, an area better known for its apple orchards than its wineries. "There is an old saying, 'If you can grow apples, you can grow grapes,'" Lykins explains. "This is proven apple country, so I knew a vineyard would work here."

Lykins undertook the restoration of the site, a farm dating back to the 1890s that became overgrown. He refurbished the historic barn with painstaking attention to detail, incorporating original materials to transform the space into the tasting barn. The goal was to create a winery that honors the setting. "I wanted to encompass as much of Southern Appalachia as I could," he says. "By growing grapes here, I want the terroir of Southern Appalachia expressed in our wines."

5704 Clear Creek Road, Ellijay (Gilmer County), 706-698-9463, www.cartecayvineyards.com

## BlackStock Vineyards and Winery

BlackStock Vineyards has one of the most diverse plantings of vinifera grapes in Georgia. There are seven varieties of grapes planted on the forty-acre vineyard: Merlot, Chardonnay, Cabernet Sauvignon, Touriga, Sangiovese, Mourvedre, and Viognier. Winemaker David Harris uses estate fruit to create wines like Reserve Touriga, red wine made from grapes grown on the side of the Dahlonega Mountains, and ACE, a family reserve that was named best red wine in Georgia and number one new and unique wine in the United States by *Wine Report*.

All ten varietals produced at the winery are served in the tasting room, which offers stunning views of the vineyard set against the backdrop of the Blue Ridge Mountains.

5400 Town Creek Road, Dahlonega (Lumpkin County), 706-219-2789, www.bsvw.com

## Cavender Creek Vineyards

Tinkerbell is supposed to be guarding the donkeys and sheep in the pasture, but instead, the fluffy Great Pyrenees is lounging on the porch of the winery, hoping for some attention from visitors. Inside the tasting room, her owners, Raymond and Donna Castleberry, pour glasses of sweet red, dry white, and muscadine wine with names like Jackass Red and Donkey Hotie Red. Although the couple just bottled their first vintages in 2010, the enthusiastic response to their wine has been overwhelming—no small feat for the retired teachers whose experience with home winemaking were, by their own admission, "horrible failures." "For such young vines, we've been very lucky with our wines," says Donna.

In the tasting room, the couple is happy to pour visitors a glass of their favorite wine or recommend new styles to try. "It doesn't matter what the wine writers or sommeliers think: Whatever YOU like is a good wine," says Raymond. "We're not wine snobs, we want you to drink the wines you like best."

In addition to planting more than 2,000 vines and building a tasting room, the couple refurbished a log cabin that dates back to the 1820s and turned it into vineyard accommodations.

3610 Cavender Creek Road, Dahlonega (Lumpkin County), 770-823-9255, www.cavendercreekvineyards.com

## All Signs Point to the Farm

The Georgia Department of Agriculture and the Georgia Department of Transportation (DOT) want to make it easier to find agritourism destinations. A partnership between the two government organizations installs road signs to help motorists find wineries, farms, corn mazes, and dairies all across the state. Agritourism operators submit applications through the Department of Agriculture and pay a small fee for the signs, which the DOT installs. Since the program started in 2008, more than 283 signs have been installed along freeways, blacktops, and rural roads across Georgia.

### Frogtown Cellars

If the weight of the medals wouldn't cause back pain or interfere with the farming equipment, it's easy to imagine Craig Kritzer wearing them around his neck for all to see. An unapologetic wine snob, Kritzer, a business-lawyer-turned-winemaker, boasts about the rewards bestowed on the fifty-seven-acre wine estate he started with his wife, Cydney, in 1999. "We are the most awarded winery outside of California in the country in major wine competitions for premium and ultra premium dry wines," he says.

Kritzer grows vinifera grapes in North Georgia and muscadine grapes in South Georgia, producing wines under five labels: Frogtown Cellars, Thirteenth Colony, Talking Rock, Southern Charm, and Helen Wine Company. All of the wines are made from estate fruit and earned an impressive seventy-three medals in 2011. Accolades aside, Kritzer believes his success boils down to one simple fact, "We have a passion for fine wine."

700 Ridge Point Drive, Dahlonega (Lumpkin County), 706-865-0687, www.frogtownwine.com

### Montaluce Winery and Estates

The vineyard is a slice of Tuscany in the heart of northeast Georgia. The wines, including Prima Luce, Dolce, Centurio, and Primoro, are blends of Bordeaux varietals. Winemaker Maria Peterson, who worked at wineries in

South Africa, France, Australia, and California before moving to Georgia, oversees the production of wines made with grapes from the fifteen-acres of vines that were planted five years ago. In 2011, Montaluce introduced Wildflower Mead, sparkling wine made from local honey, to complement their Italian-style wines. "Our wines are made from young vines; they are fresh and fruity, wines that are not meant to be serious," she says. "We're making the best wines we can from the grapes we're growing."

In the on-site restaurant, Le Vigne, executive chef Austin Rocconi was inspired by the abundance of locally grown products. He prepares Italian foods with a southern twist. Much of the produce used in dishes like heirloom tomato salad, marinated beets, and garden basil preserves come from the on-site garden. "We don't even have a freezer," Austin says. "All of the dishes are prepared with ingredients that arrived that morning or the night before."

True fans can purchase a Tuscan-inspired home in the Montaluce development for easy access to the tasting room.

501 Hightower Church Road, Dahlonega (Lumpkin County), 706-867-4060, www.montaluce.com

## Three Sisters Vineyards

Three Sisters Vineyards produces serious wines—Georgia port, Pinot Blanc, Cabernet Franc, Merlot, and Dahlonega Gold—but winemakers Doug and Sharon Paul don't take themselves too seriously. The couple also produces "fun wines" under the Fat Boy label and live by the mantra printed on a plaque in the tasting room: "Dream big dreams then put on your overalls." "There is no pretentiousness here," says Sharon.

Former broadcasters from Atlanta, Doug and Sharon planted the 15,000 vines in 1998 and set about making wines that reflect a sense of place. All of the wines, including the award-winning Merlot, are made from estate fruit. "We believe that this region is the sweet spot for growing the most varietals, and our focus is on what we can do with the grapes that are grown here," says Doug. "We're a true reflection of this property; you're tasting Georgia in our wines."

439 Vineyard Way, Dahlonega (Lumpkin County), 706-865-9463, www.threesistersvineyards.com

## Wolf Mountain Vineyards

There are no signs of the scrub pines that once dominated the landscape where Wolf Mountain Vineyards now stands. Carl and Linda Boegner cleared the timber to plant ten acres of vinefera vines in 2000. The winery sits on a hill overlooking the Chattahoochee National Forest, offering some of the most spectacular scenery in northeast Georgia. On weekends, visitors to the tasting room spill out onto the balconies to sip wine and take in the views, and guests clamor for a patio seat at the prix fixe brunch.

An increased interest in agritourism led the winery to start offering tours. During the hour-long "vineyard walks," guests learn about farming techniques and the winemaking process and tour the cask room. Tours end in the tasting room, where guests can sample the fourteen varietals made in the on-site winery.

In 2008, Wolf Mountain added French champagne to its offerings. "It's all hand produced, no part of the process is automated," says marketing director Stephen Smith. "It's all small batches, and people cherish that."

180 Wolf Mountain Trail, Dahlonega (Lumpkin County), 706-867-9862, www.wolfmountainvineyards.com

## 12 Spies Vineyards

After successful careers in the corporate world, Mike Brown and Lisa Romanello moved to North Georgia to be closer to their families. Without the grueling schedules and frequent travel that their former jobs required, the couple turned their attention to more pleasurable pursuits. "We were interested in wine and wanted to grow our knowledge, not because we wanted to own a winery, but because we had an interest," Brown explains. "Then we realized that a vineyard was a lot of work for a hobby, so we decided to get a license and do it right."

In 2005, Brown accepted a position as the executive director of the Wine Growers Association of Georgia and Romanello started working the tasting room of a local winery. As their knowledge grew, so did their desire to grow grapes and experiment with winemaking. Their first vines—Tannat and Norton, grapes that Brown believes "a lot of people are not familiar with"—were planted in 2008, and the roots for 12 Spies, named from a biblical passage about Moses sending spies to the Promised Land, took hold.

12 Spies released its first vintages in 2011. Their wines—Revelation Red, Temptation Traminette, 12 Spies Cabernet Sauvignon, and the most popular, a sweet white wine called Lordy Mercy—are served in a tasting room overlooking the vineyard. "In our community and in this industry, there have been so many people who have been willing to help us get started," Brown says. "Their guidance helped us produce wines we're really proud of."

550 Black Branch Road, Rabun Gap (Rabun County), 706-746-2097, www.12spiesvineyards.com

## Stonewall Creek Vineyards

The decision to plant grapevines helped Carl and Carla Fackler collect a lot of stamps on their passports. "We went to each of the wine regions in France and Argentina and talked to growers to learn their techniques and see how their grapes were growing," Carl recalls. In 2005, the couple transformed five acres of a former apple orchard into a vineyard. With the release of their first two varietals in 2012, Stonewall Creek also opened a tasting room. It didn't take long for the wines, Yukari, a rosé, and Boriana, a Petit Manseng named after their daughters-in-law, to sell out. "We manipulate the wines very little," says Carl. "We want our wines to be as close to natural winemaking as possible."

Carl believes the success of their initial release is a testament to the growing popularity of Georgia wines—and he couldn't be happier. Winemaking is a second career for the retired orthopedic surgeon, and he thrives on the challenge. "Instead of spending all night in the emergency room taking care of patients who were in car accidents, I'm up all night building fires in barrels in the vineyard to ward off frost," he jokes.

323 Standing Deer Lane, Tiger (Rabun County), 706-212-0584, www.stonewallcreek.com

### Tiger Mountain Vineyards

In 1995, John and Martha Ezzard bought a 100-acre farm to protect the site from development. Instead of planting corn and beans like other farmers in the county, John suggested turning the farm into a vineyard. "I thought he was having a midlife crisis," Martha recalls.

The opportunity to work the land, which has been in John's family since the 1830s, proved too tempting to resist. The first grapes were planted in 1995. With Tannat, Petit Manseng, and Malbec vines in the soil, Tiger Mountain Vineyards became the first vinifera vineyard in North Georgia. "We're big believers in teaching people that growing grapes is farming," says Martha.

As the vineyard grew, John and Martha transitioned from careers in medicine and environmental law to tending grapes. They opened a tasting room in 1999 to serve and sell wines ranging from sweet dessert wines and rosés to full-bodied reds. The couple has also been instrumental in developing the wine region in Rabun County, providing guidance and support to new winemakers and launching events like Rabun County Farm Winery Day. "We want to see a new generation of wine growers in the region," Martha says.

2592 Old Highway 441 South, Tiger (Rabun County), 706-782-4777, www.tigerwine.com

### Crane Creek Vineyards

Crane Creek Vineyards ought to be in pictures. Adirondack chairs perch on the lawn overlooking the grapevines that grow on gently sloping hills with Brasstown Bald Mountain as a backdrop. It looks like a scene from the movie *Sideways*. "Our setting it amazing," admits general manager David Sanford. The wine is just as good.

Retired U.S. Army officer Eric Seifarth developed a passion for wine while he was stationed in Italy. After retiring from the military, he returned to Georgia with a goal of making regional Appalachian wine. Seifarth planted fourteen varieties of grapes, including Norton and Catawba, which are native to North Georgia, on twenty-two acres. The winery makes thirteen wines, including Brasstown, Barn Swallow, and Mountain Harvest. All of the varietals honor the region and its terroir. Of all the wineries in Georgia, Sanford believes, Crane Creek is the farthest north and situated at one of the highest elevations. "It gives us a unique opportunity to grow good grapes," he says. "We are, first and foremost, a farm; the vineyard comes before everything else because without it, we have nothing."

The vineyard also has a thriving organic garden. It adds to the ambience and provides essential ingredients for tapas served in the tasting room on Friday evenings; guests can sample toasted zucchini, roasted eggplant dip, and caprese salads while sipping wines. "Wine is all about the enjoyment of life—and that is what we're all about," Sanford says. "We encourage people to bring picnics and spend the day enjoying the setting and the wines."

916 Crane Creek Road, Young Harris (Towns County), 706-379-1236, www.cranecreekvineyards.com

## Hightower Creek Vineyards

Like a lot of wine lovers, Sanford and Liz Green learned to make wine from a kit and produced small batches in their basement. As the number of wineries in North Georgia expanded, the couple wondered if it was time to turn their winemaking hobby into something more. "Other North Georgia wineries were seeing a lot of success, so we thought we'd give it a try," says Sanford.

Sanford sold the NAPA Auto Parts store he owned for almost two decades and Liz left a career in real estate. Even their children got involved: Their son, Travis, took on the role of winemaker, and their daughter, Heather, assumed the role of public relations manager. The first grapes were planted in 2009, and the Catawba, Pinot Gris, Merlot, and Vignoles were turned into six different wines, including Trillium, Deliverance, and Chatuga Red, all named after significant landmarks in the region. "We're still learning but we thought our first wines did really well," says Liz.

7150 Canaan Drive, Hiawassee (Towns County), 706-896-8963, www.hightowercreekvineyards.com

## Habersham Winery

Habersham Winery is one of the oldest and largest wineries in the state, producing twenty different wines under three labels: Habersham, Creekstone, and Southern Harvest. Owner Tom Slick planted his first vines in 1980. From twenty-five acres of vines, including Cabernet Sauvignon, Merlot, Vidal, and Chambourcin, Habersham Winery produces 100 tons of grapes, turning them into red, white, rosé, and muscadine wines like Scarlett, Chalet White, Cherokee Rosé, and Peach Treat. Wines from all three labels are poured in the tasting room, where a window behind the bar offers a glimpse into the production facility, making it possible for guests to peer into the barrel room or watch the bottling line while sipping samples. Tours are available by appointment.

Several local wineries credit Habersham with developing the wine region in North Georgia. "Tom [Slick] is one of the pioneers in the wine region, [and] Habersham is one of the granddaddies of the industry," says general manager Steve Gibson. "He's a proponent of getting more people involved in winemaking and keeping the industry growing." It's a motto worth toasting!

7025 South Main Street, Helen (White County), 706-878-9463,
www.habershamwinery.com

## Sautee Nacoochee Vineyards

Tracy Strickland describes the tasting room as "laid back, like being invited to a friend's house for a glass of wine." The tasting room, which is overlooks the vineyard and is just steps from the home of owners and winemakers Hue and Jane Rainey, does have a casual vibe. The wines—Cabernet Sauvignon, Merlot, rosé, white, and muscadine—are also uncomplicated, according to Strickland, the tasting room manager.

The original tasting room was in the heart of Sautee Nacoochee. Although it was a popular spot, Hue, a former real estate developer, and Jane, a school counselor, had a vision for a tasting room that overlooked the grapevines. In 2012, the couple opened one at the vineyard, where an expansive patio offers views of the vines and neighboring farms. "It's a special place," says Strickland.

1299 Highway 17, Sautee (White County), 706-878-2056,
www.sauteenacoocheevineyards.com

## Yonah Mountain Vineyards

Producing wines from estate fruit is a dream come true for Bob and Jane Miller. "We knew if we were going to [start a winery] we wanted to make the best possible wines we could," says Jane. "By growing our own grapes, we can control the quality and make better wine."

The couple started growing grapes in the North Georgia mountains in 2006 to produce Cabernet Sauvignon, Chardonnay, and their flagship red, Genesis. The wines attracted the attention of judges at the San Francisco Chronicle Wine Competition, who awarded six medals to Yonah Mountain wines, including gold medals to their Chardonnay, Genesis 2, and Traminette. "People were surprised and shocked that Georgia wine could compete against the best wines in the world," says Bob.

The vineyard produces wines under three labels, Yonah Mountain Vineyards, Serenity Cellars, and Bearly Sweet. The tasting room is located in Sautee (2454-B Georgia Highway 17), but tours of the vineyard and winery are also available on weekends as part of the Tour de la Cave and Barrel Tasting events.

1717 Highway 255, Cleveland (White County), 706-878-5522, www.yonahmountainvineyards.com

# FESTIVALS AND EVENTS

## Georgia Apple Festival

The boll weevil is not exactly popular in Georgia, but the little beetle is partially to thank for the Georgia Apple Festival, which takes place over two weekends each October. When the "evil" boll weevil swept through the South in the 1920s, infesting and destroying cotton crops, it was the apple orchards planted in North Georgia's Gilmore County that helped save the local economy. In 1971, the town of Ellijay, known as the Apple Capital of Georgia, decided to celebrate the fruit in all of its forms. The festival features twenty-three varieties of tree-ripened apples as well as apple pies, cakes, dumplings, fritters, fried pies, and caramel apples. Over 300 fine arts vendors also showcase their handcrafted items and offer demonstrations of everything from glass-blowing to candle-making. There is also live entertainment and activities ranging from rock wall climbing to pony rides.

1729 South Main Street, Ellijay (Gilmer County), 706-636-4500, www.georgiaapplefestival.org

### Chattahoochee Mountain Fair

The annual Chattahoochee Mountain Fair is a little bit country, a little bit rock and roll. On the midway, ride operators blast heavy metal tunes as passengers on the tilting and twirling rides throw their hands in the air and scream over the music. On the main stage, country crooners and bluegrass musicians sing to the masses. Held at the Habersham County Fair Grounds, the fair has been a community tradition for almost four decades and still includes some of the same activities that debuted at the first fair in 1975. One of the agricultural highlights of the fair is the livestock competition. As part of the judging, future farmers lead their four-legged charges into the ring in the hopes of earning a blue ribbon. There is nothing quite like watching a first-grader pull an uncooperative goat into the ring! A series of "Homemaker Events" pit competitors against each other in categories like Best Canned Goods and Best Pie, with coveted blue ribbons awarded to the winners.

4235 Toccoa Highway, Clarkesville (Habersham County), 706-839-0200, www.chattahoocheemountainfair.org

### Heirloom Tomato Festival

Unlike the perfect red spheres found on supermarket shelves, the tomatoes at Clarkesville's Heirloom Tomato Festival come in all shapes and sizes and a kaleidoscope of colors. Since 2003, the tiny northeast Georgia town of Clarkesville has celebrated the heirloom tomato, a fruit grown from seeds passed down through generations. The heirloom tomato is believed by many to taste sweeter than mass-produced commercial varieties, but visitors can decide for themselves at this daylong festival, held in late July. Dozens of varieties of heirlooms are available for tasting, and the tomatoes are featured in several meal options, including classic BLTs, tomato tartlets, and—of course—fried green tomatoes. Spread over a twelve-acre meadow, the festival also offers live bluegrass music, local fine arts vendors, and painting demonstrations. Admission to the festival is limited and advanced tickets are recommended. An evening buffet supper is available for an additional fee.

1789 Bear Gap Road, Clarkesville (Habersham County), 706-754-7295

## Georgia Mountains Farm Tour

To showcase the diverse farming operations in Rabun, Habersham, White, and Stephens Counties, the Soque River Watershed Association coordinated a farm tour. A total of eighteen farms participated in the inaugural tour in June 2012. Along the route, attendees had the chance to sample fresh ice cream during a creamery tour, watch horse-powered plowing demonstrations, and learn how water powers a mill. Several of the farms and community gardens on the tour are not normally open to the public, so this was a unique opportunity for tour participants to get a glimpse of what happens past the pasture gates.

www.soque.org

## Rabun County Farm Winery Day

Fine wines may possess a certain je ne sais quoi, but Rabun County's Tiger Mountain Vineyards (2592 Old Highway 441 South, Tiger, 706-782-4777, www.tigerwine.com) is eager to showcase the beverage's down-to-earth roots. That's why it started Rabun County Farm Winery Day in 2011. "Farm Winery Day highlights the fact that wine is an agricultural product. Producing a glass of wine requires research into the varieties of grapes in the region—plus sweat, dirt, and farming," says Jade Hilson, assistant wine maker at Tiger Mountain. At the annual August event, Tiger Mountain offers wine tastings, winery tours, hayrides, and live music. Hunger pangs are satisfied with snacks made from blueberries grown on the farm as well as other seasonal, regional fruits and vegetables. Other participating wineries include Stonewall Creek Vineyards (323 Standing Deer Lane, Tiger, 706-212-0584, www.stonewallcreek.com) and 12 Spies Vineyards (550 Black Branch Road, Rabun Gap, 706-746-2097, www.12spiesvineyards.com). "The idea [is] to expose different wineries in the area, to show people that Georgia wineries produce some great wines," says Lisa Romanello of 12 Spies Vineyards.

706-782-4777, www.explorerabun.com

### Crane Creek Tomato Festival

Since 2007, Crane Creek Vineyards has celebrated fruit from a different vine during its annual tomato festival. Held in August, the festival serves up samplings of Crane Creek's finest wines along with delicacies bursting with fresh tomatoes from Crane Creek's own gardens. Winery tours and wine by the glass are also available. Local farmers offer up additional food and produce samples, and local musicians provide bluegrass music. This family-friendly festival features an art tent and fishing rodeo for kids, as well as hayrides for the whole family.

916 Crane Creek Road, Young Harris (Towns County), 706-379-1236, www.cranecreekvineyards.com

### Green Bean Festival

Blairsville's Green Bean Festival sprouted up in 2010 as a way to increase tourism and promote sustainable living. The two-day festival, held in late July on the grounds of the Union County Farmer's Market, features over seventy-five booths overflowing with seasonal produce, including dozens of green bean varieties. Visitors are encouraged to chat with local famers about their produce and swap recipes and tips for preparing this versatile vegetable. Visitors can also attend seminars on growing or canning this little legume and even tour a canning plant. Other green bean festivities include a recipe contest, canning contest, green bean pizza–eating contest, "Little Miss Bean Sprout" beauty pageant, and "Green Bean Man" costume character. Non-green-bean-related activities range from face painting and live music to a quilt show, hoedown, and low-country boil.

148 Old Smokey Road, Blairsville (Union County), www.greenbeanfestival.com

### Sorghum Festival

To promote the little-known art of sorghum syrup making, the town of Blairsville hosts the annual Sorghum Festival during the first two weekends in October. Sorghum syrup, which is produced mainly in Georgia's Blue Ridge Mountains region, is created from squeezing juice from sorghum cane, filtering it, then cooking it in a copper pan before filtering it again. The festival, which started in 1969, showcases the painstaking process from start to finish and provides visitors samples of the sweet syrup, which is often slathered on biscuits. The fest also features arts and crafts, live music, square dancing, and a whole host of games and contests, including "Biskit Eatin'" (warning: it takes ten or more to win!), pole climbing, log sawing, rock throwing, tobacco spitting, and horseshoe throwing. Prizes are also awarded to the oldest person in attendance as well as the one who has traveled the farthest.

Georgia Highway 515, Blairsville (Union County), 706-745-4745, sorghum.blairsville.com

### GarlicFest

LoganBerry Farm might not be an accredited educational institution, but that doesn't stop Sharon Mauney from handing out degrees to graduates of Garlic University. To earn the certification, students participate in mini-lessons about garlic (hint: it's a variety of lily) and test their taste buds by sampling several of the fourteen varieties of the stinking rose. Between classes, chefs host cooking demonstrations and Mauney, better known as "Organic Rose," answers questions about the farm. The market barn is filled with garlic, and varieties like French Red, Italian White, German, and Loganberry Red are available for purchase alongside decorative garlic arrangements and braided garlic. The August event is one of the most popular on the farm.

2660 Adair Mill Road, Cleveland (White County), 706-348-6068, www.loganberryheritagefarm.com

### Smithgall Woods Conservation Area
### Blackberry Picking Weekends

At most state parks, rangers emphasize Leave No Trace ethics: Leave nothing but footprints, take nothing but memories. And Smithgall Woods Conservation Area is no exception—except during weekends in July when rangers encourage visitors to seek out bushes bursting with blackberries and fill their containers with ripe fruit. "The blackberries grow like weeds in the park," says Johnna Tuttle, an interpretive ranger at the park. "Letting visitors pick them is like asking them to help us control the weeds!"

Tuttle isn't certain when Blackberry Picking Weekends first started, but the event, which was launched to increase the number of visitors to the park, has been a big hit. The picturesque setting—Smithgall Woods State Park encompasses 5,550 acres—is as much a part of the draw as the fresh fruit.

The park also hosts other foodie events, including mushroom hikes and classes on edible and medicinal plants. During the fall festival, there are demonstrations on cooking with acorns. "A lot of people are interested in learning traditional skills," Tuttle says. "Often, their parents or grandparents were into these kinds of activities but they never took advantage of their knowledge, and now they want to learn [about them]."

61 Tsalaki Trail, Helen (White County), 706-878-3087, www.georgiastateparks.org/info/smithgall

## SPECIALTY SHOPS

### Naturally Georgia

From the sidewalk, the small shop on the square in historic downtown Dahlonega appears to be an art gallery—and it is. But beyond the paintings and pottery in the Bleu Art Gallery, Naturally Georgia, a shop-within-a-shop, is stocked with Georgia-grown products like cheese and honey. It also serves as a satellite tasting room for Tiger Mountain Vineyards and Crane Creek Vineyards. Wines from both farm wineries can be sampled on-site.

90 Public Square North, Dahlonega (Lumpkin County), 706-864-0832, www.naturallygeorgia.com

### Barker's Creek Mill

Although the Hambidge Center for the Creative Arts and Sciences is best known for visual art programs, farmers in the region travel to campus to take advantage of a different kind of creative skill: the lost art of milling. The campus is home to Barker's Creek Mill. The current mill, powered by a twelve-foot overshot wheel, was constructed in 1944 on the site of an older mill dating back to the 1800s.

A local teacher, Woody Malot, operates the mill with help from students from the Rabun Gap–Nacoochee School who grind corn and wheat while learning about the process of milling and its historic importance to the region. The mill produces whole wheat and buckwheat flour and corn for grits and meal using heirloom varieties of corn that are sold through the Hambidge Center. Malot also provides milling services to locals who want their corn turned into stone-ground meal. "I do a lot of custom grinding, mostly for little old ladies who come out with a pillowcase full of corn for me to grind," he says. "They want to grind their own corn [instead of buying cornmeal from the store] because that's the way they've always had it. You can taste the difference."

Barker's Creek Mill is open to the public on the first Saturday of the month. Malot, whose family has been building and operating gristmills since the 1750s, is on-site to demonstrate the workings of the mill to visitors and is eager to share his knowledge of the process. Through a partnership with the U.S. Department of Agriculture, the mill is also participating in a maize genome project to help collect, catalog, and preserve historic varieties of corn.

105 Hambidge Court, Rabun Gap (Rabun County), 706-746-5718, www.hambidge.org

## Goats on the Roof

While the shop sells gourmet products, from cheese and jam to popcorn and pasta, the goats are the main attraction. Danny Benson had the idea to put goats on the roof after seeing a television show about it. His partner, Tracy Allard, thought the idea was too crazy to consider. "I'm eating those words now," she says.

The couple decided to let the goats make their homes up high, planting grass on the rooftops of their gourmet shop and café and connecting them with a series of swinging bridges and ladders. There are ramps and bridges for climbing and a miniature red barn for shelter. The shop sells feed, which can be placed in buckets that reach the goats via pulley systems and hand cranks.

Thirty mountain goats live on their farm and take turns on the rooftop. The goats are transported back to the farm in the evenings and when the weather turns cold, but their favorite place is on the roof looking down at guests and waiting for buckets of treats to reach the roof. "The goats love being up high," says Tracy. "Probably because they're so well fed up there!"

3026 Highway 441 South, Tiger (Rabun County), 706-782-2784, www.goats-on-the-roof.com

## Nora Mill Granary

Watching the 1876 mill operate feels a little like watching reruns of *Little House on the Prairie* or recalling school field trips to pioneer villages. Miller Tommy Martin still uses the same process as the original millers to grind corn. There are no buttons or computers, just pulleys and cranks. The entire mill operates on water and gravity, grinding up to 20,000 pounds of corn per month for products like cornmeal and grits and processing popcorn. "I learned to listen to the clanks and feel the rhythm of the stones," Martin says. "You're not just milling corn, you're building a heartbeat of the mill."

The age-old process has attracted a lot of attention. Restaurants in New York, Chicago, and Atlanta serve Nora Mill grits, and the mill has been featured on the Food Network. Even the ducks wait for Martin to arrive in the morning, wading out of the Chattahoochee River and onto the rocks where Martin tosses them handfuls of spent corn.

Watching the mill in action is a big draw (Martin does special grinding demonstrations with advanced reservations), but it's the fresh products that keep customers coming back to the country store and placing online orders that are shipped across the country. "Once people try the product, they love it and refuse to buy store-bought grits and [cornmeal] anymore," Martin says.

7107 South Main Street, Helen (White County), 706-878-2375, www.noramill.com

## Old Sautee Store

When the Old Sautee Store opened in 1872, it was a source for seed and farm supplies and provisions like sugar, flour, and molasses, as well as a post office and a community gathering spot. Vestiges of the past still remain. In fact, owners Galen and Jean Greene have dedicated one side of the original store to honor its beginnings, complete with a historic cash register, scales that were used to weigh bulk goods like flour and sugar, coffee grinders, antique signs, and rusted farm implements. It looks much as it did 140 years ago, which is just how the Greenes intended it. "It's part museum, part store," one of the shopkeepers explained to a customer. In fact, shoppers are just as likely to spend time browsing through the old store (even though nothing is for sale) as they are to check out the cheese, pickles, relish, salsas, jams, and jellies made by local producers in the modern version of a general store.

2315 Georgia Highway 17, Sautee (White County), 706-878-2281,
www.oldsauteestore.com

To test the quality of cornmeal and grits he makes for Nora Mill Granary, miller Tommy Martin smells the ground corn.

## The Gourd Place

Priscilla Wilson and Janice Lymburner are living "the gourd life" in the mountains. Their passion for the often overlooked fruits led the couple to establish a gourd museum, a quirky and educational venue filled with odd-shaped gourds and utilitarian containers made out of gourds, including flutes, snuff containers, baskets, and toys from places around the globe like Zaire, Nigeria, Peru, and China. "We have such an ancient connection to gourds," says Wilson. "There is something about them that speaks to people on a deeper level."

Wilson started turning the gourds into planters and carving wildflowers onto their skins in 1976. "Ideas for new concepts kept emerging from the shape of the gourds," she recalls. The teachers-turned-artists/entrepreneurs grew their business from weekend craft fairs to a popular retail shop. In addition to the planters and carvings that helped launch their business, the shop also sells a line of gourd pottery, including bowls, plates, and mugs, made from a patented process that Wilson perfected in 2000. "I knew it was a weird idea, but I became really obsessed with it, which is a good thing because the pottery has become very popular," she says.

For decades, the couple grew their own gourds, hosting elaborate harvest parties that drew hundreds of helpers from the community, but farming and running a retail shop became too time consuming. Now they rely on farmers in Cumming and Royston to grow gourds for their projects.

2319 Duncan Bridge Road, Sautee Nacoochee (White County), 706-865-4048, www.gourdplace.com

## The Herb Crib

Echinacea, ginseng, feverfew, eucalyptus, lavender: The list of herbs that Karin Rutishauser stocks in her Union County nursery reads like the labels on expensive beauty products and natural cold remedies—and that is exactly how she planned it. Rutishauser started The Herb Crib in 2000 to serve as a source of culinary and medicinal herbs for the local community. She stocks more than 100 different varieties of herbs, wildflowers, and native plants, all certified organic. The nursery, which is open seasonally between May and October, is home to a beautiful herb garden—"Some people come here just to take pictures of the gardens or to watch the butterflies and bees," says Rutishauser—and the entire site is certified as an Appalachian Native Botanical Sanctuary. A rustic potting shed serves as a retail space where Rutishauser carries an extensive selection of deliciously scented products like hand-milled soaps, lotions, lip balms, salves, and tinctures made from herbs. "Every year, there are more plants that are new and unusual for my customers to try," she says. "I am always experimenting with new things."

2998 Track Rock Church Road, Blairsville (Union County), 706-781-6465, www.herbcrib.com

# FARM-TO-TABLE RESTAURANTS

## 2 Dog

Even though breakfast isn't served at 2 Dog, mornings are one of the busiest times in the restaurant. Chef/owner Tim Roberts gets up at dawn, brews a cup of coffee, and sets to work in the kitchen, baking bread and waiting for David White to arrive with a box of produce. White, the organic farmer who oversees production at It Began With A Seed, brings fresh produce to the restaurant every morning; Roberts chooses the eggplant, tomatoes, peppers, and onions for staple dishes like chicken cacciatore and Greek pasta and comes up with creative specials to feature the fresh bounty. "We know that getting produce that is as fresh as possible is where the flavor is," says 2 Dog co-owner Tina Roberts. "The flavor of local, organic vegetables is unbelievable."

2 Dog, which opened in 1997, is housed in a historic home that once served at various times as a hospice, a real estate agency, and a law firm. Tim added a herb garden in 2006 to have access to fresh herbs for dishes like pesto pizza. "Tim loves having access to the robust, fresh flavor of herbs that we grow ourselves," says Tina. "It changes the flavor of a dish."

317 Spring Street SE, Gainesville (Hall County), 770-287-8384, www.2dogrestaurant.com. $

## Bourbon Street Grille

The Bourbon Street Grill looks like it belongs in the French Quarter in New Orleans, not on the historic square in the heart of Dahlonega, Georgia. Beads are draped over the sign at the front door, and Mardi Gras masks hang on the walls, creating a vibe that screams, *Laissez les bons temps rouler!* Even the menu is pure Louisiana—red beans and rice, crab cakes, gumbo, and muffaletta—but the restaurant honors its Georgia roots, sourcing local ingredients for the Cajun and Creole dishes that are served up at lunch and dinner.

90 Public Square North, Dahlonega (Lumpkin County), 706-864-0086, www.thebourbonstreetgrille.com. $$

## 61 Main

Executive chef Jenna Schreiber might be preparing the meals that arrive at the table of this downtown restaurant, but she knows the farmers are the real stars. Schreiber, who attended Johnson and Wales Culinary School in Charleston and runs the restaurant with her husband, Tadd, takes time to list the names of all of the farmers whose produce, herbs, meat, cheese, and eggs are featured on the menu on a chalkboard in the dining room. She sources ingredients from farms across the state, including Dig It Farm, Talking Rock Produce, Faith Farm, and 74 Ranch. There are local beers on the menu; even the coffee is roasted locally. All of the dishes are served in the former Jasper movie theater. The historic landmark houses the only farm-to-table restaurant in town.

The couple doesn't just support farmers by purchasing farm-fresh ingredients; all of the compost that the restaurant makes is sent to local farms to help provide fertile soil for the crops.

49 South Main Street, Jasper (Pickens County), 706-253-7289, www.61main.com. $$

## Cupboard Café

There is no wilted iceberg lettuce or tomatoes trucked in from South America on the salad bar at the Cupboard Café. All of the produce is grown on local farms, harvested at peak ripeness, and delivered to the kitchen doors within hours; all of the meat used in the restaurant also comes from regional producers, and the biscuits are made from scratch. The focus on fresh, local fare has helped the restaurant earn an enthusiastic following. For restaurant owners Billy and Charlene Johnson, the approach is familiar: It's the same good southern cooking with garden-grown ingredients that the couple grew up with.

7388 U.S. Highway 441, Dillard (Rabun County), 706-746-5700. $

## Dillard House

Arthur and Carrie Dillard began serving meals and renting rooms in their 1917 farmhouse to travelers after the railroad came through the mountains of northeast Georgia. It didn't take long for word of the family-style meals and southern hospitality to spread, transforming Dillard House from a family homestead into an inn and celebrated restaurant. In addition to four cottages and ninety guestrooms spread across 300 acres, the Dillard family still rents rooms in the original farmhouse. The porches on the

Blue Ridge block of rooms overlook the stables and pasture where a rotating herd of forty horses spend the afternoon grazing. In the restaurant, the same family-style meals that were served in 1800s continue to draw crowds. "We source about 80 percent of the food served in the restaurant from local farmers, and almost all of the recipes are the same ones my grandparents and great-grandparents used," explains John Dillard Jr. "We want to keep things as much like they used to be as we can."

In fact, the Dillard House has such a strong focus on local products that in addition to purchasing cornmeal from a local mill and produce from local farms, the family cures its own meats and makes jams, jellies, and preserves in an on-site processing plant. Their homemade products are served in the restaurant and sold in the gift shop adjacent to the restaurant.

768 Franklin Street, Dillard (Rabun County), 1-800-541-0671, www.dillardhouse.com. $$

## Grapes and Beans

Sue Willis never planned to open a restaurant. But the plan to sell wine and coffee was changed before Grapes and Beans even opened. "The painter I hired told me that he knew someone who could cook and encouraged me to give her a shot," Willis recalls. "I hired her without ever tasting her food." The change of plans turned out to be a good idea.

Willis sources most of the ingredients on the menu from farmers in Rabun County. The combination of comfort foods—soup and grilled cheese sandwiches—and lighter fare—has helped to make the restaurant a destination in downtown Clayton. Since Willis opened Grapes and Beans in 2000, she believes supporting local farmers is more important than ever. "The county has been hit really hard with the economic downturn, and anything we can do to support the local community, including our farmers, is really important," she says. "The food tastes so much better because it's grown right here, and it's the right thing to do."

42 East Savannah Street, Clayton (Rabun County), 706-212-0020, www.grapesandbeans.com. $

## Lake Rabun Hotel and Restaurant

When Jamie Allred became executive chef of Lake Rabun Hotel and Restaurant in 2010, he served Spanish-inspired tapas every Thursday night. But after visiting the Simply Homegrown Farmers Market in Clayton, Allred became inspired by local farmers. He still serves small plates, but he creates them using ingredients produced by a different northeast Georgia farmer or food producer each week, including fruit and vegetable farmers, ranchers, beekeepers, and cheesemakers. He also brings in the farmers themselves, who mingle with diners and answer questions. Business has doubled since the introduction of Featured Farmer Thursdays and the accolades are pouring in. The restaurant received the website Open Table's 2011 and 2012 Diners' Choice Awards for best food, best service, best overall ambience, and great place for brunch, and it topped *Atlanta Magazine's* list of best new and noteworthy restaurants in 2009. Reservations for Thursday nights are highly recommended.

35 Andrea Lane, Lakemont (Rabun County), 706-782-4946, www.lakerabunhotel.com/restaurant.html. $$

## Nacoochee Grill

The Irvin Lumber Company donated the early-twentieth-century farmhouse to Nacoochee Village, and, after significant restoration to preserve its period details, it became a centerpiece of a development project that features restaurants and retail space. As a nod to its pastoral past, the restaurant strives to bring a taste of the farm to the table. Through relationships with regional producers like Nora Mill Granary, Springer Mountain Farms, and Mountain Fresh Creamery, executive chef Tony Williams sources ingredients for popular dishes like cornmeal-coated rainbow trout, veggie pasta, and shrimp and grits. The wine list at Nacoochee Grill features wines from another Nacoochee Village resident, Habersham Winery.

7277 South Main Street, Helen (White County), 706-878-8020, www.nacoocheegrill.com. $

## Nacoochee Village Tavern & Pizzeria

Chef Paul Rampulla knows that when he needs more flour or cornmeal for his hand-tossed pizza crusts, all he has to do is walk down the street. All of the flour and cornmeal used to make the brick-hearth pizza at Nacoochee Village Tavern & Pizzeria are sourced through Nora Mill Granary, a water-powered gristmill that dates back to 1875. "We're a classic old-school pizzeria where everything is made from scratch daily," says Rampulla. "I want to use the best ingredients I can get and those are often local ingredients."

In addition to using foraged mushrooms and tomatoes, onions, and peppers from local farms, Rampulla works with local farmers to source other farm-fresh pizza toppings as well as the ingredients for salads and sandwiches. He estimates that 90 percent of the ingredients he uses in the restaurant, especially to create the daily specials, are sourced from local growers. "We're going back to our agrarian roots, it's a very European way to make pizza—and it tastes better," he says.

7275 South Main Street, Helen (White County), 706-878-0199, villagetavernpizza.com. $

## LODGING

### Horse Creek Stable Bed and Breakfast

A thoroughbred changed the lives of Lester and Diane Aradi. The couple met Haggis, a retired racehorse that was discarded and left to starve, at an equine rescue. It was love at first sight. After adopting Haggis and moving from Florida to a thirty-six-acre farm in Georgia, Lester and Diane adopted a second horse, Atlas, and opened their barn to rescue and rehabilitate horses in need through the Georgia Equine Rescue League.

In 2009, Lester and Diane turned a quaint cabin on the working horse farm in the Blue Ridge Mountains into a bed and breakfast. Their original plan was to host travelers who wanted a place to stay with their horses, but, according to Lester, the couple quickly discovered that they had "found a niche for people who want to get away; and even if they don't have their own horses, they want to come and interact with ours."

Past guests have even pitched in with chores, helping to feed and water the horses or muck out stalls. "It's not a required part of the stay, but we've definitely had guests who were eager to help out and get more hands-on with the horses," Lester says. More commonly, guests sit on the porch and watch the horses grazing in the pasture, walk on the nature trails, or explore the vegetable garden, beehives, and chicken coops. (Sneaking a few carrots to the horses is a favorite pastime for guests!) "Haggis, being the old man, can be a little standoffish at first," says Lester, "but as soon as he sees treats, he warms up very quickly!".

574 Postell Road, Mineral Bluff (Fannin County), 706-455-3060, www.horsecreekstableandlodging.com. $$

## The Martyn House

Artist JoAnn Antonelli and photographer Rick Lucas had no intention of starting a bed and breakfast when they moved from Atlanta to Ellijay in 2007. During the renovation of the 1880s farmhouse, Antonelli, who owns an event tent business, turned one of her tents into a guesthouse. After spending the night, friends told the couple, "We'd pay to stay here," and the idea took off. Antonelli and Lucas set up four tents on the eighteen-acre homestead, decorating each with whimsical fabrics and colorful quilts. Although the tents ignite a childlike sense of wonder, the couple designed the bed and breakfast as an escape for adults (sorry, kids)!

Determined to honor the history of the home, the couple started an organic garden and partnered with local farmers to provide "welcome" suppers and farm-fresh breakfasts for their guests. "When the Martin family owned this house, they grew all of the food they ate," Antonelli explains. "Now everything we serve comes from our own backyard."

The popularity of the farm-fresh fare sparked another idea: A farm-to-table dinner series. Antonelli and Lucas partnered with local chefs, farmers, and winemakers to offer prix fixe meals at the Martyn House several times each year. "One of the reasons we do these dinners is to remind people to buy local and eat organic," Antonelli says. "We live in a small community, and it's important to support our neighbors."

912 Flat Branch Road, Ellijay (Gilmer County), 706-635-4759, www.themartynhouse.com. $$$–$$$$

## Glen Ella Springs Inn

A lifelong dream to own a bed and breakfast brought North Carolinians Ed and Lucy Kivett to northeast Georgia in 2008. After making a list of criteria, researching countless inns across the Southeast, and contacting dozens of innkeepers, the couple knew the historic sixteen-room inn would be their new home and business the minute they walked through the door. "It was almost exactly like the inn we had in our vision," Ed recalls.

The inn, listed on the National Register of Historic Places, has been a private home, orphanage, and bed and breakfast at various times since it was built in 1875. Guests began spending the night in 1890, enjoying the

## Finding Food in the Forest

Foraging is the latest foodie fixation. While there is nothing new about the practice of gathering food from wild places, creative locavores are taking the art of found food to new levels, transforming the bounty into restaurant meals, artisan beer and CSA programs.

Of course, some of the plants growing in the wild are poisonous (or just taste bad), so it's best to learn the art of foraging from an expert who can explain how to find edible foods in the wild and which plants to avoid. David and Gayle Darugh, innkeepers at Beechwood Inn, host annual Wild Foods Weekends. During the events, guests are invited to join Gayle, a former interpreter for Smoky Mountains National Park, to forage for wild herbs and mushrooms that are then transformed into an evening feast. Wild foods classes are also held at Medicine Bow, an outdoor school in Dahlonega. Director Mark Warren leads students into the woods to forage for edible plants.

picturesque surroundings and hot springs and feasting on gourmet meals made from ingredients grown on the farm and milk from the dairy. More than a century later, the farm-to-table tradition of the inn continues. The restaurant overlooks the garden that's overflowing with tomatoes, peppers, zucchini, and herbs, and Ed works with Melon Head Farm, Nora Mill Granary, and other local producers to source ingredients he can't grow on-site.

1789 Bear Gap Road, Clarkesville (Habersham County), 706-754-7295, www.glenella.com. $$$

## 74 Ranch

74 Ranch is the kind of place that makes you want to kick off your cowboy boots and stay awhile, which is just what ranchers Larry Butler and Pam Martin wanted when they opened their ranch to overnight guests in 2007. Butler grew up on a ranch before heading off to law school in Atlanta and feels just as comfortable roping and riding as he does in the courtroom. Martin, an award-winning newscaster who never set foot on a farm before meeting Butler, fell in love with ranching. "I feel so blessed to have this life," she says. "There is a reason that the Old West captures people's imaginations; it's the longing for the freedom to jump on a horse and ride into the sunset that people see in movies and books, and it comes to life when they are here."

Though the atmosphere seems laid-back, 74 Ranch is a working ranch. Located about an hour outside of Atlanta, the fifty-acre homestead is an American Quarter Horse and Corriente cattle breeding and training operation. (Though Butler sheepishly admits that the Texas longhorn cattle are oversized pets: "The first rule of ranching, never let your wife name the cows," he jokes.)

Sign up for a trail ride or roping lessons or pitch in with farm chores— an extra hand to feed and groom the livestock is always welcome. Or relax in a rocking chair overlooking the pasture and wait for the chow bell to ring: A breakfast of pancakes, bacon, eggs, and fresh fruit is hearty enough for the hungriest cowboy.

9205 Georgia Highway 53 West, Jasper (Pickens County), 706-692-0123, www.seventyfourranch.com, $–$$$

## Beechwood Inn

The kitchen at the eight-room bed and breakfast rivals the local farmers' market: A fresh batch of homemade lemon verbena ice cream is hiding in the freezer, and a basket of foraged chanterelle mushrooms sits on the counter. Outside, a kitchen garden is filled with herbs. David and Gayle Darugh use the fresh ingredients from Barker's Creek Mill, Fackler Farm, and Trillium Farm in gourmet breakfasts for guests, hors d'oeuvres at cocktail hour, and wine dinners on Saturday nights. "I grew up in the restaurant business before we had [major food distributors]," David recalls. "We'd go to the back of the restaurant and someone in a pickup truck would unload onions, tomatoes, and potatoes. We try to take the same approach here, using organic ingredients from sustainable farms."

Innkeepers David and Gayle Darugh source local ingredients like chanterelle mushrooms for farm-to-table dinners at the Beechwood Inn.

It's the food that draws guests to the inn, helping it earn a reputation as a premier accommodation in Georgia with a place on Select Registry, an association of independent innkeepers, as one of the 400 best inns in North America.

The couple bottles four private-label wines and offers farm-to-table cooking classes. During annual Wild Food Weekends, Gayle, a former interpreter for the Great Smoky Mountains National Park, takes guests into the mountains to forage for wild ingredients that are turned into a six-course dinner. Beechwood Inn also offers accommodations for the annual Georgia Mountains Farm Tour.

220 Beechwood Drive, Clayton (Rabun County), 706-782-5485, www.beechwoodinn.ws. $$$

## Sylvan Falls Inn

The blueberry scones Linda Johnson serves at breakfast are made with blueberries from her garden and flour she ground at the on-site mill just hours earlier. Remnants of the flour are still visible on the floor of the breakfast room.

Linda and her husband, Mike, purchased the four-room inn in 2001. The online listing for the property—an 1840s working mill that had been converted to a bed and breakfast—intrigued the couple. It was love at first sight. "We felt like it was just waiting for us," Mike recalls. They knew the mill worked but had no intention of making cornmeal, flour, and grits. Instead, they appreciated the historic significance and aesthetic and hoped their guests would, too. Once they got the hang of running an inn, the couple decided to experiment with milling. Five years later, most of the breakfasts served to guests are made from products milled on-site. Linda, who grinds up to 500 pounds of corn and flour per week, also sells cornmeal, grits, spelt flour, and cornbread mix through farmers' markets and online. Guests often wake up to the smell of Linda baking bread and cakes, the scents wafting into the breakfast room whetting their appetites for breakfasts of blueberry johnnycakes and fresh grits.

The food is as much of a draw as the setting. Several of their past guests have connections to the mill, including a woman in her eighties whose father was one of the original mill operators. "It's such an important part of the community and we want to preserve it," says Linda.

Taylors Chapel Road, Rabun Gap (Rabun County), 706-746-7138, www.sylvanfallsmill.com. $$

## Enota Mountain Retreat and Organic Farm

Visitors to this private, nonprofit nature reserve, located in North Georgia just a mile from the Appalachian Trail and adjacent to Chatahoochee National Forest, may feel like they're traveling back in time. Whether camping in a rented cabin or on one of the retreat's ninety tent sites or thirty-five RV sites, guests can explore sixty acres of mountain streams, waterfalls, and forests untouched by development. They can also live at least partially off the land—milking cows and gathering eggs from Enota's small farm, or catching a trout dinner from the fish pond. Guests are also free to pick peppers, squash, or berries from Enota's certified organic farm. And those who really want to get their hands dirty can apply for Enota's Work Camp program, where they can work in the garden or retreat center for up to a month in exchange for free food and lodging.

1000 Highway 180, Hiawassee (Towns County), 706-896-9966, www.enota.com. $–$$

# RECIPES

## Lavender Ice Cream

*Sneak a peek in the freezer at the Beechwood Inn, and there's a good chance you'll find a container filled with homemade ice cream. Innkeepers David and Gayle Darugh, who are known for their exquisite meals, often experiment with herbs from their kitchen garden. Turning culinary lavender into ice cream proved to be one of their most delicious discoveries.*

MAKES 1 QUART

| | |
|---|---|
| ⅓ | cup fresh culinary lavender, rinsed and dried (or 2 ½ tablespoons dried lavender) |
| 1 ½ | cups whole milk |
| 1 ½ | cups heavy whipping cream |
| ¾ | cup sugar |
| ⅛ | teaspoon salt |
| 6 | large egg yolks |
| 1 | teaspoon grated lemon zest |
| ¾ | teaspoon vanilla extract |

Place the milk, ½ cup of the cream, the sugar, and the salt in a saucepan over medium-low heat, stirring until the sugar dissolves. When it begins to simmer, add the lavender and cook at a very low simmer for another minute. Remove from the heat, cover, and steep for 45 minutes. (Steep for 20 minutes if using dried flowers.)

To make the custard, pour the remaining cream into a large bowl and put it in the refrigerator to stay cold. Strain the lavender cream through a mesh sieve into a bowl, pressing against the leaves to extract as much liquid as possible. Discard the lavender. Re-warm the lavender infusion in the saucepan. In a separate bowl, whisk the eggs yolks and slowly add the warm infusion, whisking constantly to temper the eggs.

Scrape the warmed infusion back into the saucepan and cook, stirring constantly with a heatproof spatula, until the custard leaves a trail on the spatula when you drag your finger across it. (If using a thermometer, it should read about 175 degrees F, or 79 degrees C.) Immediately strain the custard into the bowl of cold cream. Scrape the strainer to help the custard drain. Discard the solids in the strainer, and stir the custard until cool. Stir in the lemon zest and vanilla and chill completely, at least 6 hours up to overnight.

Freeze the custard in an ice-cream maker according to the manufacturer's instructions. Transfer to an airtight container and harden in the freezer. Serve in chilled bowls and garnish with fresh lavender leaves.

## Nora Mill Granary Easy Cornbread

*For as long as gristmills have been grinding corn, farmers have been noshing on cornbread. Fresh cornmeal from corn ground at Nora Mill, a historic mill in White County, makes cornbread that has visitors begging for more.*

SERVES 8

|   |   |
|---|---|
| 2 | large eggs, lightly beaten |
| ¼ | cup vegetable oil |
| ½ | cup creamed corn |
| 1 | cup sour cream |
| 1 | cup Nora Mill self-rising cornmeal |

Preheat the oven to 400 degrees. Combine the eggs, oil, creamed corn, and sour cream in a medium bowl. Add the cornmeal and mix until completely blended. Pour into a lightly greased 8-inch cast-iron pan. Bake for 25 minutes.

# AGRICULTURE 101: SOME FARM TERMS DEFINED

**Abattoir** A term used interchangeably with slaughterhouse.

**Agritourism** Short for agricultural tourism, the term is used to describe activities that bring visitors to farms, including farm tours, farm stays, and picking your own fruits or vegetables, as well as activities that connect people to farmers such as farmers' markets, agricultural fairs, and workshops.

**Biodynamic farming** A holistic approach to farming pioneered by Austrian philosopher and educator Rudolf Steiner that involves a spiritual-ethical-ecological approach to growing crops and raising animals. Proponents of biodynamic farming believe it creates a diversified, balanced ecosystem on the farm that promotes soil fertility and animal health. Biodynamic farms are organic.

**Broilers** Chickens raised specifically for their meat. Broilers are typically slaughtered between six and eight weeks of age to keep their meat tender.

**Centennial farm** Also known as a century farm, a farm that has been in operation for at least 100 years. The program was founded in 1992 by the Historic Preservation Division of the Georgia Department of Natural Resources and has recognized 426 farms across Georgia for their commitment to preserving the agricultural history of the state.

**Conservation easement** An agreement made between landowner and easement holder that restrict how the land is used. (There are fifty organizations in Georgia qualified to hold easements, including the Georgia Forestry Commission and the Department of Natural Resources.) Most easements forbid subdivision of the land or mining but allow agriculture and recreation. It protects the property from development and is binding for all future landowners.

**Community Supported Agriculture** Abbreviated CSA, a program that allows consumers to buy shares, also known as memberships or subscriptions, of a farm. In exchange for a fee, members receive a box of seasonal produce (often weekly).

**Farmstead cheese** Also called artisan cheese, it refers to small batches of cheese made from milk produced on the farm where the animals are raised.

**Feedlot** A confined area where animals, often cattle, are kept. It's a system used in industrial agriculture that keeps animals in small areas instead of letting them graze in pastures.

**Food desert** A region where residents have low access to supermarkets and grocers selling fresh, healthy foods. In rural areas, the USDA defines "low access" as distances of more than ten miles from home to the market.

**GMO** An acronym for Genetically Modified Organism, it refers to a plant that has its genetic code altered, often to improve yield or increase disease resistance.

**Grass-fed** The term is used to define cattle that eat grass on a pasture instead of grain in a feedlot. It's not a regulated term, which means sellers do not have to prove their claims.

**Heirloom varieties** Refers to older cultivars. Most gardeners agree that heirloom fruits and vegetables were introduced before 1951 when plant breeders started using hybrids. Some growers focus on varieties that date back to the 1920s. Heirloom varieties are typically grown on small-scale, sustainable farms.

**Heritage livestock breeds** Defined by the American Livestock Breeds Conservancy as a heritage breed that was introduced before 1925 and bred continuously since. Many heritage breeds are also endangered.

**Laying hens** Chickens used for egg production.

**Locavore** Someone who participates in the local food movement and eats locally grown and produced foods whenever possible.

**Muscadine** A grape native to the southeastern United States. The varieties range from bronze to black and are often used to make sweet wines.

**Native plant** Plants that are indigenous, or native, to a region. Over time, native plants have adapted to their environment, often making them more suitable for the climate.

**Permaculture** A branch of agricultural design that incorporates three key tenets: take care of the earth, take care of the people, and share the surplus. It emphasizes practicing agriculture in a way that preserves the environment.

**Row crops** Crops like cotton, corn, soybeans, and tobacco that are grown in rows. Planting crops in rows makes it easier for farmers to use tractors and other machinery in the fields.

**Sorghum syrup** Syrup made from sorghum cane.

**Sustainable** A method of harvesting or using a resource in which the resource is not depleted or permanently damaged.

**Vinifera** A variety of grape common to Europe. It's the most common grape used in wine production and the fresh fruit market.

# COUNTY-BY-COUNTY LISTINGS

# RESOURCES

There are so many great books, movies, and websites dedicated to food and farming that it's hard to narrow them down. This list is not exhaustive but will help serve as a starting point for exploring the issues.

## BOOKS

Barbara Berst Adams, *The New Agritourism* (New World Publishing, 2008)

Will Allen, *The Good Food Revolution: Growing Healthy Food, People, and Communities* (Gotham, 2012)

James C. Bonner, *A History of Georgia Agriculture: 1732–1860* (University of Georgia Press, 2009)

Diane Daniel, *Farm Fresh North Carolina* (University of North Carolina Press, 2010)

Jonathan Safran Foer, *Eating Animals* (Little, Brown and Company, 2009)

Ben Hewitt, *The Town That Food Saved: How One Community Found Vitality in Local Food* (Rodale Books, 2011)

Michael Pollan, *The Omnivore's Dilemma* (Penguin Press, 2006)

Janisse Ray, *The Seed Underground: A Growing Revolution to Save Food* (Chelsea Green Publishing, 2012)

——, *Ecology of a Cracker Childhood: The World as Home* (Milkweed Editions, 2000)

Joel Salatin, *Folks, This Ain't Normal: A Farmer's Advice for Happier Hens, Healthier People, and a Better World* (Center Street, 2012)

——, *You Can Farm: The Entrepreneur's Guide to Start and Succeed in a Farming Enterprise* (Polyface, 1998)

## FILMS

*CUD* (directed by Joe York, 2009)
*Food, Inc.* (directed by Robert Kenner, 2008)
*Fresh* (directed by Ana Sofia Jones, 2009)
*Grow!* (directed by Christine Anthony and Owen Masterson, 2011)
*King Corn* (directed by Aaron Woolf, 2007)
*Sustainable Table: What's On Your Plate* (directed by Mischa Hedges, 2006)
*Troublesome Creek: A Midwestern* (directed by Jeanne Jordan and
    Steven Ascher, 1996)

## WEBSITES

### Georgia Directories and Information

www.agr.georgia.gov
www.exploregeorgia.org
www.extension.uga.edu/agriculture
www.gachristmastree.com
www.georgia-agritourism.com
www.georgiagrown.com
www.georgiaorganics.org
www.georgiawine.com
www.georgiawinecountry.com
www.gfb.org
www.slowfoodatlanta.org

### National Directories

www.eatwellguide.org
www.localharvest.org
www.pickyourown.org
www.rodaleinstitute.org/farm_locator

### Promoting Sustainable Family Farms

www.albc-usa.org
www.animalwelfareapproved.org
www.attra.org
www.certifiedhumane.org
www.farmland.org
www.farmtoschool.org
www.growingpower.org
www.sare.org
www.slowfoodusa.org
www.southernfoodways.com
www.wwoof.org

# BOUNTIFUL APPRECIATION

Just like a farmer relies on the sun, soil, and seeds to turn a fallow field into a bountiful harvest, I relied on the support of countless folks to bring an idea to life.

*Farm Fresh Georgia* would not have come together without Diane Daniel. As the author of *Farm Fresh North Carolina*, the book that started it all, I was fortunate to benefit not just from the concept but from her introductions to the team at UNC Press, immeasurable support during the research and writing of the book, and, most of all, her friendship. Dank je vriend! Elaine Maisner and the entire team at UNC Press for believing in the series, and in me, and allowing me the amazing opportunity to spend a year on a grand adventure through Georgia that I will not soon forget.

All of the gals at the Georgia Department of Economic Development: Stefanie Paupeck, Maggie Potter, Lori Hennesy, Janet Cochran, Cheryl Smith, Brittney Gray, Mandy McCullough, and Carey Ferrara have my endless gratitude. I have traveled the world and never met a more helpful group of tourism contacts. Your eagerness to share the agricultural treasures in Georgia helped shape this book.

I was also fortunate to benefit from the knowledge and hospitality of numerous regional tourism contacts across the state. Thank you!

Heather Rice Brooks, my Farm Tour 2012 companion, thanks for keeping me company on the road, serving as my dinner date for countless farm-fresh meals, consulting Janice, the GPS, to make sure we stayed on track, taking notes, and acting as the best unpaid assistant and worst photographer a friend could ask for.

Without Lori Hile, researcher and writer extraordinaire, and Nicole Anthony, who turned a jumble of Word documents into a single, organized file, *Farm Fresh Georgia* would never have come together. Andria Gaskins, an award-winning chef and new friend, tackled the task of testing all of the recipes in the book. I'm grateful for your delicious work!

I'm so blessed to have the support of friends like Polly Campbell, Rosie Molinary, Heather Rice Brooks, Amanda Cash, Caroline Tiger, Kate Hanley, Page Leggett, and Megan Bame who cheered me on during countless research trips and late-night, caffeine-fueled writing marathons. And, of course, my family, Hank and Dianne Helmer, Shannon, Ryan, and Charlotte McKinnon, and Judy Sands who remind me every day that I am loved. I will spend a lifetime thanking my partner, Jerry Porter. I never imagined that a serendipitous encounter at a pet store would lead to such an adventure. Your patience, kindness, support, sense of humor, and love are a constant source of amazement. Thank you for believing that love survives countless out-of-state trips, bad cell phone connections, and deadline stress; for tending to the vegetable gardens and the "Thundering Herd" while I was on the road; and, always, for welcoming me home with open arms. I love loving you.

And, always, to the farmers. I was so fortunate to be welcomed by farmers, ranchers, winemakers, and chefs all over the state who shared their stories (and, often, their harvests) helping bring *Farm Fresh Georgia* to life. For your insights and your time, I am grateful.

# INDEX

## ABOUT THE AUTHOR

 Born and raised in the suburbs of Toronto, Jodi Helmer began saying "y'all" instead of "eh" when she moved to North Carolina in 2007. With a passion for food, farming, and the environment, Helmer spends her weekends tending to her vegetable garden, sampling fresh produce at local farmers' markets, learning to make mozzarella, scouring flea markets for vintage treasures, and assisting the resident handyman with home improvement projects; she is also the proud mama of a pack of rescue dogs.

As a freelance journalist and author, Helmer specializes in writing about travel and sustainable living. On assignment for magazines like *National Geographic Traveler*, *AAA Living*, *American Way*, *Urban Farm*, and *Hemispheres*, she has corralled calves, helped boil maple syrup, kissed an alpaca, eaten snake soup, and tried hang gliding. Helmer is also the author of three books, including *The Green Year: 365 Small Things You Can Do to Make a Big Difference* (Alpha, 2008) and *Moon Charlotte* (Avalon Travel, 2010), a travel guidebook to the Queen City.

# Other **Southern Gateways Guides** you might enjoy

**Farm Fresh North Carolina** The Go-To Guide to Great Farmers' Markets, Farm Stands, Farms, Apple Orchards, U-Picks, Kids' Activities, Lodging, Dining, Choose-and-Cut Christmas Trees, Vineyards and Wineries, and More **DIANE DANIEL**

*The one and only guidebook to North Carolina's farms and fresh foods*

"*Farm Fresh North Carolina* is indispensable not only to us who live in the Tar Heel State but also to the millions who visit each year. . . .[it] belongs in every house and every car. . . . I can't wait to hit the road."
—*Jean Anderson Cooks* blog

**Farm Fresh Tennessee** The Go-To Guide to Great Farmers' Markets, Farm Stands, Farms, U-Picks, Kids' Activities, Lodging, Dining, Wineries, Breweries, Distilleries, Festivals, and More **PAUL AND ANGELA KNIPPLE**

*Featuring 13 Fresh Local Recipes*

"If local simply suits your style, then you may want to take a look at a new Southern Gateways Guide by Paul and Angela Knipple. . . . The first guidebook of its kind for Tennessee, it leads food lovers, families, locals and tourists on a lively tour of more than 360 farms and farm-related attractions."
—*Chattanooga Magazine*

Available at bookstores, by phone at **1-800-848-6224**, or on the web at **www.uncpress.unc.edu**

MIX
Paper from
responsible sources
FSC® C013483